Mining Industry Association at Multiple Levels of Governance

Mining Industry Association at Multiple Levels of Governance:

Drilling Down

By

Aynsley Kellow and Marian Simms

Cambridge
Scholars
Publishing

Mining Industry Association at Multiple Levels of Governance:
Drilling Down

By Aynsley Kellow and Marian Simms

This book first published 2022

Cambridge Scholars Publishing

Lady Stephenson Library, Newcastle upon Tyne, NE6 2PA, UK

British Library Cataloguing in Publication Data
A catalogue record for this book is available from the British Library

ISBN (10): 1-5275-7691-4
ISBN (13): 978-1-5275-7691-9

For our students – from whom we learned so much.

CONTENTS

PREFACE

This book has had a long gestation. Longer than we would have preferred. We secured a grant from the Australian Research Council in 2000 to undertake the research for it, but it really had its origins in 1994, when David Hughes, Environment Affairs Manager at MIM Holdings (now part of Glencore) commissioned me to undertake a consultancy examining the emerging global environmental policy agenda—especially on the risks of toxic substances—and the organisation of the mining industry to engage with this regulatory agenda.

That project opened numerous doors: to the International Council on Metals and the Environment; various metals commodity associations; representatives of mining companies; risk management officials in agencies in Canada, the United States, the United Kingdom, Sweden and Australia; similar staff in international organisations such as the OECD and UNEP and the then GATT. It also led to further work, including preparing instructional materials on risk management of nickel and copper for WMC Resources, which was staffed overwhelmingly by geologists and mining engineers who were largely unaware that the products they mined were toxic substances—like most substances, at specific doses. (As Paracelsus put it, the dose makes the poison). And I found myself on two Australian Delegations to OECD Workshops on Risk Reduction for Existing Chemicals in Rome in 1995 and 1996.

All this led to three prongs of work. First, a book on global risk policy, *International Toxic Risk Management: Ideals, Interests and Implementation* with Cambridge University Press in 1999. That touched upon the problems of the poor organisation of the mining industry in engaging with the global agenda, and so the present project really evolved out of that. But my exposure to the OECD made me aware of how little scholarly literature there was on that international organisation, a view I discovered that was shared with my colleague Peter Carroll. The resulting ARC funded project has yielded three books and numerous articles and chapters. That was something of a diversion, as were the changes of position by Marian, who went from the Australian National University to Otago, then to Deakin and then to the Australian Research Council.

The subjects of our study were not standing still all the while. Particularly significant was the failed introduction of a "Resource Super Profits Tax" that the Australian Government attempted to introduce in 2010, bungling the introduction of a tax that the industry initially supported, but eventually opposed vehemently, resulting in a reinvigoration of the Minerals Council of Australia. Then the Minerals Council came under assault from some of its larger members over its stand on climate change issues.

The bulk of the research for this book was undertaken in the period 2000-2005, and was able to capture the significant changes that saw the Global Mining Initiative, including the review of industry associations that led to the establishment of the International Council on Mining and Metals, the first industry-wide association formed at the international level. The research involved both documentary research and interviews with key participants.

Interviews were conducted with Sir Robert Wilson (Executive Chairman, Rio Tinto) and Doug Yearley (CEO of Phelps Dodge) and a conversation with Hugh Morgan at an early stage in the GMI process (October 1999) at which the intentions of the main founders for the process were enunciated was also of great assistance.

Interviews were also conducted with a number of the "Sherpas", appointed by the CEOs to progress negotiations for the formation of the ICMM. These were: Andy Vickerman, Rio Tinto; Gordon Drake, then with WMC Resources, and formerly with BHP; John Groom, Anglo American; Dave Rodier, Noranda; and Ian Wood, BHP Billiton. Interviews were also conducted with key players in the GMI: Eric Derobert, Vice-President, World Business Council for Sustainable Development; Tim Duncan, Hintons Ltd and formerly with Rio Tinto; George Littlewood, Allens Consulting, and formerly with Rio Tinto; Anita Roper, ICMM, formerly with WMC, and then with Alcoa; Richard Sandbrook, International Institute of Environment and Development; Ivor Kirman, Nickel Development Institute; Kathryn Tayles, formerly with Rio Tinto and then with UNEP, Paris; Doug Horswill, Teck Cominco and Chairman, Canadian Mining Association; Jack Whelan, International Chamber of Commerce; Millie Edwards, International Chamber of Commerce, Australia Committee. Mick Buffier of Glencore, then Chairman of the World Coal Association, also shared his insights into the tensions over coal in the Minerals Council.

Overwhelmingly, these were used to reconstruct the history of the GMI, rather than to seek opinions or assessment of the initiative, and these oral history accounts have been triangulated with both the recollections of others and documentary sources such as the MMSD report.

Extensive documentation was available on the Minerals Council of Australia and state chamber of mines, but this was supplemented with interviews with key informants: Mitch Hooke, MCA; Dick Wells, formerly with the MCA; Ian Satchwell, MCA, and later Chamber of Minerals and Energy of Western Australia (and previously with the Tasmanian Chamber); Tim Shanahan, Chamber of Minerals and Energy of Western Australia; Karen Grady, Business Council of Australia and formerly MCA; Nikki Edwards, NSW Minerals Council; Chris Fraser, Victorian Minerals and Energy Council; Michael Pinnock, Queensland Resources Council; and Phil Sutherland, South Australian Chamber of Minerals and Energy.

We are grateful to them all for sharing their insights and inside knowledge of the processes we seek to describe, without which we could not have provided as much empirical depth.

We are also grateful to Ted Lowi, who was there at the commencement as a Partner Investigator and who provided conceptual guidance. Ted collaborated on a theoretical paper at the beginning (Kellow, Lowi and Simms, 2000) and then provided advice and criticism of early drafts during visits to Hobart in 2001 (which allowed a workshop with Marian) and the summer of 2008-09 when he taught a summer school with Phil Schmitter on a related topic "Governance in the 21st Century". Phil's views also helped adumbrate the topic. Unfortunately, Ted passed away in early 2017.

Also of great sadness was the sudden passing of my co-author, Marian Simms, in 2021 as we were finalising the manuscript. Just as the book drew on my knowledge of the mining industry and its engagement with environmental issues, Marian's knowledge, in particular, of interest groups, trade unions, the land rights issue and Australian politics were vital to the project. We spent many hours on the fringes of conferences we both attended and enjoyed many lively email discussions, and the final product is fully the fruit of her work. As she was not available to sign off on the final manuscript, any mistakes are inevitably mine.

Aynsley Kellow, Hobart, September 2021.

CHAPTER 1

PUSHING BACK THE TIDE: GLOBAL POLITICS AND THE MINING INDUSTRY

Business has long been a global actor, but the international representation of business is problematic. Transnational corporations have long been a feature on the global landscape, but as governance has become increasingly global in character, the manner in which business engages with global governance institutions has varied according to the kind of policy in question and from sector to sector.

Global governance institutions have become increasingly complex and problematic. On the one hand, they show signs of 'licensing' civil society groups to undertake the provision of public goods, in an interesting parallel to the actions of nation-states, which under neo-liberalism often license community groups to undertake welfare functions (Kamat 2004). On the other hand, there are growing concerns about the legitimacy of such civil society groups. Global governance institutions extend from the United Nations (UN), which often seeks a regulatory function, to the so-called 'Bretton Woods' institutions—the World Bank and the International Monetary Fund (IMF)—and the World Trade Organization (WTO). Non-Governmental Organizations (NGOs) licensed by the UN include both Business International NGOs (BINGOs) and those sometimes called Public Interest NGOs or PINGOs, that have generally sought greater regulation and compliance to new international norms. The UN strategy is often two-pronged: the promulgation of UN Conventions, which may then be implemented to varying degrees at the national level; and, the creation of international NGO conferences.

Formal provision for NGOs is made within the UN system, with article 71 of the UN Charter providing for 'suitable arrangements' to be made for consultation with NGOs concerned with matters within its competence. ECOSOC Resolution 1296 (XLIV) of 23 May 1968 governs these arrangements. It went on to define NGOs as providing specific relationships '....between civil organizations and the intergovernmental process' (UNRISD 1997, 11).

Four topics have become prominent since the 1970s within the UN umbrella: gender relations, including the abolition of sexual trafficking; labour regulation, including prohibitions against the labour of children; development and post-colonialism, known in the 1990s as the "North-South" dialogue; and environmental sustainability. The last-named topic has generated activism by both capital and labour.

The global sustainability agenda started with UN Conference on the Human Environment (Stockholm) 1972, and, in many ways peaked with the UN Conference on Environment and Development (Rio De Janeiro) 1992. The Kyoto Protocol to the Framework Convention on Climate Change was adopted in 1997. The movement towards globally-sanctioned regulation, on pollution in general, and carbon dioxide emissions in particular, led to a range of responses by business. The prominence of environmental NGOs such as Greenpeace created a 'countervailing' response from business. A socially-responsible business agenda emerged both in the formation of BINGOs and in the development of company level campaigns.

Business is represented globally by a peak business group, the International Chamber of Commerce, but this has its limitations, and the whole question of business representation in international politics raises important questions about how interest groups are affected by different jurisdictional levels as suggested by Lowi (2001), from the macro-level realm of international relations down to the micro-level well below the meso-level of the nation-state. In this book we discuss these questions, focusing on one sector—mining and metals—and one country—Australia—where that sector is especially important and where the presence of a federal polity allows us to examine how that sector organises at each level, and how it relates to peak associations of business and labour. Mining was chosen because at the start of the period we examine it had no international business association at the international level. We explore why this was the case.

We identify the factors which have made the international arena more propitious for the mining industry since then, such that it overcame its reluctance and organized at that level. We also ask: What was the role of countervailing groups in the formation of a more well-organized mining industry group at the international level? It is important to define the many meanings of the 'international'. It includes peak associations, BINGOs, and media campaigns by those plus individual firms designed to sway the opinion of middle class consumers, to purchase their products and to resist the ideas and views of world-wide NGOs such as Greenpeace. This question regarding international activities takes on a heightened importance because environmental NGOs are more influential relative to business at that level than they are at the domestic level (Levy and Egan 1998; Kellow 2002), and because their influence was amplified by the use of the Sustainable Development agenda by the trade union movement internationally. This was largely in response to changes in Australian industrial relations (IR) law which encouraged the unions to socialize their conflict by going global and making linkages with environment and development groups.

We ask whether countervailing groups or some other factors have driven this increase in the associability of unions and business.

Globalization has been a significant factor, with the emergence of a global middle class of consumers, as well as greater investment opportunities fostered by the WTO, but a further question is raised, as follows: If the associability of the sector was increasing at the international level, what was happening to national and sub-national mining industry associations? National associations appear to have become less-and-less relevant for the chemicals sector, and sub-national chemicals associations appear *never* to have been significant. In the Australian states, for example, there is no sign that state chemicals associations have ever existed. We wish to explore, therefore, the changing patterns of interest association in the mining sector, and the sector's changing relationship with peak associations and labour groups at the international, national and sub-national levels.

Our research questions focus on why the sector belatedly began organizing internationally; how associations changed at the sub-national and national levels; whether factors within the industry, the emergence of countervailing groups, and/or shifts in the policy '*compétences*' at each level drove the changes; what the relationship was between the sector and peak business associations at each level of governance; how the sector's relationship with labour at each level changed, and what part (if any) this played in the formation of an international association. In short, we examine associability at multiple levels. First, in Chapter 2, we turn to a consideration of why the mining industry had not formed a business association.

The period we study covers primarily from 1990 to 2008, because the mining and minerals industry came under increased pressure in the 1990s to improve its social, developmental, and environmental performance.

(We also note some developments before 1990 and after 2008). Previously, it had little organized presence in global politics, and its sub-national organizational forms developed as the *compétences* of state and national governments changed, again largely in response to UN and other global initiatives, especially in relation to environment and development issues, brought together under the rubric of 'sustainable development.' These developments have both required business to organize globally, and changed the nature of the constitutional balance between the states and territories, on the one hand, and the Australian national government, on the other, especially in ways that have also required mining industry associations to change. Here we track how these policy changes have impacted on mining industry associations as they have sought to deal with new challenges in a globalized world.

The challenges faced by the mining industry over this period have been many-faceted, as can be illustrated by the experience of the industry in one country, Papua New Guinea. The Panguna copper mine on the island of Bougainville operated by Conzinc Riotinto of Australia (CRA, then a subsidiary of, but since 1995 a part of Rio Tinto) became caught at the center of a separatist movement seeking independence from Papua New Guinea, motivated at least in part by a desire for better returns for Bougainville denizens from the mine, which ironically closed—perhaps never to reopen—as a result of the conflict.

The Papua New Guinea government, pressured by the loss of taxation revenues and foreign exchange earnings, was then caught in a poacher-gamekeeper dilemma over its equity holding in the Ok Tedi copper and gold mine, majority-owned by BHP. BHP had originally preferred to exploit only the gold-rich ore that sat atop the larger copper-gold deposit. The PNG government had insisted as a condition of developing the mine that BHP develop the whole deposit, giving rise to considerably more mine tailings than would have resulted from a gold-only operation. The area had very difficult terrain, peppered with limestone caves, and was subject to tropical rainfall. An attempt was made (at a cost of tens of millions of dollars) to construct a tailings dam under these difficult conditions, but a flood washed it away.

The PNG government had taken equity in the project, and was thus doubly compromised: not only did it benefit from foreign exchange earnings, taxation and the purchase of labour and other services by the mine, but it had a direct interest in the profitability of the mine. When the question arose as to whether Ok Tedi should be permitted to continue to operate without a tailings dam, the PNG government not just permitted it, but actively encouraged this course. After the loss of Panguna in 1989, Ok Tedi was even more important to the PNG economy, as a source of both foreign exchange and tax revenue. Operating Ok Tedi without a tailings dam had a devastating impact on a large section of the Fly River, and gave rise to a class action by landholders in the Australian courts, which BHP settled out of court, later quitting its interest in the mine (which nevertheless continued to operate) and placing its compensation payment for landholders into an independently administered trust fund.

Similar problems became apparent with mining activities elsewhere, especially but not exclusively in the developing world. Gold mining, which almost universally relies on the use of cyanide in ore treatment, was especially problematic, with tailings dams failing at Omai in Guyana in 1995 and at the Esmeralda mine in Romania in 2000, causing widespread fish kills. Esmeralda, a small Australian-owned company, went into liquidation when faced with the clean-up costs from the disaster, which killed fish downstream in Hungary. The emergence of the sustainable development agenda internationally focused attention on both environmental performance and community relations, especially with the indigenous people who often inhabited the land under which mineral ores were to be found. Moreover, more traditional countervailing groups such as trade unions were willing to build coalitions to exploit such issues for their own ends, as we can see with a brief case study that raises questions (central to our theoretical concerns) about whether the belated formation of a mining industry association at the global level was a response to such campaigns, or a response to the salience of policies developed at that level.

The Campaign Against Rio Tinto

In February 1998 a visiting group of Dyak people attended a stop-work meeting of coal miners, members of the Construction, Forestry, Mining and Energy Union (or CFMEU) in the Hunter Valley in Australia, seeking support for their grievances over the impact of Rio Tinto's mining operations in Kalimantan, Indonesia on their environment and their traditional lifestyle. Their translator put their case, and the Australian workers followed the presentation with a thunderous chant of 'The workers, united, will never be defeated!' The Dyaks initially recoiled, intimidated by this chant, but—according to a report in the *Newcastle Herald* (February 3, 1998)—eventually they seemed to understand its meaning and began raising their fists in defiance, bringing further cheers from the crowd.

This unlikely clash of cultures was one of the first public manifestations of a global campaign against Rio Tinto over its environmental performance and treatment of indigenous people. It came after a meeting in November 1997 between the CFMEU and Vic Thorpe, general secretary of the International Federation of Chemical, Energy, Mine and General Workers Union (ICEM), where it was agreed to devise a strategy to attack Rio Tinto. The Australian union and its international counterpart considered a range of environmental, consumer and land rights issues they believed had the potential to embarrass the London-based Rio Tinto. No definitive policy decisions were taken at this November meeting, but it was decided to hold a three-day meeting in Johannesburg in January 1998 to further canvass the issues. In South Africa, former Australian Labor prime minister (and former union leader) Bob Hawke addressed the 45 delegates from 14 countries attending the anti-Rio Tinto planning meeting.

Later in 1998, during Metals Week, an annual gathering and dinner every October associated with the London Metal Exchange,[1] ten of the world's largest mining companies established the Global Mining Initiative (GMI) to explore how the industry could engage with the sustainable development agenda. Within a year, these companies and some 20 others commissioned the International Institute for Environment and Development (IIED) in London, through the World Business Council for Sustainable Development (WBCSD), to conduct what was named the Mining, Minerals and Sustainable Development (MMSD) project. This was an independent two-year project which sought to involve relevant stakeholders to try to develop an understanding of how the sector could make a transition to sustainability. A parallel process in the GMI saw a review of industry associations, culminating in the establishment in October 2001 of the first broad-based sector organization at the international level, the International Council on Mining and Metals (ICMM), which would be charged with developing an industry response to the issues of sustainable development.

---

[1] The London Metal Exchange (LME) is a market in which refined copper, aluminium, nickel, lead, zinc, tin, and silver are bought and sold, for delivery either immediately or at fixed dates in the future. LME prices are used world-wide as the basis price for transactions in these metals (with the exception of silver), and for products upstream (such as ores and concentrates) and for downstream products, and even scrap prices. Most LME contracts are hedging transactions and only an estimated 5 percent of the metals produced annually are physically traded through the LME, with most metal normally sold directly or through merchants. The total value of the trade was historically around $US 12 trillion annually. (Clow 1992).

To what extent, if any, were these developments linked? Was the GMI a response to the campaign against Rio? Certainly, Rio Chairman Sir Robert Wilson was identified as playing a prominent role not just in these events, but in responding in order to blunt developments at the Johannesburg meeting in 1998 and in playing a leading role in the industry response, and Rio seemed to be the prominent target of this and similar campaigns. Rio Tinto's Kelian gold mine in Kalimantan, from whence the Dyaks came, had twice been shut by blockades by protestors, which had trimmed its returns. It also had a 14 percent stake in Freeport Indonesia, the operator of Grasberg, the world's largest gold mine, and a 40 percent stake in some of its lucrative expansion activities, including Kucing Liar (*Weekend Australian* 27-28 May 2000). Freeport was the target of international campaigns and became intertwined with the separatist politics of the Free Papua Movement (OPM). The Rainforest Action Network and Project Underground ran a campaign against Freeport-McMoRan from 1995 which Manheim (2000, 342) suggests might have been related to the Rio campaign.

Campaigns initiated by unions had also been conducted against other mining companies, including Phelps Dodge (1983, 1998), Agip mining subsidiary ENI (1988-89), and Kaiser Aluminium (1998), so Rio was not alone, but it was one of the global mining giants. The GMI and the increased level of organization of the industry at the international level thus appeared at least to come in response to the activities of 'countervailing groups'. This would suggest that a society-centred explanation of interest group formation might be preferred to those which seek to explain this in terms of the characteristics of the state (or some similar 'reciprocating agent' at the international level). The question of interest group formation and maintenance in an increasingly globalised world is thus one which demands more detailed analysis. Relationships between firms and groups representing their industrial sectors, between sectors and countervailing groups, and between peak associations of business and labour now occur at sub-national, national, and transnational levels, and they require explanation.

As we shall see, as with these other campaigns, the international campaign against Rio had more to do with the campaigners' weakness in domestic-level industrial relations than with environment and development, and while Sir Robert Wilson was an important player, others were as, if not more, instrumental in initiating and driving the GMI, which was more a response to an emergent policy agenda advanced by international governance structures than a direct response to NGO campaigns. Further, the GMI had as much to do with issues of improving industry financial performance as with sustainable development. The debate over sustainable development therefore was not solely about reconciling development in the Third World with environmental concerns, but also served as a medium through which other agendas were addressed, by both labour and capital, rather than an issue solely of concern on its own merits. It provided the basis for an expansion in the scope of industrial conflict, which was in the interests of the unions.

For the unions, sustainable development provided a means whereby their weakness in the industrial relations arena nationally could be remedied by a campaign which was not just socialised, but globalised. It was an extension to the global stage of Schattschneider's (1960) dictum that the loser in any conflict will socialise the conflict to draw in other participants to change the balance of power. While any issue is likely to see the 'whirlpooling' of different agendas being drawn into the maelstrom, the process is not random and actors seek to expand or limit the scope of conflict by making or breaking linkages with other issues.[2] For the industry, sustainable development was an agenda which was important for its continued financial performance (which had been historically poor) and its continued 'licence to operate' (a concept that emerged in the mining industry in the mid-1990s). This is not to say that there was not concern on both sides for the issues of environment and development (especially as they relate to indigenous people) which come together under the rubric of sustainable development. Rather, the point is that sustainable development also meant other things to each side, and there was at best a somewhat incidental connection through sustainable development which gave the illusion that the GMI was a response to the union campaign against Rio and (to a lesser extent) others.

The meeting of Dyaks and miners in the Hunter Valley clearly indicated that a linkage had been made between industrial relations and the issues concerning indigenous people which are part of the sustainable development agenda. The campaign against Rio Tinto gave prominence to its corporate conduct in the Third World, but these were in reality concerns added to the traditional issues of industrial relations that were of greater concern to the trade union movement. The 'local' (in the form of industrial relations at a Hunter Valley mine) now had the potential to 'go global.' The mining industry, however, found itself both without a global champion (in the form of an industry association) and ill-equipped to contest those things

---

[2] While the notion of 'whirlpooling' is usually attributed to Henning (1970), it should be noted that he attributed the concept to Ernest S. Griffith (1956, 127).

that might do it harm at a sectoral level, rather than just at the level of the individual firm.

Ultimately, as the Rio case shows, there was potential to link such issues to what can be called 'redistributive' issues, which involve capital and labour in peak associations (Lowi, 1964). For this reason, we will consider later not just the association of firms into sector groups at state, national and international levels, but the relationship between these organizations and peak business groups—*and* we must also consider briefly what was happening with organised labour.

The extent to which the concerns about Rio's performance in the Third World were secondary to the issues of industrial relations can be seen by asking just how serious the threat Rio posed to the Third World was. And, reversing the question, by asking how serious the threat of a campaign based on Third World concerns was to Rio. It is easy to overestimate the importance of both threats, as Rio had relatively *little* exposure to developing countries. Rio's assets were located 45 percent in Australia, 40 percent in North America and 3 percent in Europe—88 percent in 'old' (First and Second World), politically stable areas. Only 3 percent of Rio's assets were in Africa and 5 percent in South America (Gottliebsen 2002). Industrial relations in Australia, the location of the largest share of its assets, was a much more significant factor, though there was good prospectivity outside its traditional areas of investment, and its reputation in these areas was important.

Rio had gained a reputation for aggressive industrial relations at its iron ore mines in the Pilbara region of Western Australia. The rewards for the company were significant: Rio had improved vastly the productivity of its Hamersley Iron subsidiary in the Pilbara, with tonnes per employee rising 4.5 times over 20 years (Gottliebsen 2002), and it had acquired Robe River where aggressive labour relations had been pioneered in the 1980s. A key to this had been the introduction of individual employment contracts under the Western Australian (Richard) Court government's industrial relations policy, which effectively shut the unions out of the mines.

The election of a Liberal-National coalition government and the defeat of the Australian Labor Party (ALP) nationally in 1996 heralded a new era in industrial relations in Australia, which provided Rio with an opportunity to bring its industrial relations practices from its iron ore mines in the West to its coal mines in the East. This was largely because the new legislation (the *Workplace Relations Act 1996*) not only provided for individual work contracts but prohibited so-called secondary boycotts on the threat of substantial penalties and the possibility of damages being awarded against unions. Secondary boycotts had previously limited attempts at industrial relations reform in the coal industry because, in the event of an industrial dispute involving the coal mining union (the CFMEU), the waterfronts would likely be closed down under secondary boycotts by the maritime unions, inflicting heavy costs on the substantially export-oriented industry. Ironically, the first major test of the 1996 legislation involved the dockworkers of the Maritime Union of Australia (MUA), breaking restrictive work practices which had previously resulted in poor 'lift rates' in container cargo terminals, after a bitter dispute.

The MUA set a precedent for the CFMEU campaign against Rio in the 1997 waterfront dispute when it received support from the International Transport Workers Federation (ITWF) to threaten an international ban on shipping. The ICEM was briefed subsequently by the ITWF on the strategy of international campaigns. The resort by the MUA to international support in itself indicated the new realities, because its power to close ports in the days before the *Workplace Relations Act* usually would have sufficed. Economic liberalisation on cabotage also meant fewer crews on ships involved in international trade from Australian ports were now Australian nationals and were therefore not likely to be MUA members. The new industrial laws on secondary boycotts meant the MUA was forced to pursue an international campaign.

The international campaign against Rio Tinto followed immediately from the failure of the CFMEU to get Rio to change its industrial relations policies at the Hunter Valley No 1 mine. The CFMEU was forced to seek allies offshore because it could not win the battle on the ground or in the Industrial Relations Commission, after a full bench verdict overturned a decision to arbitrate the Hunter Valley No 1 dispute. The CFMEU attempted to portray Rio Tinto internationally as a pariah because the company was seeking reform of work practices while attempting to sideline the CFMEU. Individual work contracts posed a threat not so much to workers' incomes as to the union itself, since the company was seeking better productivity by weakening restrictive work practices rather than wage cuts, and individual contracts between the company and workers would have sidelined the CFMEU.

Restrictive work practices in place in the Hunter Valley included: restrictions on freedom to use contractors, part-time, temporary or casual labour on any work as required; restrictions on the right to allocate overtime at management's discretion, rather than through a union seniority list; the right to hire and fire on 'merit' as decided by the company in place of recruitment from a union list of retrenched miners; and retrenchment on a 'last on, first off' basis. The company offered a substantial $10,000 a year pay rise as an inducement as well as concessions in superannuation and medical benefits to anyone accepting an individual contract, but all but seven of the 430 workers at the Mt Thorley mine refused the contracts, insisting instead on a collective agreement, and commencing a five week strike which ended with Rio securing reform, but the CFMEU securing continued representation.

So in the extension of individual work contracts from the Pilbara to the coal mines of the Hunter Valley the CFMEU was seriously weakened by the secondary boycotts provisions of the *Workplace Relations Act*. The eventual gains for the company were even more spectacular than they had been in the Pilbara, with new Rio CEO Leigh Clifford achieving similar gains in coal mine productivity over five years to those that had been achieved in iron ore over a decade, with productivity increasing 3.5-fold at the Blair Athol mine and a similar increase over five years at the Mt Thorley mine (Gottliebsen 2002).

This occurred in a context where the labour movement in Australia was already in some trouble, in both its political and industrial wings. The poor performance of the ALP federally over the decade until 2007 is well-enough known, and its membership had also been in decline. Just as important was the decline in membership of the trade union movement, with which it is formally affiliated (on a state and territory basis).

In a column published in the *Weekend Australian* on 3-4 June 2000, the newspaper's political correspondent, Ian Henderson—a former assistant national secretary of the ALP—pointed out just how significant had been the decline in trade union membership in Australia. In August 1999 1,878,200 people were recorded as trade union members in an official survey. This represented only 25.7 percent of employees overall. Membership was a mere 19.6 percent of employees in the private sector workforce, and it continued to fall to 19.1 percent in 2000 and 17.6 percent by 2003. By August 2003, only one in five female employees and less than one in four males were members of a trade union, although almost 47 percent of public sector employees were (ABS Series 6310.0). By 2106, membership was only 10.4 percent in the private sector and 38.5 percent in the public sector. The changing face of unionism is reflected in the fact that the then president of the peak Australian Council of Trade Unions (ACTU) was a woman who rose through the teaching sector. Gone were the days of blue-singleted blokes dominating unions; service unions were now the powerbases, and the services were more likely *public* services at that. However, a number of senior male union officials, who identified strongly with blue collar workers, rose to national prominence after 2005, largely through media campaigns, and this provided a platform for entry into national politics, via ALP endorsement. By way of contrast, 40.6 percent of the adult workforce were direct shareholders in 1999 and 54 percent were shareholders when indirect shareholding in superannuation and managed funds was taken into account. The number of direct shareholders was 5.7 million—three times the number of union members.

This changed the face of politics, with large numbers of people having interests not just in maximising income and wealth through wages and salaries, but through the profitability of business. Unions, particularly those in traditionally strong sectors such as extractive industries, came under threat. The CFMEU, in particular, was thus angered by the use of individual work contracts by Rio and its plans to change work practices at its Hunter Valley coal mines, and this is a fundamentally important factor in understanding why it and its brother unions sought to expand the conflict internationally, and to the additional domains of human rights, environment and indigenous rights.

The Rio Campaign Goes Global

As noted above, the first signs of the union-led campaign against Rio came in 1998, when ICEM held a meeting in Johannesburg and decided to target Rio. ICEM represented 467 industrial trade unions in 132 countries, covering 20 million workers. Many of these were employed in the mining industry. A key activity of ICEM was negotiating and monitoring global agreements with multinational companies.

This meeting had the objectives of developing a global profile of the company, establishing an international framework for unions dealing with it, and devising a strategy for pressuring Rio Tinto. In a report on this meeting, ICEM focused not just on industrial relations issues but included human rights, environment and indigenous people issues. It then produced two 'white papers' (*Rio Tinto—Tainted Titan* and *Rio Tinto—Behind the Facade*) for the company's 1998 and 1999 annual meetings. In order to take the campaign to the shareholders, CFMEU national secretary, Mr John

Maitland,[3] and ICEM General Secretary, Mr Vic Thorpe, had purchased shares in the conglomerate to gain a voice at the meeting (*Australian Financial Review* 25 May 1998). Maitland and Thorpe, criticized Rio's record on indigenous land rights, environmental management and relations with unions at the London AGM, accusing it of a systematic campaign to undermine collective bargaining.

The campaign also included a complaint to the OECD under its Guidelines for Multinational Enterprises, and a video, 'Naked into the Jungle'. Manheim (2000, 128) describes ICEM's Rio campaign as 'the prototype for the transposition of the corporate campaign from the domestic U.S. arena into the international economic system.' Manheim does not discuss, however, the extent to which it was the extension of an industrial relations campaign from Australia to the international arena, although his appendix summarising union-led campaigns makes a brief reference to these factors (Manheim 2000, 334). At the conference in South Africa in 1998 former Australian Prime Minster and union leader Bob Hawke and former South African President Nelson Mandela were photographed with CFMEU secretary John Maitland to highlight human rights issues. This aspect of the campaign was quickly blunted by Rio; Chairman Sir Robert Wilson was able to undercut the campaign by producing letters at the subsequent Rio annual meeting from Mandela and Amnesty International disassociating themselves from the protest.

The CFMEU then organized the first proxy fight mounted by an Australian trade union. This style of action was being led by the then ACTU Secretary Greg Combet—who went on to be elected to the national parliament for the ALP. Union delegates from Rio operations around the world met in Canberra in February 2000 to plan the campaign. In March 2000 the global proxy campaign was launched with the formation of the Rio Tinto Shareholders Coalition, backed by the AFL-CIO in the US, Trade Union Congress in the UK, and the ICEM, as well as the CFMEU and the ACTU. Then they gave Rio its first fully-fledged proxy fight at the annual meeting of Rio Tinto in Brisbane in May 2000. The union global campaign managed to get the Australian Securities and Investments Commission to order nominee companies to disclose to the coalition the names of shareholders on whose behalf they were acting, the first time this had

[3] Maitland was later convicted of corruption in 2017 over the granting of coal leases by his friend, Resources Minister Ian Macdonald in the NSW ALP government, but both were freed on appeal in February 2019 and a retrial ordered which remains pending at the time of writing.

occurred outside the context of a corporate takeover. The unions also secured the assistance of former ALP minister Susan Ryan, who was president of the Australian Superannuation Trustees Association at the time, to solicit shareholder support within Australia.

Ryan ran an argument that profitability depended on good corporate governance, under which she included good industrial relations, and that superannuation (retirement benefits) fund managers concerned with returns should support the union proxy fight. Since many such funds are industry funds with union representatives on their boards (established under reforms initiated by ALP Treasurer, later Prime Minister, Paul Keating, and promoted by former ACTU secretary Bill Kelty), many were only too willing to accept Ryan's argument. One of the resolutions put to the Rio meeting called on Rio to develop an industrial relations code of conduct which enshrined the rights of collective bargaining and trade union representation in line with ILO standards, and to have its compliance independently verified. Ryan used a cover story in the magazine of the Australian Institute of Company Directors (AICD) to argue that if the company ran down its 'industrial relations infrastructure' it might not be able to retain the workforce to maintain shareholder value. The unions then mounted an investor campaign portraying Rio as a poor performer, underperforming the Dow Jones mining diversified index for the preceding two years. The other resolution put to the meeting sponsored by the coalition would have required Rio's deputy chair to be a non-executive position.

Ryan's role was the signature of a classic corporate campaign, in which a person with good personal credentials had been selected to become the public face of the campaign, masking the identity of the real authors—John Maitland and Tony Maher of the CFMEU. Ryan's job was to widen the campaign and approach audiences valued by the target company, just as Hawke had tried three years earlier to secure Nelson Mandela's support for the Hunter Valley CFMEU. Rio's then general manager corporate affairs, Tim Duncan, maintained that Ryan played the role so well that the AICD missed entirely the point that she was ultimately working for the CFMEU. The industrial relations resolution won 17 percent of the approximately one-third of the total capital which voted, and the corporate governance resolution 20 percent. Duncan argued that most of those voting saw through the resolutions as really being about 'very narrow industrial issues located in the coal fields of the upper Hunter Valley' (Uren 2000).

Ultimately, however, the coal disputes were settled with union representation continuing in the Hunter Valley, but with sweeping reform of work practices that yielded Rio the productivity gains it sought. One observer remarked that there was now less of an ideological emphasis on industrial relations in Rio than there had been in the past, and a much greater focus on outcomes beneficial for shareholders. After that, the global campaign against Rio subsided at least so far as substantial union involvement was concerned. This is hardly surprising: mine workers are in the highest paid sector in Australia, and are after all, ultimately supportive of the industry which employs them, and the alliance with groups which were essentially opposed to mining was unlikely to be more than a tactical one for the unions. The ability of the unions to create alliances and build a global campaign, however, did highlight the lack of an organizational basis for the industry to counter such campaigns in future. While the GMI had a wider base than just the campaign against Rio, the campaign did underscore the need for the industry to get its act together.

The coalition of the unions with environment and indigenous groups was an alliance of convenience, not one based on fundamentals, and was therefore vulnerable to countermeasures. The environment and development NGOs were able, with union funding, to produce better publications and to enhance their visibility, but some NGOs were fundamentally anti-mining whereas ICEM was fundamentally committed to mining. Rio engaged with the union movement at the highest level, and talked with ICEM about the possibility of a global agreement. Some of the union leadership at the international level wanted it. Fred Higgs (ICEM general secretary) and ICEM played a key role in MMSD, with Reg Green representing ICEM on the MMSD Assurance Group. Higgs' view was that unions had a big stake in the mining industry and he was to differentiate his stance from the NGOs during the MMSD process. The CFMEU's John Maitland continued to be disgruntled, but Rio wanted outcomes, so yielded on the question of union agreements to achieve the productivity improvements it wanted.

Rio had also moved on a different front to help divide the union and environment movements, committing $1.4m over four years to WWF to fund a frog conservation program (Burton 2000). This provoked an angry response from John Maitland, who wrote to WWF Australian CEO Dr David Butcher, pointing out that Rio Tinto was the focus of an international campaign on human rights, and its environmental record and occupational health and safety performance and arguing that it was 'stunning' that WWF could associate itself with the company and allow its PR machine to assert how wonderful the company was because it had a partnership with WWF (Moody 2001).

So the international campaign changed little on the ground. It helped focus attention within Rio on productivity outcomes, rather than on ending union representation and thus moved aside some ideologues in Rio. It also encouraged Rio to engage more actively with the investment community, moving it to take a more proactive role in response to the shareholder proxy battle. But the GMI was to be driven by a number of companies, not just Rio, and WMC Resources and Phelps Dodge were marginally ahead of Rio in the vanguard of the GMI, which was fundamentally a response to 'the licence to operate' issue. The industry feared it was being driven out of markets and off land because of perceptions about its behaviour.

At best, the Rio campaign was a catalyst, helping accelerate the move to openness and recognition of the need to engage with stakeholders, but Rio did so by focusing on the key stakeholders—unions and communities, more so than environment and development NGOs—engaging them separately and leaving the more extreme groups to one side. But these developments were well under way in Rio before the union campaign commenced in 1998.

The threat to the licence to operate was greatest for the global players, because they had global reputations to defend. It was not the campaign by unions and its allies against the industry in the form of an international social movement that was to prove important in driving the GMI response, but concerns over access to ground for prospecting and mining development (matters within the *compétence* of national and subnational governments) by companies with global reputations, together with the emergence of an international regulatory agenda that threatened markets for products that were largely undifferentiated. The unions were largely with Rio while on their home ground, but had an interest in making more difficult access to ground in other jurisdictions where production costs (including labour) might be lower. Both these factors reflected to some extent the activities of NGOs, but the main driver was the changing nature of governmental and intergovernmental policy—in short, of governance—rather than the need to respond to the competition of NGOs as participants in social movements, supporting a top-down rather than bottom-up view of the factors driving interest group formation.

And ironically, just as the CFMEU used the Sustainable Development agenda as the basis for globalising its campaign because of threats to its organizational base, the industry quite selectively chose Sustainable Development as its organizing focus because it would maximize associability, carefully avoiding those issues which might have divided the industry.

The Global Mining Industry at the End of the Millennium

The mining industry was not the only sector to be targeted by global social movements at this time. Other corporate sectors also came under pressure during this period to improve their 'corporate social responsibility', but in the mining and metals sector, companies were also coming under increasing pressure over their poor financial performance. In short, the sector was failing to earn the real cost of its capital, meaning that investors would have earned higher returns had they invested in bonds. Rio Tinto CEO Leigh Clifford stated in 2002 that while average annual returns of business globally were 7.35 percent and a slightly higher 8.6 percent in the oil and gas sector, mining was at the bottom with returns on capital of only 4.67 percent (Gottliebsen 2002).

Globalisation had exacerbated the predicament of the mining sector. Not only did an end to the Cold War result in substantial privatization of assets (such as copper producer ZCCM in Zambia, tin producer Comibol in Bolivia, copper producer Tintaya in Peru, and Karaganda Steelworks in Kazakhstan) and the opening up of new areas for exploration, but the competition between the large global players for access to these new exploration and development opportunities brought into sharper focus the important role played by reputation in the granting by governments of a 'licence to operate'. Increasing pressures surrounding existing operations on social and environmental grounds meant that the 'licence to operate' could no longer be taken for granted in any jurisdiction, but a good corporate reputation came to be seen as an almost 'bankable' asset in securing access to new prospects and projects.[4] Privatization did moderate a perennial problem for the industry however: the continuation of mining at below cost at nationalized mines which contributed to low profitability and unstable commodity price cycles.

The industry, led by the large global players with global reputations to defend, was to develop an effectively self-regulatory approach in response to these challenges, raising industry performance through the development of codes of practice. This was sound business, of course, because not only did this response address social concerns, but — inasmuch as higher standards became the norm — raised the costs of entry of new

[4] The concept of a 'social licence to operate' was enunciated by James Cooney, the Vice President of External Relations for Placer Dome Inc., a Vancouver-based Canadian gold mining company, in 1997. In 1996 Placer Dome received criticism after the failure of one its tailings dams in the Philippines.

players. Large, global corporations could spread reputation management costs across a large number of mines; small companies were faced with higher marginal costs of securing their reputations. Just as the widespread cessation of national ownership would make the bottom of commodity cycles more shallow, regulation (albeit self-regulation) would make more costly the entry of new producers that might clip the peaks off the top of the cycle.

Transnational ownership of the largest global players accentuated the willingness of NGOs to criticize corporate behaviour, because, as Mary Douglas (2002) pointed out), many of the complaints about the environmental risks associated with large corporations are essentially attacks on their power and influence. But transnational ownership of the industry leaders could also help drive pressures for a 'race to the top.' The large global players actually had global reputations to worry about—in the manner described by Leonard (1988)—whereas the smaller players frequently had only one or two mines, often located within a single jurisdiction, and were immune from the damage that criticism of their operations might mean for government approvals in other jurisdictions.

The problem for the industry was, many mining operations could be commenced by smaller players, particularly in the gold sector, where operations could start and stop according to gold price movements. Whereas state-owned enterprises wrought havoc on supply and demand when prices were low by continuing to mine below cost, small and artisanal mining clipped returns at the top of commodity cycles. The Esmeralda disaster seemed to typify another problem, because a small undercapitalized operation did serious harm to the reputation of the sector as a whole, which was also dependent on the use of cyanide extraction methods. In an industry which is fundamentally a price taker, this ability for small players to either continue with less than 'best practice' approaches to environmental or indigenous people's issues, or to enter the market with minimal standards was a serious problem as it both limited the ability of any players to bring external diseconomies within their cost structure, and threatened to undermine any pressures for a race to the top among the larger global players, since they were vulnerable to reputational damage at the sectoral level as a result of the practices of the smaller players. Each firm could work on its own reputation, but there was a class of issues which were sectoral in their impact, so that the large players could be harmed by the performance of the small players mining the same product, such as Esmeralda.

These industry characteristics are important. Considered in a global context, the minerals industry is relatively small, despite the appearance that they are large players in countries such as Australia, and despite also the central importance of a range of mined products, especially metals, to many other industrial sectors. In September 2001, the top 150 international minerals companies had a combined market capitalization of only $US224 billion. This was less than the capitalization of single companies in other sectors, such as General Electric ($US469 billion), ExxonMobil ($US289 billion) and Wal-Mart ($US241 billion). The top 10 mining companies had a combined capitalization of $92 billion, with Alcoa valued at $US26 billion, BHP-Billiton at $US25 billion, Anglo-American $US17.5 billion, and Norsk Hydro at $US10 billion. The mining sector represented only 0.6 percent of the value of the capital in the United States (as measured by the S&P 500 index) and 6 percent of the value of the Toronto Stock Exchange 300. It was more significant in Australia, but even there had declined from 26 percent of the value of the All Ordinaries Index in 1996 to 12 percent in 2000 (Allen Consulting Group 2000, 7). By 2008, BHP-Billiton (thanks to acquisitions and organic growth) was valued at $US130 billion, having briefly touched $US160 billion, and had issued a takeover bid for the $US50 billion Rio Tinto.

By the late 1990s, the mining industry was declining in size and significance, and it was not particularly well-organized to affect its fate. Ineffective participation at the United Nations Conference on Sustainable Development at Rio de Janiero in 1992 had seen the adoption of a work program in Agenda 21, Chapter 19 that was to address chemicals that were persistent, toxic, and bioaccumulative, and this included almost every non-ferrous and non-precious metal. There were about 30-40 large multinational corporations which explored, mined, smelted, refined, and sold metal concentrates and metals on world markets. Low commodity prices and poor returns among the big players produced greater concentration in the late 1990s. Mergers included BHP and Billiton, Cominco and Teck, and the acquisition of Asarco by Grupo Mexico, CRA and North Ltd by Rio Tinto, and MIM Holdings by Xstrata. Political association was, for various reasons, more problematic. Of great significance were the differences between firms producing different commodities.

The degree of concentration of ownership varied significantly across of producers of metals and minerals. Steel had a relatively dispersed structure, with the 10 largest firms producing less than 30 percent of global output, but the ten largest producers of aluminium accounted for more than 90 percent of global output. There was little vertical integration in iron and steel and, of the top five iron ore producers, only Rio Tinto was active in as many as three countries. In aluminium, the industry was highly vertically-integrated, but this was atypical of the sector. Co-products were often significant. For example, firms producing nickel from sulphide ores (such as Inco, Norilsk, and Falconbridge) derived significant by-product revenues from copper, cobalt, and precious metals. This meant that there was significant trade in non-ferrous metal concentrates and residues, many of which were potentially classifiable as hazardous wastes, which was why the industry became concerned over the proposal to adopt a trade ban under the Basel Convention (Kellow 1999a). There were thus also numerous small traders, fabricators and recyclers in non-ferrous metals, although there were some exceptions, such as the fully integrated multinational copper producer Phelps Dodge, which was involved in all stages of copper production from mining to wire making.

The large multinational companies were highly visible and thus relatively well-aware of the need for a 'licence to operate'. Many had developed codes of practice, business plans, and reporting procedures in response to environmental and social concerns. They were more likely to make a substantial effort to assess, minimize, and mitigate many of the environmental and social impacts of a new mine development, to develop an effective closure plan, and to seek to engage with the local community. This was driven by their concern with global reputation, and they could more readily afford to meet the costs of such improved behaviour. Smaller companies could buy in consultant expertise to deal with development approval issues such as environment or indigenous rights, but these concerns were necessarily less well-embedded in such companies. They were vulnerable to competition from those not globally-focused, who might not need to be overly concerned with global reputation, and were more likely to be able to rely upon structural power within a jurisdiction to reduce the costs of regulation.

This included intermediate companies operating several small to medium-sized (typically gold or base metal) mines in one or a few countries selling concentrates to a trader or custom smelter, but also companies known as 'juniors', which might be involved exclusively in mineral exploration, negotiating agreements with larger players for the development of an ore body they had discovered, or perhaps trying to exploit the ore body themselves. Canada had more than 1,000 junior companies (compared with about only 100 in the United States), and they were also active in Latin America, Africa, the Pacific Rim, Europe, and Australia — where they are referred to colloquially as 'dirt diggers' and 'rock kickers.'

While some intermediate and junior companies met the highest environmental and social standards, they were arguably in a minority, and many considered sustainable development to be a 'big company game' that had little relevance to them, as they had less financial capacity to meet higher standards and fewer reputational reasons to want to do so. Regulation, be it state-imposed or self-regulation through an industry code of practice, was likely to raise the costs of their doing business, and disadvantage them relative to the global players.

While there had been considerable privatization over the previous 20 years there were still many state-owned companies, though they were concentrated in a few countries, such as China, although in Chile, the large copper-molybdenum producer Codelco was state-owned. The state took a minority share in mining activities in a number of countries, such as Papua New Guinea, Botswana, and Namibia. India still had huge state-owned companies: coal producer CIL, steel producer Sail, Hindustan Copper and Hindustan Zinc, and aluminium company Nalco. Many of these were small by global standards, had few reputational concerns (especially as they operated in a single jurisdiction) and enjoyed a privileged position in relation to the state which, as owner, was caught in a classic poacher-gamekeeper problem.

Conclusion and Prospect

With the tenth anniversary of the Rio Earth Summit in mind, in late 1998 ten of the largest mining companies decided to embark on a new initiative intended to achieve a serious change in the way industry approached contemporary problems. They called this the Global Mining Initiative. It included a program of internal reform, a review of the various associations they belonged to, and a rigorous study of the societal issues they had to face. Through the World Business Council for Sustainable Development (WBCSD), they commissioned the International Institute of Environment and Development (IIED) to undertake a scoping study in May 1999 to set out the global challenge of sustainable development facing the mining sector and to propose the scope of a two-year process of participatory analysis to explore the role of the sector in the transition to sustainable development. A team of IIED researchers reviewed existing initiatives and materials, and consulted over 150 separate individuals and organizations to understand their views of how the minerals sector's contribution to sustainable development could be improved and to develop a more detailed framework for the process.

This process led to the formation for the first time of a comprehensive mining and metals NGO at the international level, replacing a much more limited predecessor. Prior to this, the mining industry had simply not organized effectively at the international level. This was partly because of the complex industry structure described above, but also because Lindblom's 'privileged position of business' does not translate well to the international level. As a result, the international level is less propitious for business, and it tends to invest less at the international level than at the national level, so its greater ability to mobilize resources relative to non-business groups is less relevant (see Kellow 2002).

Our research questions, explored in this book, are these:

Why did the sector begin organizing internationally? How did associations change at the sub-national and national levels? Did factors within the industry, the emergence of countervailing groups, or shifts in the policy '*compétences*' at each level drive the changes?

What is its relationship with peak business associations at each level of governance?

How has the sector's relationship with labour at each level changed and what part (if any) has this played in the formation of an international association?

We shall later explore some of these issues by mapping interest groups and governance structures at various levels in the final chapter. To anticipate that discussion, we would argue that this study is a unique attempt to do so, for—while others have sought to account for developments in interest group formation at various levels (nations, the European Union, and so on)—we seek to capture and account for simultaneous developments at three levels in a way that promises rich insight into some significant theoretical perspectives on interest groups. Our national and sub-national level foci will be Australia and the Australian states and territories—partly out of convenience (for that is where we are based, and the system with which we are familiar), but partly, too, because Australian actors played significant roles in the processes we seek to study. But mining is a much more significant sector in the Australian economy than it is in Canada or the US (which might also have served as case studies, since they also possess federal constitutions); mining enjoys greater (though declining) structural power in Australia, and this change is one which we thought might have important consequences.

Our focus, then, is Australia and its states and their state chambers of mines, and the formation of an international sector association, though we will make some comparative comments along the way about the state of the play elsewhere and provide some insight into other industrial sectors.

CHAPTER 2

EXPLAINING THE ABSENCE OF AN INTERNATIONAL MINING ASSOCIATION

We can see from the snapshot in Chapter 1 that the mining industry globally, while producing products of great significance for industry, was relatively small in sheer size and was highly fragmented and lacking in vertical integration. This explains a little of why the industry was not well-organised internationally, but there are other industries that have been more highly organised globally for much longer than mining. The challenge is to explain this 'arrested development' of the mining industry.

We must begin this discussion by noting that the organization of business as a whole at the international level is more problematic than at the national level, which is the level on which traditional studies of interest groups focus, and the reason for this is that international arenas are less propitious than national arenas. We can explain why this is so by pointing out why business is influential at the national level. Lindblom suggested that business enjoys a 'privileged position' in politics, but this privilege is confined mostly to the domestic level and does not transfer well to the international level. Lindblom's analysis of the power of business identifies three factors which give it such a degree of influence that he concludes it enjoys a 'privileged' position (Lindblom 1977).

The first factor relates to the structural dependence of the state on business; the second, is its knowledge and expertise; and the third, is its superior ability to organize and mobilize resources. Structural dependency theory suggests that the state enjoys a degree of autonomy from business power, but in a market system is structurally dependent on private sector profitability. Governments increasingly depend on popular support and legitimacy, which in turn relies on jobs and prosperity in the private sector and the ability to fund programs from taxation revenue. In an era of globally mobile capital, nation-states have to compete to attract investment, and thus are driven 'to act on behalf of, rather than at the behest of, business' (Levy and Egan 1998, 342) which gives business its 'privileged position'. International organizations are not subject to these structural dependencies and are not open to influence to the same extent. For this reason, they constitute less attractive targets for business influence, and when business does attempt to exert its influence in international negotiations it is often to try to contest regulation at the national level (Levy and Egan 1998, 343).

International organisations such as the UN are not directly dependent for revenues upon healthy national economies and are above any competition to attract capital, and thus they are insulated from the economic consequences of international policies to the extent that this is a source of concern to some observers (Levy and Egan 1998, 347). Levy and Egan note that despite the vast resources potentially available to business groups, their influence has not overwhelmed that of environmental NGOs at international negotiations (Levy and Egan 1998, 345). Their influence is also weakened by the diversity of industry interests which prevents business from acting as a cohesive bloc (Levy and Egan 1998, 346), a point to which we shall return.

While the rhetoric in environmental politics at the international level sounds redistributive—something which is accentuated by linkage with development and human rights issues—the policies adopted are usually regulatory, and thus they divide business along sectoral lines (Lowi 1964). Peak business groups such as the International Chamber of Commerce are frequently split along sectoral lines and even within sectors the interests of fossil fuel industries such as coal, oil and gas producers are substantially different when confronted by climate change policies, since they each give rise to progressively fewer emissions, with fuel switching to gas providing the easiest way of achieving substantial emission reductions. Intergovernmental organizations (IGOs) often expect business to speak with a single voice on issues on which no single position is possible (and on which national governments would not expect to hear anything other than a discordant chorus), and so business often says little of consequence. The secretariat of the Framework Convention on Climate Change (FCCC) expected the International Chamber of Commerce to speak for all business, for example.

The second factor to which Lindblom attributes the superior bargaining resources held by business is its command over the knowledge and practical expertise which is necessary to the development and implementation of effective policy. But IGOs are not responsible for the implementation of international policies, so the effectiveness of this leverage is diminished in the international arena. As Underdal (1980) observed, global policy is often marked by a 'vertical disintegration' to which the differential influence of business at international and national levels contributes. This points to a perennial problem with the relationship between the development and implementation of global policy, captured by the observation by Joseph Weiler (1988) that in the EEC those first to agree were usually those least likely to implement. Indeed, the poor implementation of multilateral environmental agreements (MEAs) is an area of considerable concern. Implementation is a task which is undertaken by nation-states, which continue to guard jealously their sovereignty in the face of any proposals for implementation by international actors—to an extent often overlooked by those tending to overestimate the extent of globalisation. (The ability of NGOs to report instances of default to IGOs is for this reason one of the factors which gives them influence).

The third factor is the superior ability of business to mobilize resources when compared with other groups. This factor does not appear to hold with regard to international environment politics, where PINGOs have substantial budgets which not only are comparable to or larger than those of business groups, but are also larger than many relevant intergovernmental organisations, such as UNEP. In part, this reluctance of business to commit resources in the international arena probably reflects the other two factors which make this arena relatively less propitious than the domestic route. (See Kellow 2002).

NGOs are therefore more likely to be transnational actors than are corporations. Levy and Egan (1998, 355) maintain that NGOs advocate international regulation because they recognize that many states would not take strong action without international agreement because of the structural dependence of the state on capital, and unilateral action is likely to result in high costs for little environmental benefit, so they promise to spread the pain of regulation by imposing it on all nations. This, however, ignores Vogel's (1997) analysis of the *advantages* which might lie in a 'first mover' strategy if only domestic approaches can subsequently be successfully internationalised, and the more general point that regulation creates winners *and* losers, and is by no means universally opposed. For this reason, business groups can frequently be found supporting international regulation which internationalises their domestic regulatory disadvantage, which either ensures that international competitors face the same disadvantage or that export opportunities are created for those who can meet the new international standards because they have been required to do so domestically. As Sandbrook (1997, 649) noted, transnational corporations often want rules to be harmonised, and have an interest in spreading effective international regulation to avoid being undercut on environmental costs. He saw a need to enhance business participation in international negotiation processes—to 'bring the private sector into the discourse' (1997, 649). Environment NGOs are more likely to be international actors not only because the arena is less propitious for its business opponents, but because it is also more favourable for them.

The international arena is more favourable to NGOs because the functions they can perform for IGOs translate into influence (they can exchange 'access goods'). ENGOs are able to provide lobbying not just at international meetings, but at the national level, where UNEP cannot lobby without violating Article 2(7) of the UN Charter which forbids intervention in matters essentially within the domestic jurisdiction of any state. Even without this impediment to domestic level lobbying in its constitution, however, it is doubtful whether an agency like UNEP possesses either the resources or the capacity to be effective in such a role since it faces problems of severe overload. The transnational activities of ENGOs are (for this reason) important to the development of MEAs, and they assist UNEP greatly by being able to campaign for proposals where UNEP cannot go.

At the international level, therefore, the relative advantage of environment and business groups is the reverse of that which obtains at the domestic level. Business interests have good relations with some national delegations in the climate change arena, but these are based primarily on congruence of interests between industries and nation-states (Levy and Egan 1998, 344). The climate change case suggests that, while business is active at the international level in trying to influence regulatory outcomes, 'such action in this arena, rather than eclipsing the national state, is largely channelled through it, and is frequently directed toward blocking strong international action' (Levy and Egan 1998, 348).

The environment NGOs also enjoy an advantage in 'discursive power' in the international arena, where 'blame and shame' rhetoric is often employed, assisted by the linkage forged with international redistributive politics. Sandbrook noted that in the Commission for Sustainable Development, 'attendance is made up of environment ministries or the UN representatives who play out the same games in every forum. There is very little evidence of the finance or big economic players' (Sandbrook 1997, 646). Sandbrook was critical of the populist writing which sees corporate players as villains.[1] Rather than excluding business, he saw a need to 'bring the private sector into the discourse' (Sandbrook 1997, 649). Yet the redistributive rhetoric is more amenable to the tactics of 'blame and shame' employed by environment NGOs than the interest-based claims of business,

[1] Sandbrook cites as an example of this perspective David Korten, *When Corporations Rule the World.* London, Earthscan, 1996.

and the expectation by IGOs that business must speak with one voice on what are essentially regulatory matters masquerading as redistributive issues almost guarantees that business will (in a relative sense at least) strike its tent and organise elsewhere to maximise influence.

In contrast to the chemicals sector, the mining industry is generally well-represented by industry associations at the national and subnational levels, but has lacked effective international representation. Chemicals companies want international harmonisation of risk management and licensing approvals and patent protection. Most mining industry associations have been overwhelmingly concerned with *production*—with access to prospects, mine site approvals, and issues of royalties and sovereign risk. National or subnational governments distribute property rights (rights for exploration and exploitation) to produce a product indistinguishable from those of other firms and other countries and so continue to be significant agents for interaction by firms or associations, but whether the state enjoys relatively greater power because of the fixed nature of resources (Krasner 1995, 268) is questionable, because capital is mobile and prospects are numerous. Any patents are confined to production processes. Environmental concerns, when they emerged, centred largely on the impact of mining and site rehabilitation. These were clearly national level concerns, and there was little need for engagement at the international level (aside from reputational concerns).

As we noted earlier, there is also an absence of vertical integration. Aluminium aside, producers of metals have been organised quite separately from those who used metals and who were exposed to consumer issues, and there is generally a clear division between the mining and refining sector and the metals manufacturing and fabricating sector. In the US, the Copper and Brass Fabricators split from the copper mining industry over thirty years previously, largely over trade, issues such as protection from imports, and these interests continue to diverge. For example, restrictions on exports of copper scrap advantage fabricators, since the US is a net exporter and a ban would drive down prices for fabricators.

At the international level the degree of organisation of the industry has been low, except in numerous commodity associations focussing on information exchange and publications, research and development, conference and seminar provision, and product promotion. Such groups included the International Copper Association, International Magnesium Association, International Manganese Institute, Nickel Development Institute, European Lead Development Committee, Lead Development Association, Cadmium

Association, and Zinc Development Association. There was a greater focus on chemical hazards within the nickel sector, largely as the result of the association of some species of nickel compounds with occupational cancer and the acute toxicity of one compound (nickel carbonyl). The Nickel Development Institute (NiDI, which promotes nickel products) was augmented by the Nickel Producers Environmental Research Association (NiPERA).

The most significant development in the representation of the mining and metals industry in the emerging international environmental policy arena was the formation in 1991 of the International Council on Metals and the Environment (ICME), largely in response to the holding of UNCED in Rio in 1992. Remarkably, ICME was the first and only sector-wide group in the non-ferrous metals sector, the only organization in which businesses in the sector came together on a sectoral rather than a commodity basis. ICME was formed out of the major industry players which were members of the London Metal Exchange, which meet each October for an industry conference and dinner—until ICME, the only regular point of global contact for the industry players. (See, for example, Clow 1992).

ICME had a limited impact, and the leading companies at the turn of the millennium undertook the Global Mining Initiative outside the auspices of ICME, although at the lead of the then current ICME President. The purpose of this book is to explore this contrast between chemicals and mining and metals, by asking what drove such reluctant associates as the metals industry together at the international level. Mining industry associations at the international level are much weaker than chemicals. The sector has been more fragmented, and it organised at the sectoral level only belatedly. In addressing this puzzle, we provide some insight into the global organization of business more generally.

The International Council on Metals and the Environment - 1991

To highlight the significance of the GMI, it is worth looking at its main precursors. In doing so, we will draw upon a review conducted (for MIM) in late 1994,[2] updated by the addition of more contemporary material on

[2] One of the present authors (Kellow) conducted this review for MIM Holdings Ltd, which later withdrew from membership of ICME (Kellow 1994). This was not recommended in the report, but the report was critical of the adequacy of the then existing structures, the environmental performance of the mining industry, and its

associations which still exist, since this account serves two purposes, the historical and the contextual.

Prior to the GMI, the most significant development in the representation of the mining and metals industry in the emerging international environmental policy arena had been the formation in 1991 of the International Council on Metals and the Environment (ICME). In the view of one industry association insider, ICME had been set up by Gerry Ellis and Hugh Morgan, then CEOs of BHP and WMC respectively, but despite these antipodean origins, it was later seen as being too close to the Canadian and US companies, with the ICME Secretary-General Gary Nash being regarded by some as close to Bob Muth from ASARCO.

ICME was focused more on consumption issues (metal toxicity and safety) rather than production issues (indigenous people, mine site rehabilitation, tailings dams and the other parts of the sustainability debate), though its work in these areas grew over the 1990s. Gary Nash came from an industry association background in asbestos, and there was a fear behind ICME that toxics regulation might limit markets, rather than a concern with getting access to ground.

The formation of ICME was encouraged particularly by the moves against lead in the United States and reflected a desire on the part of the major non-ferrous metals producers to be more effective politically at the international level (Kellow, 1999). It must be stated, however, that the motivation of some companies in joining was questionable. Some European companies were seen to join to prevent a North American dominance, and—perhaps more importantly—some joined to prevent ICME from 'doing harm' by submitting voluntarily to regulation, as the chemical industry had tended to do. ICME was therefore limited in its effectiveness somewhat by this lack of clarity over its role.

ICME was governed by a Board of Directors comprising senior executives from each of the member companies, essentially the major non-ferrous metals producers internationally. It was based in Ottawa and operated in 1994 on a budget of only $Can1.5m pa with a staff of four (plus

---

poor commitment to supporting both those associations then in existence and what could be termed the sustainable development agenda. There was nothing in that project brief that limited the independence or scope of the report's author, but (in the interests of disclosure) the reader should be aware of how interest in the current work was sparked. Conducting that review undoubtedly gave the author insights and contacts which have helped the current research.

secretarial support). It operated four standing committees: Environmental Stewardship; Safe Use of Metals; Health; and Communications.

The model for the formation of ICME was the chemical industry with its ‘Responsible Care®’ program developed after the Bhopal disaster in India. Responsible Care® was a Canadian concept, which was picked up enthusiastically by the CEOs of the large chemical companies. For this reason, CEOs were seen as the appropriate people to be involved in ICME, since they were able to commit their companies on the spot at Board meetings. When Greenpeace launched a campaign against chlorine, for example, chemical industry CEOs committed $60m over five years on the spot to respond to the campaign. Middle management would be unable to do this, and such a rapid response would not be possible in a federation of national associations, which would each need to consult its members. Ironically, by targeting chlorine (and thus a large number of organochlorines) Greenpeace provided an associational basis for the whole industry, since all companies had products containing chlorine. It was always a struggle for ICME to get a similar level of engagement from mining industry CEOs, and membership was overwhelmingly of larger companies. We argue here that the origins of ICME were only partly motivated by countervailing factors, related to consumption issues such as toxicity.

The concern over those issues had emerged via what were widely considered as losses for the industry: Chapter 19 of Agenda 21 coming out of the UN’s Rio conference in 1992, and the ban amendment to the Basel Convention. While Agenda 21 was merely ‘noted’ by governments at Rio, rather than adopted as a binding commitment, it had assumed some epistemic hegemony and Chapter 19 included the aim of phasing out chemicals which were ‘toxic, persistent and bioaccumulative’— a description which fitted almost all metals under some circumstances. Metals were elements, so they were necessarily persistent. Most were also toxic at some dosage, despite the fact that many (such as copper, zinc, iron) were also essential minerals in human nutrition. And many were bioaccumulative: some species bioaccumulated nickel, for example, though this caused them no obvious harm. Bioaccumulation was taken as a proxy in Agenda 21 for the more worrying biomagnification, or the increasing concentration of chemicals up trophic levels. Moves, led particularly by the Nordic nations, in the OECD and European Union to put Chapter 19 of Agenda 21 into effect were seen by the metals industry as a significant threat to its markets.

Morgan, together with Gerry Ellis, then CEO of BHP, had played a key role in the establishment of ICME, but its remit was seen as ‘too narrow’ and it was increasingly seen by the Australians and South Africans as too close to the US and the Canadians. Secretary-General of ICME, Gary Nash, was seen by some as resisting a broader role and a location closer than Ottawa to significant intergovernmental organizations. Nash saw advantages in an Ottawa location because of the access to information his contacts gave him. He maintained that his contacts with insiders in the Canadian government gave him access to information at the international level. He may well have been correct, but the question for the industry leaders was whether this access outweighed the locational disadvantages of Ottawa.

The activities of ICME reflected these origins, with much of its effort being directed to promoting sound environmental practice in the mining industry. Its small budget limited the ability of ICME to play an effective role as an interest group at the international level, which was essentially its other main function. It identified common policy issues, helped develop consensus positions on these and provided members and national associations with information which allowed them to play this role more effectively, but it operated under considerable resource constraints.

In comparison with the chemicals industry organisation at the international level, ICME was clearly limited by not including the ferrous and aluminium sectors and by providing for only informal liaison with national industry associations and international commodity associations. This limited the resource base and the coherence of the Council. The scope of ICME was narrow, but it had never been intended that it have a broader scope.

ICME tried to play a greater coordinating role by involving the international commodity associations as active participants in its committees and on one or two occasions each year it brought the key national associations together. The formalisation of links would have helped build a sense of community within the industry, but this was rejected by the Council, as was the suggestion of associate membership for the steel industry. Invitations to aluminium companies to join were rejected by those companies.

Some of the impetus for the GMI was born out of frustration with what could be achieved by ICME, which had a limited mandate, tended to produce lowest common denominator responses, and suffered from a lack of willingness by members to expand its budget (though it did double over the decade).

Some reported that Gary Nash resisted a wider role for ICME, and there was an element of US and Canada vs Australia and South Africa in the push for review, but Hugh Morgan was ICME president at the time the GMI was established, and one insider at the formative stage of GMI was insistent that Nash was cooperative with the GMI and the review of industry associations. Nash had been badgering members for years over the need for CEO involvement, so was clearly in favour of some kind of change, though did not favour the move away from Ottawa (where his contacts lay) that was to come. The architects of the GMI knew they needed to go beyond ICME with its now $3m budget, but they did not want the reform process to be seen as another industry association push.

European Associability

In addition to ICME, there were numerous metals associations operating at the international level in the mid-1990s, but most of these were focused on particular commodities, rather than being multi-metal sector groups. The one exception (though it operated only at the European level) was Eurometaux (the European Association of Metals). Eurometaux is the classic example of an association forming in response to factors associated with governance structures—that is, 'top-down' factors. It was established in 1957 pursuant to the Rome Treaty, and was known initially as the Comité de Liaison des Industries de Métaux Non Ferreux de la Communauté Economique Européenne. In 1988 it was constituted as an international association governed by Belgian law under the name of Eurometaux when the way in which Community legislation and its policies were developing called for an enlarged and reinforced industry presence at European level.

Eurometaux saw itself as providing the interface between the European non-ferrous metals industry and the European authorities as well as international or intergovernmental bodies. It was committed to establishing dialogue with the international or intergovernmental bodies in order to ensure early consultation in all fields of policy and legislation that might affect industry and to represent the sector's views and positions in this respect. It therefore adopted a role of representation outside Europe. Eurometaux also incorporated the views of the diversity of each of different subsectors through its metal groups (Copper, Lead, Nickel, Precious Metals) and its members which were international commodity groups (European Aluminium Association, IZA-Europe, OECAM). It also networked with sector-related international or European organisations (such as BIR, ILZRO, ECI, ICA, IZA, the Cobalt Institute, NiDI, the International Cadmium Association, and NiPERA). In all, Eurometaux had thirteen company members, eight international members and metal groups, and 22 national members.

Eurometaux grouped together the trade associations of the twelve Member States of the European Communities and the seven States of the European Free Trade Association, representing the interests of the national mining and non-ferrous metals industries. The Commission of the European Communities (CEC), enjoyed close cooperation with Eurometaux, which coordinated data collection among members and provided a single point of contact between the industry and the Commission. A similarly close working relationship also existed between the Commission and Euromines on mining issues, but there is now little mining activity in Europe. The budget of Eurometaux was around 50 million Belgian Francs in 1994 ($US1.5m—increased to about $2m by 2001), employing 12 people (compared with four in ICME with a similar budget at that time). By way of comparison, the European Chemical Industries Council (CEFIC) had an undisclosed budget, but employed a staff of 85, in addition to the participation of many staff from member companies on various projects.

Eurometaux had both vertical (specific metals) and horizontal (specific issues) committees and began paying increased attention to the 'horizontal' issues. Committees included Research and Development, Energy, Communication, and Environment, which included their Health and Safety Working Parties. Eurometaux was becoming increasingly involved in environmental policy discussions. As the Association noted:

> In certain specific fields, the [European] Commission is gradually becoming more anxious to have a constructive dialogue with the industry. It has just announced the setting-up of an 'Advisory Forum on the Environment'. Various industry associations, including Eurometaux, have accepted the Commission's invitation to discuss with the latter 'lasting development policies' for implementation at Community level.
>
> The generalization of these problems should somewhat reassure the industry...
>
> The actual impact of this generalization of environment policy on the industry will depend to a large extent on the quality of the replies which it is capable of giving to the many basic questions put to it. In this context, it is important for the non-ferrous metals industry to be constructive, united and credible in its choices.[3]

[3]Kellow 1994, 20-21.

While Eurometaux focused on metals, the European Association of Mining Industries (Euromines) was the recognised representative of the European metals and minerals mining industry in Europe, primarily from the mining end. Its primary objective was to promote the industry and maintained relations with European institutions at all levels. It also provided services to its members with regard to EU policy and a network for information exchange and co-operation throughout the mining sector within Europe. Euromines also had an international outlook, and fostered contacts with other parts of the mining community throughout the world.

The membership of Euromines was comprised a federation of nine national mining federations (Austria, France, Germany, Greece, Ireland, Finland, Sweden, the United Kingdom and Turkey), sixteen direct company members and five associate members. Euromines represented large and small companies and subsidiaries in Europe and elsewhere. Based in Brussels, it held membership meetings twice a year, with working committees and groups meeting more frequently throughout the year. Its major activities cover the areas of environment, health & safety, R&D, communication, and international co-operation.

International commodity associations

The International Copper Association is a trade association whose major goal is to promote the use of copper worldwide by implementing projects targeting various end-use applications and geographic markets. Its members were corporations, both producers and fabricators. With a budget of over US$10 million in 1993, the association was one of the largest in the sector. The ICA was also expanding rapidly. Its budget had increased by 150 percent since 1989, funded almost entirely through increased members' dues.[4] The ICA was regarded as a good model for commodity associations in terms of fee structure. Fees were based on production tonnages and members only paid once. The ICA then paid national development associations, so a single fee cascaded down. By the turn of the century it had an annual budget of $30m.

The ICA was developing environmental programmes, but they remained secondary to the Association's market and product development activities. The Association appeared to have been forced into a defensive position by the internationalisation of environmental regulation. Thus, the ICA stated that its Environmental Service activities 'aim to dispel

[4]International Copper Association Ltd. 1993 Annual Report.

misconceptions about copper in the environment possessed by the public, the business community and governments throughout the world.'[5]

The International Primary Aluminium Institute (IPAI) represented aluminium producers globally, with membership made up of companies. The Association had around 40 members in over 20 countries. Though having only a small staff, it produced a range of publications, and appeared to focus on information gathering and exchange. It had a number of committees including Environmental and Health Committees. (Aluminum had been implicated as a possible factor in Alzheimer's disease). The aluminium industry, like the iron and steel industry, was strongly integrated vertically, with the same firms often involved from bauxite mining through refining, smelting and fabrication, and thus maintained its own representative association, and was less involved with 'horizontal' issues or with sector associations than either non-ferrous or precious metal producers.

There was a range of Iron & Steel Institutes and Associations, international, regional and national in scope. They represented producers but also users and included the International Iron and Steel Institute (IISI), the Latin American Iron & Steel Institute, South East Asia Iron & Steel Institute, and BCIRA (previously British Cast Iron Research Association), among others. Between them, these organisations represented considerable resources and membership. BCIRA alone, for example, had a budget around US$5 million and a staff of 100. These organisations dealt largely in research and development, information exchange and members' interests. The IISI had an Environmental Affairs Committee.

Groups in this industry included:

- International Iron and Steel Institute: 165 members, 20 staff.
- Latin American Iron & Steel Institute: 178 members, 22 staff.
- South East Asia Iron & Steel Institute (Companies, ministerial representatives from 9 countries):18 staff.
- BCIRA. 400 members, 100 staff.
- European Independent Steelworks Association. 10 members, 2 staff.
- Federation of Indonesian Iron and Steel Manufacturers. 104 members.
- Iron and Steel Institute of Japan.
- Swedish Steel Producers Association. 24 members, 30 staff.

---

[5]ICA 1993, 10.

A range of other associations existed in the sector, overwhelmingly organised vertically, and focussing on information exchange and publications, research and development, conference and seminar provision, and product promotion. Some of these were:

- International Lead & Zinc Study Group. 32 members, including governments and industry advisers. 32 countries.
- International Magnesium Association. Based in the USA. 80 members in 20 countries.
- International Manganese Institute (previously the Manganese Centre). 40 members.
- Nickel Development Institute (NiDI). 16 members in 7 countries.
- European Lead Development Committee. 8 members in 8 countries.
- Lead Development Association. 20 members in 10 countries. Budget of £300,000.
- International Cadmium Association. 34 members. Budget of £100,000.
- Zinc Development Association. 16 members.

These were only some of the international commodity-based associations. Their full extent revealed just how fragmented the sector was, because to the above list could be added the following: Cobalt Development Association, Cobalt Institute, Gold Institute, Industrial Minerals Association, International Cadmium Association, International Chromium Development Association, International Lead Zinc Research Organisation, International Molybdenum Association, International Tin Research Institute, International Tungsten Industry Association, International Wrought Copper Council, International Zinc Association, Lead Industries Association, Nickel Producers Environmental Research Association, Silver Institute, Uranium Institute, World Coal Institute, World Gold Council,

Each of these associations were separate and distinct, whereas in the chemicals sector (for example) commodity groups were integrated into national and international chemicals industry associations. Regional networks or associations (other than Eurometaux and Euromines) were notable by their relative absence. Representation to international forums did not generally occur at the level of the mining industry. Most activities were conducted at the commodity level, or through broader associations, such as the International Chamber of Commerce, dealing with horizontal issues that extended beyond the minerals sector. (Membership of the ICC was through its national committees).

The principal exceptions were Eurometaux and Euromines, which had ongoing roles in EU consultative frameworks. Other exceptions included the ASEAN Federation of Mining Associations which was small and had no permanent staff, and the Council of Mining & Metallurgical Institutions (CMMI), which had 11 association members from 5 Commonwealth countries. In addition, there were or had been a number of associations of mineral exporting countries of which nation states were members, some initially modelled (somewhat hopefully) on OPEC, but none as successful. These included:

- Association of Iron Ore Exporting Countries (presently inactive) (nine members)
- Association of Tin Producing Countries (seven members)
- Intergovernmental Council of Copper Exporting Countries (five members)
- International Bauxite Association (ten members).

National Mining Industry Associations.

In the US, the National Mining Association (NMA) was formed from the 1995 merger of the National Coal Association (NCA) and the American Mining Congress (AMC), which had been founded in 1917 and 1897 respectively. The NMA is the only national trade organization representing the interests of the mining industry at the national level. Its membership of more than 325 included corporations from all mining sectors including coal, metal and industrial mineral producers, mineral processors, equipment manufacturers, bulk transporters, engineering firms, consultants, financial institutions and other companies that supply goods and services to the mining industry. It also included thirteen state or regional associations, ten state or regional coal associations, plus the American Coal Council and Lignite Energy Council. The NMA provided a single sector group for domestic mining representation.

The first Chamber of Mines in South Africa, the Chamber of Mines in Johannesburg, was formed on 7 December 1887 and was succeeded by the predecessor of the modern Chamber in October 1889, the Witwatersrand Chamber of Mines (1889-1896). The various incarnations of the South African Chamber reflect the history of the country, changing first during the Boer rebellion against the British to Chamber of Mines of the South African Republic (1897-1901), then the Transvaal Chamber of Mines (1902-1952), Transvaal and Orange Free State Chamber of Mines (1953-1967), and finally the Chamber of Mines of South Africa (1968-). The categories of membership and numbers reflected the predominance of gold, platinum, diamond and coal mining in South Africa. There were twelve Gold Mining members, ten Coal Mining members, two Diamond Mining members, six Platinum members, one Base and Industrial member, and eleven in the 'other' category.

The Mining Association of Canada (MAC), the national organization of the Canadian mining industry, was formed in 1935. It comprised companies engaged in mineral exploration, mining, smelting, refining and semi-fabrication, accounting for the majority of Canada's output of metals and major industrial materials. MAC's mission is essentially to promote the interests of the industry nationally and (unlike the NMA) internationally. It worked closely with provincial and other industry groups across Canada and in other countries, but the primary role of MAC was the presentation of industry information and views to the federal government of its members throughout Canada and internationally. (The MAC code is binding on those who adopt it). Neither the MAC nor the NMA appears to have had the focus on indigenous affairs of the Minerals Council of Australia. Membership was open to all firms (subject to the approval of the Board of Directors) in mining and related businesses, and most companies with producing mines and plants were members. There was a special category of Associate Member for suppliers. Provincial and territorial mining associations and chambers of mines were represented by means of their elected representatives being invited to serve as Honorary Directors. It had 26 members and 28 associate members.

The Japan Mining Industry Association was typical in structure of many national associations. Membership was of companies (59 in 1994), with an extensive committee structure, including an Environmental Control Committee. The organisation also had an Environmental and Safety Department, and a budget of ¥420 million. While the Japanese Association, and others like it, focused on intra-industry matters including information exchange and market monitoring and development, lobbying was also as an important activity. Similar organizations existed in Brazil (Instituto Brasileiro de Mineracao, or IBRAM), Sweden (Svenska Gruvföreningen, the Swedish Mining Association), Chile (Sociodad Nacional de Mineria, or SONAMI), Mexico (Camara Minera de Mexico, Consejo Minero a.g., Sociedad Nacional Minera y Petroleo or SNMPE), India (Federation of Indian Mineral Industries), Indonesia (Indonesian Mining Association), Bulgarian Mining Chamber, Austria (Association of the Mining and Steel Producing Industry), France (Fédération des Chambres Syndicales des Minerais, Minéraux Industriels et Métaux Non-Ferreux), Germany

(Wirtschaftsvereinigung Bergbau), Greece (Greek Mining Enterprises Association), and similar mining associations in Ireland, Finland, the United Kingdom and Turkey.

As this analysis shows, the mining industry was highly fragmented internationally. National associations were generally well-organised, but associability was highly problematic beyond the level of the nation state, and largely limited to a concern with marketing matters. The associations formed to promote the use of particular commodities were the best organised, and those commodities where the industry demonstrated strong vertical integration (steel and aluminium) demonstrated the most highly developed organization. But the non-ferrous metals mining sector, where there was little vertical integration and many commodities are competitive (that is, they are directly substitutable) was poorly organised.

CHAPTER 3

THE GLOBAL MINING INITIATIVE AND THE INTERNATIONAL REORGANISATION OF THE MINING INDUSTRY

In 1999 the mining industry established the Global Mining Initiative, part of which saw a review of industry associations. This led to the creation of a new international group, the International Council on Mining and Metals (ICMM), in 2001, and was the first serious collective global initiative of the world's largest mining companies. By the late 1990s, it was widely recognised that the performance of the mining industry, both in its ability to affect international agendas of concern to it and its return on capital, was poor. Its reputation on social and environmental issues was seen as contributing to the situation where it was not earning the cost of its capital—that is, returns on capital in the industry were lower than could have been obtained by investing in interest-bearing bonds. Increased regulatory costs and costs associated with access to ground were seen as stemming from a poor shared global reputation for mining.

The Global Mining Initiative, was an ambitious attempt to change this state of affairs, involving a three tracks approach: towards improving industry representation and reputation (track one); improving social and environmental performance through a Mining Minerals and Sustainable Development project (track two); leading into a conference for securing commitment for the way forward (track three).

Rio Tinto was a major player in this process, so it might appear that it came in direct response to the global campaign against it. Rio Chairman Sir Robert Wilson did play an important role in the initiation of the GMI, but this was essentially at the invitation of Hugh Morgan, CEO of WMC Resources, and Doug Yearley, CEO of Phelps Dodge, who took the initiative, but recognised that they needed Rio Tinto on board and recruited Wilson. (George Littlewood, a former Rio public affairs executive who was working out of the Melbourne company Allens Consulting, also assisted this process). All three companies were members of the World Business Council for Sustainable Development. The three issued a joint invitation to 12 mining CEOs to a meeting in London in October (during as 'LME Week'), emphasising their view that they were destroying shareholder value by not engaging proactively with the issues of market contraction due to the regulation of toxic substances and the difficulties they were facing in getting access to new land for exploration and mine development, especially in developing countries.

There were three major 'drivers' of this development. First, it was a response to the initiatives on environmental regulation emerging under the UN umbrella; second, it showed an overt concern with 'reputational issues' after a spate of disasters associated with mining and chemical industries; and third, it reflected the leadership role of larger companies based upon a real vulnerability to the lowering of standards created by smaller companies and state owned companies. A lowering of standards could lead to a race to the bottom, and a serious loss of future investment possibilities, because many mining operations used the same methods, adapted to the particular circumstances which varied from mine to mine. Such generic issues impacted on the sector as a whole, and there was perhaps no clearer example of this than cyanide extraction methods in gold mining, which are used almost universally by mining operations.

The 1995 cyanide spill from the Omai gold mine in Guyana thus impacted upon the reputation of the gold sector around the globe. This created a challenge for the industry, especially because of the large number of small operators in this sector: the conduct of any small, undercapitalised player can impact upon the reputation of the largest, most responsible operator. Moreover, small miners operating within a single jurisdiction are relatively indifferent to their global reputation; they have only to meet the expectations and requirements of the government in whose territory they operate. This governing authority is quite likely to be structurally dependent on the economic benefits (royalties, wages, taxes, foreign exchange) provided by the mine, and is therefore more likely to be compromised when it comes to regulating on issues of social or environmental impact. This is especially so when the state owns the mining operation.

These factors can encourage a kind of reputational indifference among the smaller players, which can be damaging for the larger transnational players. This was exemplified with the cyanide spill from the Esmeralda gold mine in Romania in 2000, which again focused international attention on the use of cyanide in the sector, especially as it caused fish kills downstream across the Hungarian border. Lightly capitalised, Esmeralda simply went into liquidation when faced with liability for the clean-up costs, but the incident affected the gold sector as a whole.

The Global Mining Initiative was set up preparatory to the UN's important 10th anniversary conference post-Rio, scheduled for Johannesburg in 2002. Given the timing of the GMI and the importance of the environmental NGOs around this process, and the international union campaign underway against Rio Tinto, it is tempting to see the formation of the GMI as an instance of countervailing politics. This chapter argues instead that those three drivers are best explained as relating to issues of market share and state licensing. Under globalisation, negative stories were played out via environmental NGOs in a global fashion, particularly via new media networks; and investment opportunities in former 'iron curtain' countries could be curtailed by regulation. The origins of the GMI and thus the ICMM go much deeper than the international campaign against Rio Tinto, and lie in production issues largely concerning sustainability.

Rio Tinto (initially as CRA, with whom it merged in 1995) was undoubtedly a leader in this process, having already adopted a progressive approach to indigenous issues in Australia under CRA CEO Leon Davis, and chastened by its experience with Bougainville Copper, after the loss of which it set itself the ambitious task of only ever operating with the consent of the local people. Just how seriously it took this soon became apparent when it abandoned its Century Zinc project (sold to Pasminco) after activist Murrandoo Yanner threatened action over the slurry pipeline to carry concentrates to port. Similarly, it later abandoned the Jabiluka uranium mine that it acquired with its takeover of North Ltd on the basis of the same principle, though it must be said this decision probably came easier as uranium was not as close to its core business as had been zinc.

The appearance of the lead role being played by Rio Tinto—and thus the appearance that the GMI came in response to the international union campaign—was enhanced by the important role in facilitating the GMI played by George Littlewood. In fact, Littlewood's engagement came from a less likely source, as he was hired by Australian miner WMC Resources. The surprise lay in the fact that WMC was headed by Hugh Morgan, who had a reputation for being not just a laggard on environmental and indigenous issues, but a combative critic of both these movements and their agendas.

Morgan played a role few who know his reputation would credit. The stimulus for the change was a very public ticking-off of Morgan by his then chairman, Sir Arvi Parbo in the early 1990s which led to a transformation within WMC throughout the decade, with commitments to improved performance on environmental and indigenous issues, exemplified by the institution of reporting on both these issues under the oversight of external reference groups. Atypical in an industry where mining engineers tend to dominate, Morgan was a lawyer, and he recruited Chris Leptos from the communications sector as an agent of change as General Manager-Corporate Development.[3] One observer stated quite unequivocally that the GMI was Hugh Morgan's idea—'he sold it to Wilson [of Rio Tinto] and then got other support—got it away from the Canadians. Hugh Morgan gave the GMI idea to the English companies—he wanted to get the Canadians out.'

Explaining the Global Mining Initiative

CEOs from ten companies (Anglo American, BHP, Billiton, Codelco, Newmont, Noranda, Phelps Dodge, Placer Dome, Rio Tinto, WMC Resources) accepted the invitation to attend the London meeting, which was jointly chaired by Morgan and Yearley. (The number of GMI sponsors was subsequently reduced to nine with the merger of BHP and Billiton in 2001 to form BHP-Billiton). American company Asarco was initially included, but it became distracted with a takeover by Gruppo Mexico in 1999. After the initial meeting at the LME in October, the CEOs of the participating companies met in New York in December 1998 and the establishment of the GMI followed.

There was a shared recognition that the industry was facing a 'trust deficit' and the existing industry associations were ineffective. One insider put it that whenever CEOs would meet previously at the London Metal Exchange (LME), they would constantly swap 'war stories', with the industry always on the wrong side of issues that were difficult to defend, and bemoan the ineffectiveness of industry associations.

It seemed to the CEOs that the Sustainable Development agenda covered all the major issues which concerned them, so they decided to make it the focus, influenced by Tom Burke from Friends of the Earth, who had previously advised the Conservative government in the UK and was now doing so for Rio Tinto. Investor perceptions were also important at this stage

---

[3] Kellow was engaged as a consultant to WMC at this time, advising on risk management issues related to products such as nickel and copper as part of corporate development of staff who were overwhelmingly geologists and mining engineers.

and input from the Pension Investment Research Council and groups like Henderson's Ethical Investment Funds also informed the process.

The Sustainable Development issue was chosen as a theme rather carefully, both because the lead companies saw the Rio+10 WSSD conference in Johannesburg as an end point and to provide the best basis for associability, and they had in mind the poor outcomes for the industry from Rio de Janeiro in 1992. In July 2001, the World Bank commenced an Extractive Industries Review which provided further impetus for global cooperation.

A matrix of issues was developed, plotting mining, refining, use, and rehabilitation on the local, regional and international levels. The CEOs agreed that Sustainable Development had become the context for IGOs, NGOs and, increasingly, companies, but it was also recognised that Sustainable Development was essentially both a non-competitive issue for potential members and one that companies could not engage with alone. Individual companies could only go so far on Sustainable Development without being held back by the performance of the industry as a whole. There were still competitive factors such as the desire to differentiate the leaders from the rest and individual companies from the pack: Rio Tinto, for example, aspired to be seen as the 'preferred developer'. There were also competitive pressures between metal commodities which were substitutes, especially between aluminium and steel. There was also a higher degree of vertical integration in aluminium and steel than existed in the non-ferrous metals sector, and this was a potential problem.

The GMI (and thus the MMSD exercise) also deliberately excluded climate change on the grounds that it was a potentially competitive issue, with different implications for coal and uranium producers and metals such as aluminium which were more energy-intensive in their production processes.

Similarly, that part of the uranium cycle downstream from mining was excluded 'because the issues of weapons proliferation, security, and waste disposal are so complex and controversial that adequate attention to them all was beyond the available resources.' Also excluded were minerals traded primarily in local markets, such as construction materials (aggregates, sand and gravel) and cement (which was being considered in its own WBCSD-sponsored process). The scope therefore limited the range of issues covered in such a way that a major possible line of cleavage (coal vs atomic energy) was avoided, and the focus would tend to exclude those issues where an absence of trade or some other international dimension would otherwise have brought in those less concerned with the international agenda.

It was decided the process needed 'Sherpas' who would carry the process forward. The sherpas were the personal representatives of CEOs—individually responsible to the CEOs and able to act in their names to prepare the way. The CEOs agreed to meet again in Davos in January 1999 at the World Economic Forum. Andy Vickerman from Rio Tinto was to chair a Sherpas' meeting in the meantime. At Davos, the three tracks of the GMI were established: the review of industry associations, the MMSD process and the conference to be held in Toronto in May 2002, all with the intention of playing a positive and more effective role at WSSD at Johannesburg in 2002. The Sherpas held four meetings each year and it was agreed that the CEOs would meet again at LME week in 1999, 2000 and 2001. This they did for around four hours each meeting, with Sherpas' chair Andy Vickerman and Richard Sandbrook, who was appointed Project Coordinator for MMSD, in attendance.

Richard Sandbrook had been a founder member of Friends of the Earth International, Earthscan Publications Ltd., UNEP-UK and the European Environment Bureau as well as co-founder of Friends of the Earth (UK). In 1976, he joined the London office of the International Institute for Environment and Development (IIED), and eventually served as Executive Director between 1989 and August 1999. He had over twenty-five years' experience in conservation and environmental sciences, with broad experience in development, having been involved in the financial and personnel management of many environmental projects, both in Europe and in developing countries. He had practical experience with the agricultural, forestry and fisheries sectors, environmental economics and urban poverty, working with bilateral and multilateral donor agencies. More recently he had worked with firms from the mining, oil and gas sectors and the forestry and paper sectors, most significantly a project on this sector for the WBCSD which served as something of a model for the MMSD project. He had served on a variety of Boards and committees, including the UK Round Table for Sustainable Development, the IUCN Council for Western Europe and the Earth Council Institute Costa Rica.

In May 1999 a scoping study for MMSD was commissioned. IIED was engaged through the auspices of the WBCSD, for which it (and Sandbrook) had conducted the paper industry study. (Several of the leading mining companies were WBCSD members). The scoping study was accepted at the 1999 LME week meeting of the CEOs. At the 2000 meeting the industry association restructure was agreed to, and in 2001 a commitment was made to hold the Toronto Conference in May 2002.

The Industry Associations Review

One lesson from the forestry project for WBCSD was that it would throw up problems requiring further action. Forestry had had no institutional mechanism for actioning these items, so it became all the more important to review the industry associations and address the question of how the outcomes from the MMSD process might be carried forward. ICME had fallen below expectations, and Secretary-General Gary Nash had perennially struggled to get both CEO commitment and resources sufficient for the task. The aim now was to try to get an organization with three or four times ICME's budget, and with CEOs centrally involved in the exercise

George Littlewood, formerly of Rio Tinto, but then at Allens Consulting in Melbourne, worked for WMC in getting things moving, and Anita Roper from WMC was seconded to the GMI to work out of Rio's office in London. Roper had a background in industry associations outside the mining industry, having previously worked for the Victorian Chamber of Manufactures in Australia. (See Littlewood 2000).

The GMI involved the commissioning of two reports on the subject of mining industry associations. The first, by Arthur D. Little, reviewed existing associations, finding that the companies participating in their survey were paying about $US50m pa in subscriptions.[11] The commodity associations, which were primarily concerned with market research and market expansion (with some attention directed to environment and health issues), received 75 to 80 percent of these funds, national or regional associations 10-15 percent, and only 5-10 percent to the categories they defined as 'public policy' and 'technically driven lobbying associations.' (The 'public policy' category included non-sectoral groups such as the ICC and WBCSD). Only 2 percent of funding was going to the international 'technically driven lobbying associations': Eurometaux, Euromines and ICME (Arthur D. Little 2000, 6-7).

[11] The survey included 27 respondents representing the companies initially involved with the GMI, including CEOs, Vice-Presidents, public affairs personnel, business managers and environmental, health and safety executives.

There were several instances of duplication of effort by various associations. For example, the ICME, International Copper Association and Eurometaux were all working on copper and the environment. ICME, WBCSD, Eurometaux and the Minerals Council of Australia were all working on sustainable development issues. Socially responsible business practices were being addressed by state and national mining associations in Australia plus ICME and the WBCSD. State mining chambers in Australia were each seeking to engage with communities to communicate a positive impression of the industry to the quality of life (Arthur D. Little 2000, 8). The Little Report recommended greater networking among existing associations to meet the emerging global challenges facing the industry, but it also recommended mobilizing industry associations and a more detailed review of the structure and function of associations both within and beyond the mining sector to assess the institutional expertise needed.

That more detailed review came in a report prepared by the Allen Consulting Group in Melbourne (for which George Littlewood had been working), presented in September 2000 (Allen Consulting Group 2000). Allens conducted a review of industry associations, which highlighted what everyone knew: that the representation of the industry was fragmented and ineffective. As one observer put it: ‘The norm in the industry was to set up nine new associations to deal with an issue they agree on which the others don’t share—they never scrap one.’ There were around 100 industry associations from around the world which gathered around the LME. In addition, however, commodity prices had been flat, and there had been much downsizing: most companies had one third the corporate staff they had had five years previously, so there was diminishing public affairs capacity at the level of the individual firm.

The Allen Consulting report saw the problems essentially as threefold. First, there was fragmentation and duplication of effort, most notably on sustainable development issues. This was seen as being exacerbated by inadequate coordination and networking. Second, public policy makers did not know where to go for an authoritative strategic view. Finally, there was insufficient strategic policy making and decision making, and CEO leadership and engagement was needed for industry association positions to be regarded as authoritative (Allen Consulting Group 2000, 4).

The need for the industry was seen as being (Allen Consulting Group 2000, 5):

> To create an effective and co-ordinated network of external representation for the mining, minerals and metals industry, including a highly focused peak body to provide strategic global leadership . . . working with other, existing bodies the peak body [would] need to:
>
> - engage CEOs directly;
> - guide the strategic direction for industry advocacy;
> - represent the industry effectively at the highest international levels;
> - anticipate trends of importance;
> - understand and manage long-term perspectives;
> - marshal persuasive and rigorous advocacy programmes;
> - project a positive industry reputation; and
> - support and contribute to the necessary engagement processes.

The aim was to achieve this without increasing either the number of associations or the total resource cost of participation. There was no intention to create a single industry association but to ensure the various groups were aligned with the purposes of GMI/MMSD to ensure delivery on outcomes, and global CEO leadership in the development and acceptance of the new sustainable development paradigm inherent in MMSD. ICME was seen as the most appropriate existing platform to move from, but it needed a broader focus, a re-orientation from secretariat leadership to member leadership and new location closer to where major issues are resolved (and to reduce its Canadian focus). It was recognised that the GMI presented a rare opportunity for a comprehensive review of the industry, of a kind that might be possible only once in every 20 years or so. The CEOs in particular wanted to consider a 'clean sheet of paper' option to articulate ideal arrangements, 'uncontaminated by what we have, and current politics surrounding these issues' (Allen Consulting Group 2000, 5). The Report was quite clear that the 'association of associations' model was not favoured. It was seen as slow and politically complex and incapable of meeting the globalisation of issues and the particular circumstances of the industry.

The industry was seen as being no longer able to rely on its economic power to influence governments, partly because of a loss of reputational leverage, but particularly because its relative structural importance was small and shrinking. As noted in Chapter 1, the mining sector represented only 0.6 percent of the value of the S&P 500 index in the US and 6 percent of the value of the Toronto Stock Exchange 300. It was more significant in

Australia, but even there had declined from 26 percent of the All Ordinaries Index in 1996 to 12 percent in 2000 (Allen Consulting Group 2000, 7).

The Allen Report noted the inevitable tensions between companies and associations. It also noted that association executives pointed to cases where company executives engaging in representative advocacy on behalf of associations often sought to maximise their corporate advantage, and sought to exploit associations in doing so (Allen Consulting Group 2000, 11). Turf wars between associations were also seen as having been obstacles to coordination and effective collaboration in the sector for some time, although there had been recent improvements as the result of changes in personnel and pressure from association members. The keys to minimising this problem were seen as strong member leadership, more effective arrangements for cross-associational collaboration and reward structures which facilitate this.

It was recognised that globalisation of issues had challenged the national associations. In the late 1990s attempts were made develop 'lead house' approaches to some issues which transcended national boundaries, whereby one national association would agree to assume carriage of an activity such as data collection or the preparation of advocacy on behalf of the national associations collectively. As the report noted, this was ultimately not particularly successful. On some issues, and in an *ad hoc* manner, this gap was filled where ICME saw an alignment of interest; however, the aspirations of national associations driving this approach were frustrated—most 'lead house' initiatives failed because the work was simply not done, reflecting the natural tendency for national associations to respond to urgent domestic priorities (Allen Consulting Group 2000, 12). Some national associations had also attempted to build programs of coordinated political action across national borders, but, again, success was less than was deemed satisfactory. ICME also had a brief to facilitate coordination of national associations, but this had fallen short of aspirations. As a result, it was noted that 'The lack of an effective forum in which national organizations feel they have voice, can develop ideas collaboratively, and can get things done collectively at an international level leaves an important gap . . . .' (Allen Consulting Group 2000, 12).

The report also recognised that there were companies which operated largely within national borders and which were more reluctant to engage in international processes, content instead to free-ride on the activity of transnational players. Further, there were regional groupings within countries that were not linked by governance structures to national associations, and a number of smaller companies that did not participate in any associations at any level and were therefore difficult to influence. The national associations also lacked a consistent coverage, as some included and others excluded ferrous metals, hydrocarbons or quarrying of construction minerals. It noted that past attempts by CEOs to rationalise and strengthen organisational linkages between sectoral and regional associations had been vigorously resisted by threatened association executives and had failed.

In its review of associations, the Allen Report treated Eurometaux and Euromines, as well as fledgling transnational regional associations such as the Mining Industry Associations of Southern Africa (MIASA) and the Inter-American Mining Association (SIM), as essentially national associations (Allen Consulting Group 2000, 14). This was essentially because of the way in which they were recognised by the European Commission, which saw Eurometaux and Euromines as the appropriate means for it to engage the industry in Europe. The somewhat ambiguous nature of the EU (as perhaps more than just an economic integration organization, but not quite a sovereign federal political system) had caused some confusion and had led to some competitive behaviour between Eurometaux and ICME. This had resulted in an agreement at the turn of the century to divide leadership on international activity between Eurometaux (the EU and its agencies) and ICME (UN agencies, OECD, World Bank, and other multilateral organizations) (Allen Consulting Group 2000, 14).

The commodity associations had largely been built around marketing considerations: the need for collaborative market development; the pursuit of new or defence of old uses of metals; and research to strengthen market applications. They were well-funded, usually on a scale-based formula, and were essentially competitive with other commodity associations. Analysis subsequent to the Little Report revealed that very little of the 75-80 percent of industry funding going to commodity associations had been directed to 'a defence of regulatory intervention' (Allen Consulting Group 2000, 14). This level of funding was regarded as being too high, compared with that going to regulatory-related policy analysis, science and advocacy (Allen Consulting Group 2000, 19). There had been little consideration behind funding allocations, with resource decisions tending to come from different functional centres in companies and usually locked in via funding formulas based on scale of production or some similar measure.

The emergence of attacks on the use of commodities on the basis of health and environmental impacts had resulted in greater attention to policy-relevant research and advocacy being added to market development functions, but the balance of resource allocations between associations, the growth of secretariat bureaucracies in commodity associations, lack of familiarity with political strategy and stakeholder engagement, and the commonality of skills such as risk assessment across commodities were seen as issues. The advantages of collaboration across commodities had been demonstrated by the success of the establishment of an Ecotoxicity Advisory Panel (ETAP) across copper, nickel, lead and zinc.

The costs of the absence of coordination across associations were widely accepted. These included not just inefficiencies and a lack of cohesion, but more basic multi-organisational problems such as the scheduling of related meetings that made a call on the time of the same executives in different parts of the world simultaneously.

Many of the commodity associations had direct membership for downstream processors, which were largely about commercial marketing applications, rather than science-based policy advocacy. On the other hand, while it was recognised that each metal had its own characteristics and problems, there were considerable synergies between commodities on health and environmental issues. Pooling these activities could provide critical mass, with more efficient resource use, and facilitate access to the best scientists. It was therefore considered that commodity associations should be left with market-related competencies, while health and environment competencies were substantially pooled.

One obstacle to reform was the stake the many existing associations had in the status quo. The first report on industry associations 'went down like a lead balloon' (in the words of one Sherpa) but the second fared a little better. At an informal meeting of commodities association staffers in Toronto in November 1999, all had been concerned with defending turf. The same occurred with 20-25 company representatives from Associations who went to LME week in October 2000. There was a perception that the GMI was going to take over the commodity associations, and one key to securing reform was to limit the scope of ICMM, which effectively took on 'about 80 percent of the issues,' leaving the remainder for the commodity groups and national associations.

Forming ICMM

In May 2001, members decided to reorganise ICME into a new body. ICMM therefore replaced ICME and took over most of its concerns (one ICMM document described it as having been 'transitioned' to ICMM), with renewed emphasis on the 'licence to operate' issues of sustainable development, but ICME was the only organization of any real substance that was sacrificed in the rationalisation of associations in the industry, although more were predicted for the future. The Australian Minerals and Energy Environment Foundation (AMEEF) was the only other organization disbanded (but that had a solely Australian operation), and WMC withdrew from NiPERA, but there was little rationalisation even where it was needed, such as the considerable overlap between ILZRO, IZA and LDA. ICMM was intended not to touch single commodity issues, which would be left to the commodity associations.

ICMM was a bold initiative, but it was less bold than what might have been achieved. The Allen Consulting Report had canvassed four models for addressing the associational problems confronting the sector, including one which entailed little change from the status quo. The preferred option was for the establishment of an 'International Federation of Mining and Metals', with direct corporate membership as well as national and commodity associations. An ambitious option (an ideal which ignored the politics of the status quo) was for a fully-integrated global mining and metals association, with national or regional organizations effectively branches or divisions, managed by decentralised committees of the international organization. The international organization would take the policy-related science and advocacy work (to be handled in a series of committees), leaving the commodity associations to pursue (potentially competitive) marketing activities.

A third, 'modified reform option', would have left all current functions (including policy-related science and advocacy) with commodity associations, but established an international body. ICMM was close to this option, but it took on most of the policy-related science and advocacy work. There would be corporate membership, associate membership for national associations, an annual forum, a governing council and a small executive committee.

It was agreed that the ICA fee structure would not be followed with ICMM. Rather, membership of national associations and ICMM were to be considered separate matters, which meant that ICMM was destined to be a large-firm club, and this was consistent with the leadership role which was mapped out for it. The more substantial budget which was considered necessary perform the task set for ICMM also meant a substantial rise in subscriptions, also shaking off the smaller companies. For individual membership, the fees rose from $50,000 pa under ICME to a minimum of $100,000 and as much as $250,000 pa for ICMM.

All associations were invited onto the council for a nominal fee of $2,000 p.a., and six were invited to be on the executive, but they had be industry executives, not staff members of the associations, reflecting a reluctance to let ICMM open up to 'bureaucrats'. The low membership fees for associations were intended to ensure there was a channel into ICMM open to smaller firms. Previously, ICME provided information only to members, and smaller non-members were effectively excluded, not just from deliberative processes, but from information flows. Some such as INCO were predominantly single commodity companies (nickel) and did not see the value of a multi-metals association. INCO was regarded in the industry as 'owning' NiDI, and that gave it all the representation it needed.

The association fee level was set on the basis that the major companies would be direct members of ICMM. Barrick and INCO, which subsequently withdrew, felt that they could get access to ICMM through the Mining Association of Canada. However, ICMM was moving towards differentiation between the leadership group and those represented through associations, which could not bind their members, and therefore could not commit companies to policy decisions adopted by ICMM, so Barrick and INCO were (as one observer put it) 'left out in the cold.' Associations had no voting rights in the ICMM structure.

The initial course of ICMM was not smooth. Three new Japanese companies joined, as did Alcoa, but INCO and Barrick withdrew, indicating that they thought there was no focused work program that gave them benefit. Some wanted to continue the old ICME. The mid-sized firms began questioning whether ICMM was 'a big boys' club.' There were problems at what was effectively the first Council Meeting in October 2001. Consensus was difficult to achieve and many things had to be voted on. The South Americans (Codelco) and Europeans (Metaleurop) were holding back from wholehearted support and apparently saw ICMM as primarily a game dominated by an Australian/Anglo/American axis.

The October 2002 Council Meeting was later described as a 'disaster that had to happen.'[12] At this meeting a number of resignations occurred—by Barrick, INCO, Codelco, Phelps Dodge, and Metaleurop. That of

[12] Kellow attended several public functions surrounding this meeting and undertook several interviews on the sidelines to the meeting.

Metaleurop appears to have been for financial reasons, and it is possible this might have also been a factor for Phelps Dodge, which also resigned from the WBCSD, and the perception there was that they were cutting non-essential costs. (Placer Dome also withdrew from WBCSD). Phelps Dodge had indicated basically 'We don't think we agree with your definition of sustainable development,' but it was widely thought that financial pressures lay behind the decision. The decisions had been made in July and August, but under the constitution they had to wait until the AGM. Codelco and Phelps Dodge had a view that 'only the big guys were being listened to.' One observer thought it was partly cultural. 'They contributed so much to the development of the principles; they got 90 percent, but not 100 percent of what they wanted.' They were upset that there were some late changes that had gone to the ICMM Council for approval, rather than to members, but they were considered to be only essentially editorial in nature. Apparently, however, Codelco objected to the partnership being developed with IUCN.

Codelco was 100 percent owned by the government of Chile, and largely operated in that single jurisdiction, and so they felt they needed less to engage with any international body. Similarly, the Brazilian iron ore miner CVRD did not join. The South Africans and Canadians felt they had to be conforming to have a licence to operate. Alcan and Alcoa hardly played during MMSD, but came on board with ICMM later. (As one participant put it, they were 'a bit sniffy'). Similarly Otukumpu and Metaleurop had been reluctant to engage.

There was a 7am Executive meeting on 9 October 2002 which led to a closed Council meeting to discuss whether ICMM should even continue. It was decided to persist with ICMM, but CEO Jay Hair was charged with developing a more focused work program with a decreased budget by November—the next month. Two weeks later, Hair was in hospital with multiple myeloma from which he was subsequently to die, and his deputy, Anita Roper, had to carry on as acting CEO. The new work program was submitted and approved in November, and for the first time ICMM had the authority carry out any work and Roper was left to implement the work program when Hair died. (Roper left, voluntarily, in October 2003 and took up a position with Alcoa).

ICMM at Work

ICMM established a series of programs: Biodiversity; Tailings; Health and Safety; Community; Integrated Materials Management; Sustainable Development Framework; and International Representation. On the

Sustainable Development Framework, the Council adopted ten principles which were binding on the membership and against which they were required to report progress. They developed a memorandum of understanding to facilitate this with the Global Reporting Initiative, a multiple stakeholder consultation group developed as a partnership between UNCTAD and UNEP. ICMM also developed a position paper on Biodiversity in dialogue with the IUCN, engaged in a World Bank project in South Africa as part of its program, and commenced work on life cycle risk assessment for metals.

ICMM is governed by its membership with the key governing body being the Council. The Council is the governing body of the organisation, comprising all members of the organisation. It sets general directions, policies and priorities, and approves the business plan and budget of the organisation. An Executive Committee was elected by the Council to oversee the day-to-day implementation of Council policy and the business plan. It comprised nine members appointed at the annual meeting. The Executive Working Group comprised nominated representatives (known as Principal Liaisons) from each of the corporate and association members. This group was to facilitate input from members on cross-cutting issues and ensure the effective implementation of the ICMM work programme. Task force chairs were appointed from this group.

Committees and Task Forces were appointed by the Council to develop policy and pursue programmes as required. The Task Forces were:

- Key International Fora
- Integrated Materials Management
- Community and Social Development
- Health and Safety
- Biodiversity
- Tailings Management Guidelines

The Co-ordination Committee of Associations provided a vehicle for associations to discuss common strategic issues, while an annual forum was held to ensure that all members of the organisation could provide broad-based discussion and evaluation of the issues before the Council.

The 15 members of the ICMM Council once membership settled down (and BHP and Billiton merged) were: Alcoa; Anglo American plc; AngloGold Limited; BHP-Billiton; Freeport-McMoRan Copper & Gold Inc; Mitsubishi Materials Corporation; Newmont Mining Corporation;

Nippon Mining and Metals; Noranda Inc; Pasminco Limited; Placer Dome Inc; Rio Tinto plc; Sumitomo Metal Mining; Umicore; and WMC Limited (which was later taken over by BHP-Billiton in 2005).

The associations which joined included both national associations and international commodity groups: Camara Minera de Mexico; Chamber of Mines of South Africa; Consejo Minero a.g.; Eurometaux; Euromines; Federation of Indian Mineral Industries; Indonesian Mining Association; Industrial Minerals Association-Europe; Instituto Brasileiro de Mineracao; International Aluminium Institute; International Cadmium Association; International Copper Association (ICA); International Lead Zinc Research Organization (ILZRO); International Wrought Copper Council; International Zinc Association; Japan Mining Industry Association; Minerals Council of Australia; Mining Association of Canada; Mining Industries Associations of Southern Africa; Nickel Development Institute (NiDI); Nickel Producers Environmental Research Association (NiPERA); Prospectors and Developers Association of Canada; Sociedad Nacional Minera y Petroleo (SNMPE); Sociedad Nacional de Mineria (SONAMI); Swedish Mining Association; The Cobalt Development Institute; World Coal Institute.

The governance structure was still bedding down in 2002 and there were some tensions evident between staff and the CEOs. The first meetings of ICMM committees were held on Monday 7 and Tuesday 8 October 2002; previously, there were simply interim Task Forces. At the Council Meeting on 9 October 2002 strong CEO commitment to ICMM was evident, but they wanted to assert greater ownership. They wanted more vision and strategy, setting direction, focussing effort from work programs down.

ICMM was 'now trying to get on with it as an industry leadership group,' as one observer put it, but it depended upon the commitment of the companies who were members and their CEOs. It is a CEO-led organization, so their level of commitment was vital. The CEOs were engaged and were attending and chairing meetings. Almost 20 attended the October 2002 Council Meeting, whereas ICME meetings had always struggled to get CEOs to attend. A large test (passed with some success) was the May 2003 Council Meeting, which was held outside LME Metals Week, but there were some pitfalls ahead. By October 2002 there were only three left of the original nine CEOs who had launched the GMI. A change in CEO at Phelps Dodge might well have made it easier for that company to withdraw.

There were some tensions within ICMM over the exclusion of representatives of regional associations from the Council. Council membership is restricted to companies and those attending must be CEOs, a rule designed to ensure that (unlike ICME) CEOs were committed to the organization, and could commit their companies on the spot. For example, Barry Cusack, President of the MCA was kept outside, despite the fact that he was a former managing director of Rio Tinto in Australia. Similarly, a delegate from Placer Dome was also excluded because he was not a CEO. The attendance of CEOs probably improved because they were now much more international in outlook, and were less prepared to participate in national and regional bodies. Therefore, ICMM has company membership and Associations are only associates. It was deliberately designed not to be a federation, so that it can play a leadership role, unbound by the need for consensus and the lowest common denominator decision making that brings.

The biggest challenges identified were 'getting the process right' and recruiting good staff. ICMM was unfortunate in its initial choice of Secretary-General, with Jay Hair, with extensive experience in the international environmental movement, being recruited from the Assurance Group of the MMSD process, only to fall seriously ill from (ultimately fatal) multiple myeloma. His deputy, Anita Roper, who had been seconded out of WMC to run the GMI, therefore had to carry forward the work of ICMM through its difficult beginnings. Then Paul Mitchell was recruited from CARE Australia in the aid NGO sector.

ICMM, as we have seen, lost some members, and the outer 30 companies which did not participate in the formation of ICMM remained sceptical. But ICMM was focused more on providing leadership for the industry than attempting to achieve comprehensive coverage of the industry. As one interviewee put it, 'Increasing membership was not a KPI for [ICMM Chairman] Wilson.' ICMM became more focused, leaner, and involved the 'hard hitters'—global players who will expect things to move,' as it was put.

ICMM adopted a policy on sustainable development, formed a partnership with IUCN, institutionalised an Ecotoxicity Advisory Panel, and looked for further partnerships—for example, with the trade union movement through ICEM. To get this far, it had to overcome much territorial behaviour focused on the survival of the multifarious existing metals associations at various levels.

An analysis of the industry throws interesting light on the extent to which ICMM provided coverage of the industry, but also some light on the extent to which a global spread of activities (and thus outlook) might have driven companies to join ICMM.

As the following tables indicate, the global distribution of the industry by value of mining assets was overwhelmingly concentrated in North America, South America, Australia, Africa (especially South Africa), and Europe. Two thirds of production by value was comprised of precious metals, base metals and aluminium.

A matrix can be constructed showing the membership affiliations of the leading global companies (by market capitalization), which suggests the hypothesis that a global outlook (indicated by number of memberships in national or regional associations) facilitated participation in ICMM. For these purposes, the following membership indicators have been adopted: North America, membership of MAC and NMA; for South America, membership of IBRAM; for Australia, membership of MCA; for South Africa, membership of SACM, for Europe, membership of Eurometaux and Euromines.

Table 3.1: Distribution of Mineral Assets 2002

	By region	
	Enterprise Value US$billion	**%**
North America	67	25%
South America	38	14%
Asia	19	7%
Australia	50	19%
Africa	41	15%
Europe	55	20%
Totals:	270	100%

	By commodity grouping	
	Enterprise Value US$billion	**%**
Precious Metals	60	23%
Base Metals	50	20%
Aluminium	60	22%
Industrial Minerals	40	15%
Bulk Commodities	60	22%
	270	100%

Source: ICMM, The Mining and Metals Industries: Progress in Contributing to Sustainable Development, Working Paper, 27 February 2002; 9.

Table 3.2 Association Memberships of Largest Mining Companies 2002 (Ranked by Size, Descending Order)

Company	Associations
Alcoa	Eurometaux,
BHP-Billiton	Euromines, MAC, NMA, MCA, SACM, IBRAM
Rio Tinto	Eurometaux, Euromines, MCA, IBRAM
Anglo American	Eurometaux, Euromines, MCA, SACM, IBRAM
Norsk Hydro	
Alcan	Eurometaux, IBRAM
CVRD (now Vale)	IBRAM
Anglo Americam Platinum	SACM
Barrick Gold Corporation*	MAC, NMA, MCA
Newmont Mining	MAC, MCA, NMA
WMC Resources	MCA
Placer Dome	MAC, SACM, MCA, NMA
Anglo Gold	SACM, MCA, IBRAM
Pechiney	Eurometaux
Potash Corp (of Saskatchewan)	
Homestake Mining	(Merged with Barrick, December 2001)
Norilsk Nickel (Nickel - Russia)	
Impala Platinum	
Franco Nevada Mining (Gold)	
INCO*	MAC
Noranda	MAC
Lonmin (platinum)	SACM
Phelps Dodge*	NMA, IBRAM
Gold Fields	SACM
Mitsubishi Materials	
Sumitomo Metal Mining	
Falconbridge (Nickel)	MAC
Normandy Mining	(Merged with Newmont, Feb, 2002)
Freeport-McMoRan (Copper&Gold)	NMA
Imerys (French, specialty minerals)	
Mitsui Mining and Smelting	
Buenaventura (Peru - gold, silver)	
Cameco (Canada - Uranium, Gold)	
Antofagasta Holdings	
Teck Cominco	MAC
Gencor (asphalt)	
Dowa Mining	
Outokumpu Oyi	Eurometaux

Coal and Allied	
Goldcorp	SACM
Boliden	Eurometaux, MAC, Swedish Mining Association
De Beers	MAC, SACM, IBRAM
Pasminco	MCA, NMA
Umicore	Eurometaux,
Xstrata Coal	SACM, MCA
Codelco* (not market listed)	

NMA= National Mining Association (US); MAC= Mining Association of Canada; MCA= Minerals Council of Australia; SACME= South African Chamber of Mines; IBRAM= Instituto Brasileiro de Mineracao. Companies which joined ICMM shown in **bold** type. *Those which subsequently resigned from ICMM

Those companies which joined ICMM at formation tended to be not only the larger companies, but those exposed to multiple jurisdictions (as indicated by national association memberships). Those which were large in terms of market capitalisation which did not join, or which resigned after joining initially, tended to be those with more limited transnational exposure and/or greater specialisation in a limited number of metals or even a single metal or mineral. This is certainly the case with the ICMM resignations—Barrick (gold), INCO (nickel), and Phelps Dodge (copper). But a closer examination of those companies which did not come on board reveals that each represents an exception to this generalisation.

For example, Norsk Hydro is primarily Norwegian in orientation, with operations also in Sweden and the United Kingdom, but its assets were mostly in oil and energy, with some holdings in the (vertically integrated) aluminium industry. Alcan and Pechiney were also solely aluminium companies, and CVRD (Cia. Vale do Rio Doce, now Vale) was both largely Brazilian focused and limited to (vertically integrated) iron and steel. Anglo American Platinum, Impala Platinum and Lonmin were platinum specialists; Norilsk Nickel and Falconbridge (like INCO) were nickel specialists; Franco Nevada Mining, Gold Fields, and Goldcorp were gold miners. Virtually all the remaining companies of considerable size were specialists with limited international exposure: Buenaventura was a gold and silver miner in Peru; the name of Potash Corporation of Saskatchewan speaks for itself; so too do Coal and Allied and Xstrata Coal; Imerys is a French company focused on specialty minerals; Gencor is an asphalt specialist; De Beers is synonymous with diamonds; Outokumpu Oyi is concentrated in Finland; Boliden has some holdings in Canada, but is primarily based in Sweden.

Those companies located primarily in a single jurisdiction have less reason to be concerned with their global reputation. This is probably especially the case, as with the MAC, where their national mining association had previously adopted an international outlook. Part of the reason for this is that such companies often enjoy structural power in their home jurisdiction, and are probably used to lobbying successfully at the individual firm level. This is exacerbated with those few large players which are publicly owned, since governments are caught in extreme poacher-gamekeeper situations. Codelco is the most significant example of this: it is owned in its entirety by the Chilean government; its market capitalisation is therefore unknown, but it has no real reason to be concerned with its global reputation.

A similar associational logic applies with single commodity companies. Those companies which produce mostly a single commodity are more likely to find a commodity-based association a sufficient means of securing representation at the international level. Multi-metal producers are more likely to see the limitations of paying the costs of multiple participation in several commodity groups, and the problems which result from fragmented effort in international arenas. There is therefore a geological reason why some companies might be more interested in forming an international sector group like ICMM: the non-ferrous industry frequently mines ores which produce several metals as co-products. If a company is mining a lead-zinc-silver ore (Broken Hill in New South Wales), or copper-gold (Ok Tedi in Papua New Guinea), or copper-uranium-gold (Olympic Dam in South Australia), it is more likely to be amenable to joining an international sector group than a company mining nickel ore, or gold ore, or even an ore body which is predominantly copper. (Many ores produce quantities of other metals which are minor co-products—in quantities so small as to not characterise the ore as anything other than copper, or gold).

This observation would appear to explain what appears to be an anomaly in the list of the largest companies: WMC Resources. WMC did have prospects in other jurisdictions, but its resources were predominantly located within Australia. It was not a member of any national associations other the MCA. Why would it not just join ICMM, but play a leading role in its formation? Part of the answer is certainly the personal leadership role of Hugh Morgan, WMC CEO. But another factor is surely the diversity of WMC's asset portfolio at that time: nickel, copper, gold, uranium, bauxite, alumina, aluminium, phosphate and fertiliser.[13] It could belong to at least half a dozen commodity associations, and therefore had a greater reason to question the cost-benefit of multiple membership of commodity associations.

ICMM has therefore established itself as a sectorally-based leadership group for the mining industry at the international level. While it is a 'large firm' leadership group, quite deliberately so in an attempt to rise above lowest common denominator approaches, it sought to provide 'a window' for SMEs in the sector through its linkages with national, regional and commodity mining associations.

ICMM developed a charter on sustainable development and it made a substantial contribution, as had been its aim, at the World Summit on Sustainable Development (WSSD) held in Johannesburg, South Africa, from 26 August to 4 September 2002. As we shall see, that contribution at Johannesburg had to be made in association with peak business groups (because of the way in which participation was structured by the UN), which necessitates some discussion of the relationship between ICMM and the peak international business group, the International Chamber of Commerce.

First, however, it is valuable to look at the relationship between ICMM and the MMSD project, which had been continuing while ICMM was being formed and was developing. Recall, the three strands of the GMI were the review of industry organization, MMSD and the multi-stakeholder engagement conference held in Toronto (May 12-15, 2002) involving the industry and stakeholders to discuss the way forward, using the MMSD report as a basis for discussion. MMSD had deliberately been established at arm's length from the industry, and it is important to bear in mind that ICMM became essentially just another stakeholder in the MMSD process, albeit one representing many of the MMSD Sponsors Group. But ICMM made strongly-argued inputs into the final MMSD report, and we will turn now, before considering the ICMM participation at Johannesburg, to examine the remainder of the GMI process, and particularly the participation of ICMM in that process.

[13] WMC was later to divest itself of some of these assets, especially splitting off its aluminium assets into a separate corporate entity, Alumina. In 2005 it was taken over by BHP-Billiton, which became BHP in 2015 when it split off assets (some former Billiton) into 32 South.

MMSD

Richard Sandbrook was of the view that the MMSD process was too rushed. He felt that WSSD in Johannesburg provided a target that was too close, and too much time was wasted trying to raise funds for the project, largely because the industry was reluctant to commit the resources necessary. IIED had indicated it would need \$7m to undertake the project, but the GMI players decided to try to do it for \$5m, of which the nine players put up \$3m with instructions to find another \$2m. This target was never achieved, despite the expansion of the original nine members of the Sponsors Group to 28 companies and the participation of four consulting groups, although there were various in-kind contributions to the project. (See Appendix at the end of the Chapter). A total of 28 companies committed at least \$150,000 each to the Project and thus a total of a minimum of \$4.2m, but the Assurance Group was informed in May 2002 that the project was likely to cost about \$8.5 million (MMSD Assurance Group 2000).

MMSD also had a variety of non-commercial sponsors—ranging from governments (Australia, Canada, the United Kingdom), foundations and labour unions—who made cash or in-kind contributions towards Project activities. Sandbrook put this reluctance to fund the project in context by pointing out that at about this time, the International Cricket Council was spending \$10m investigating corruption in cricket. The aim had been to achieve 20 percent of funding from outside the industry, but ultimately only 15 percent came from external sources.

The urgency imposed by the Johannesburg deadline impacted on the project, in Sandbrook's view. Much commissioned research was less valuable than it might have been because of boundary overlaps. Scenarios such as life without mines were not explored. The Report was edited by half in the last three months of the project and it might have done more to explore the 'degrees of self-destruction' which occurred by companies over-investing in the wrong stages of cycles. And Sandbrook saw it as a 'big mistake' that everyone was too ready to close it down: it had a very good assurance group, and it might have been valuable to reassemble it and ask it for an industry report card at some later date.

ICMM made a detailed response to the draft MMSD report (ICMM, 2002), demonstrating both the extent to which MMSD was independent and the risks to the industry in allowing such independence, and the need it saw (through ICMM) to correct errors, limit any damage, and maximize the positive view of the industry it presented. ICMM considered the lack of meaningful engagement with some key governmental and civil society interests represented 'a significant deficiency in the MMSD process.' It recognized that this situation was partly beyond the control of those running MMSD, but felt it resulted in important limitations regarding certain aspects of the draft Report. These included 'the lack of case studies demonstrating how to effectively and actively engage the wide range of interests who need to be thoughtfully involved in relevant engagement processes in the future.'

ICMM also thought that the treatment of the metals portion of the minerals cycle and its contribution to sustainable development was inadequate. It made a number of suggestions for priority topics that should be addressed in the future, suggesting that it was very important they be included in the final version of the MMSD Report. It also argued that there was a need for the final MMSD Report to draw a distinction between the proper roles and responsibilities of industry, government and civil society. It submitted there was an imbalance in requiring much more responsibility from industry than from other relevant actors. ICMM believed it was inappropriate for industry or civil society to assume the role of government, 'as suggested in many parts of the draft MMSD Report.' It also believed there needed to be much more emphasis on 'capacity building, transparency and accountability for all parties—including governmental and non-governmental organizations—at all levels of society.'

ICMM acknowledged that specific examples of poor performance existed and had been identified in the draft Report, but it failed to mention many more examples of good, improving and improved performance, which detracted from the overall quality of the Report.

ICMM also argued that while there were a number of critical governance related issues that need to be addressed, the draft report had an unnecessarily negative tone towards the capacities and *compétence* of the governmental sector, which appeared to challenge directly the sovereignty of national governments, and might well impede 'the effective engagement of the governmental sector as active and effective partners in the future, particularly on those recommendations within their areas of jurisdictional responsibility.' Governments, ICMM noted, play key roles in the governance aspects essential to sustainable development, so it argued that the MMSD final report should recognise that responsibilities must be pursued primarily by governmental entities.

ICMM noted the draft Report provided a strong emphasis on certification of industry performance to demonstrate compliance with global standards which were as yet unidentified. It stated that 'While this may be laudable in concept, the value of such efforts could easily be lost in the maze of differing regulations, community expectations, and project specific circumstances.' Further, it noted that the value of independent certification had yet to be demonstrated for any activity anywhere in the world.

ICMM also criticized the draft report for its lack of citation of the many major, peer-reviewed publications which had been produced by the various commodity associations and by ICME. Only two such publications were listed in the references of the draft report, and ICMM pointed to several relevant ICME reports it considered should have been referred to because of their relevance to the MMSD project: *A World of Metals*; *Mining and Indigenous Peoples*; *The Management of Cyanide in Gold Extraction*; *Eco-Efficiency and Materials*; *Tailings Management*; *Recycling of Non-Ferrous Metals*; *Hazard and Risk Assessment Methodologies*. ICMM argued that 'To not reference such obvious and relevant documents to the mining and metals industry casts doubt on the extent to which the MMSD Report objectively covered the respective topics.'

The ICMM was clearly prepared to assert the industry's interests into the MMSD process. While the theme of the whole GMI exercise (and certainly MMSD) was one of positive engagement with stakeholders, that did not mean that the industry was not prepared to project influence by expressing its newfound voice in ICMM. It was quite prepared to contest the draft MMSD report in quite strong terms; and was concerned that the Report was inflammatory with phrases such as 'drift down to the lowest common denominator' and 'willing to take short cuts' which 'should be removed where they cannot be substantiated.' (ICMM, 2002a, p24).

The GMI had some obvious deficiencies, It primarily involved mining companies, together with some metal producers. But it did not include downstream industries, like galvanisers, and if anything it represented something of an overcorrection to one of the limitations of ICME: a focus on metals rather than mining, or the whole product cycle. MMSD failed to engage broadly with all NGOs, particularly in 'northern' countries such as Australia and the US. The Minerals Policy Centre withheld participation and this eventually escalated to a global mining campaign. Friends of the Earth (North America), Oxfam (in America), and Mining Watch Canada decided not to criticise the process, but to watch. Friends of the Earth in the United Kingdom, in contrast to its US branch, did engage. There was, however, more extensive engagement at the Toronto Conference, where a promising Declaration was adopted.

The Toronto Conference was a near-run thing, inasmuch the MMSD report was completed only the week before. There was a great deal of interest in MMSD evident at the conference. The organisers thought they would struggle to get 300 to attend in Toronto, but they got 575 registrations and 520 showed up, including all 22 CEOs, who stayed for four days. Industry representatives comprised fewer than half of the attendees, who also came from 20 governments, the ILO, numerous IGOs and the finance sector. Some green NGOs which had not engaged in MMSD did so in Toronto, including the Minerals Policy Centre in a plenary. Stakeholders wanted to talk about their views, work they had done, and their views on the way forward. There were 30-odd different workshops involving industry, NGOs and government agencies.

The success of the GMI would depend ultimately upon several factors, not least the effectiveness of ICMM. It recognised that it took a decade for the outcomes of the similar exercise in the pulp and paper sector to take effect. One problem identified there had been the absence of any institutionalisation of the process to give effect to recommendations, and ICMM was created at least in part to ensure there was an organization to carry the MMSD agenda forward. As noted above, Sandbrook thought the sponsors were too keen to close down the MMSD project, and the risks to the process in the longer term were real. One key question was how much the commitment of members to ICMM and the MMSD outcomes depended upon the personalities of the CEOs involved. Morgan was soon gone from WMC, Gilbertson from BHP-Billiton, and Yearley from Phelps Dodge. Phelps Dodge's commitment to ICMM did not survive far beyond Yearley's tenure (though it later returned), an ominous sign, since the success of ICMM depends crucially upon the willingness of CEOs to make a commitment to it. On the other hand, it was recognised that new CEOs might bring even greater levels of commitment.

Conclusion

This account of the GMI is highly partial: the focus has been very much on the representation of the mining industry, rather than on the effects of the process on the adoption and internalisation by companies of improved environmental and social practice, except inasmuch as the MMSD and the Toronto Conference impacted upon the formation of ICMM. This neglect of the other two streams of the GMI should not be taken to minimise their importance; rather, it is to say that the current focus is on interest groups, and the MMSD and Toronto Conference (as vehicles for raising industry performance) merit study on their own account.

Given the present focus on interest groups, we can now ponder what the drivers of associability appear to have been at the international level. The most obvious driver would appear to have been the increasing importance of governance at the international level, especially as manifested by UNCED in 1992 and WSSD in 2002, but also the World Bank's Extractive Industries Review. The internationalisation of governance has not necessarily entailed intergovernmental organizations, but also the tendency for national governments to take into account the global reputation of companies in being granted a 'licence to operate' under conditions which affect their financial viability.

There was a further driver encouraging the taking of a leadership role by larger players, especially if they were essentially locked into adherence to higher standards by global reputational pressures. That is that they are always vulnerable to competition from smaller players or state-owned players where poacher-gamekeeper problems have led to lower standards for occupational health and safety or environmental protection (and thus lower production costs than would otherwise be the case). Many small miners can enter production relatively easily, and this helps moderate prices received by the larger producers. Higher standards raise expectations and thus increase the cost of entry for smaller players, and thus help protect prices, so the larger players would be perfectly happy if environmental best practice (and thus higher production costs) could be imposed on the smaller players. Thus regulation—even self-regulation—not only helps the TNCs reputationally, it helps their bottom line by acting as a barrier to market entry.

The situation was summarised in an interview by a company Sherpa who had extensive involvement in the GMI process:

> There was a raft of issues on which the industry found itself in competition with conservationists—access to land, indigenous issues—plus a raft of legislation (in Europe especially) which was nibbling at the edges of markets. They were losing market opportunities—niches and larger chunks. These were driven by the toxicity of metals—plus their persistence and bioaccumulative properties, which had featured in Agenda 21.
>
> The issues were being badly handled. The intergovernmental organisations were not engaging (or were not willing to engage). The

> emerging agendas were bad for the industry. The legacy of issues and accidents left the industry with a pretty poor story to tell. The CEOs had to change the way we did business. They needed to perform. It was not solvable by public relations. They were spending large but unknown quantities of money. Why was it not working?

The reference to 'large but unknown quantities of money' related to the fact that the companies that comprised the industry were paying out substantial sums in subscriptions to various industry associations, but had little idea of how much was being spent. The subsequent review of industry associations indicated that the top nine companies (the initial sponsors of the GMI) were paying out more than $US50m each year in trade association subscriptions. Former Minerals Council of Australia Executive Director Dick Wells stated that somewhere between $US260-400m was being spent on industry associations globally, spread between about 200 organisations. Many of these were national level associations of one kind or another, with around 100 with a more international outlook clustering around the LME. In fact, this is probably a significant underestimate of the number of mining and metals associations globally. In September 2004 the trade magazine *MetalWorld* listed 289 metals associations on its website, and this number did not include many of the sub-national, national and international associations which are central to the present study.

Even smaller players like Australian company MIM Holdings were spending $1m annually on belonging to associations, and with the internationalisation of environmental policy which was accelerated by UNCED at Rio in 1992, they increasingly began to wonder what value they were getting for their money. MIM was concerned about issues such as the threat to its lead market posed by moves (in the OECD, but drawing impetus from Chapter 19 of Agenda 21) to regulate lead internationally and the proposed amendment to the Basel Convention which would ban international trade in hazardous waste even for recovery and recycling (Kellow 1999). To MIM, pressed by low commodity prices and a tight balance sheet, it was not clear that its investment in influence was paying much of a dividend.

This affected the global, multi-metal players and the smaller, single metal nationals differentially, and this was thus a driver which involved to some extent industry characteristics as well as governance system factors. But most of the important characteristics of the industry which affect associability (the 'bottom up' factors) in the industry appear to be negative factors, or impediments to association: variability of size; fragmentation; lack of vertical integration in base metals; and relative lack of an interest in harmonised approaches to risk management (such as applies with chemicals thanks to intellectual property considerations).

The development of policy initiatives overwhelmingly drove the formation of ICMM. For example, the move by the EU to regulate the use of cyanide by the gold sector after the Esmeralda spill not only helped make international organization more sensible for gold miners, and thus drove associability for ICMM, but it helped keep the 'dirt digging' gold miners at the subnational level in Western Australia interested in both the ICMM and the MCA and its Minerals Code (see Chapter 4).

As long as there were policy measures which affected the industry as a whole (or something approaching that) at the international level, there was therefore likely to be support for ICMM and its engagement strategies, not just among the larger companies which have longer-term investments and perspectives, but among the smaller 'dirt diggers' with a three-year outlook and little interest in best practice and the costs of achieving it.

The 30-odd companies immediately outside the ICMM fold were reportedly still sceptical about the whole enterprise. And probably understandably so. This is a price-taking industry selling undifferentiated products, where internalising the externalities, in the short run at least, simply eats into profits; and rates of profit had been below the cost of capital. Reputation might be a bankable commodity, but there are economies of scale here, and its value is greatest per dollar invested for the large global players. There is much less incentive for the smaller nationals to adopt international best practice, and more reason for them to view the voluntary spread of best practice by ICMM as a limitation on the ability of smaller players like them to enter the market. Such regulation (even if only self-regulation) can work to the advantage of the larger players. If externalities are to be internalised, those who can internalise at least-cost will win, and the reputational economies of scale favour the large firms, and the new operations which can be designed *de novo* to meet new standards.

So there is a tension present which suggests that the success in establishing ICMM and progress on the sustainable development agenda is somewhat fragile. The reputation of the industry is determined by the performance of the worst companies. Inevitably, the standards developed by ICMM became the expectations and formalised standards of the communities in which the industry operates. But the challenge lay in how to get greater engagement among the smaller companies. ICMM initiatives might lead to recognition by governments and juniors of what constitutes 'good practice', but ICMM cannot really deal with artisanal mining. And as Richard Sandbrook observed, 'People don't realise how small and how pivotal this sector is. It is still very dispersed, with a long tail of activity. Seventy percent of marketed gems are dug by artisanal miners.'

It is possible that some kind of product certification might come ultimately with some sort of 'Certificate of Responsible Mining', such was suggested by Michael Rae at WWF. And consumers might be prepared to pay a little more for copper or zinc or gold so certified in preference to that not certified. But probably only if the cost was marginal, and the large companies which are more likely to participate in developing such a scheme and promulgating it through ICMM will always be susceptible to being undercut by juniors and artisanal producers whose activities might take place at a lower standard, but one which (because of sheer size considerations) is less likely, and which (because they are single country operations) is unlikely to engender concerns by such producers over reputational capital, but which are likely to harm the reputation of the industry as a whole the next time a tailings dam fails or a cyanide spill occurs.

Appendix A

List of Sponsors MMSD

Alcan Inc
Alcoa Inc
Anglo American
Anglovaal Mining Limited (Avmin) Inc
BHP-Billiton
Caterpillar Inc
Cedar Products Ltd
Chilean Copper Commission
Colorado School of Mines
Conservation International
Corporación Nacional del Cobre-Codelco
CRU International Ltd
DFID, Government of UK
Environment Australia, Government of Australia
Freeport-McMoRan Copper and Gold Inc
Global Reporting Initiative
Gold Fields Ltd
HATCH Associates Ltd
ICEM
IUCN - The World Conservation Union
KPMG
Lonmin plc
M.I.M. Holdings Ltd
Mackay School of Mines
Mitsubishi Materials Corporation/Mitsubishi Corporation
Mitsui Mining and Smelting Co. Ltd
Newmont Mining Corporation
Nippon Mining & Metals Co., Ltd
Noranda Inc
Norsk Hydro ASA
NRCan, Government of Canada
Pasminco Ltd
Phelps Dodge Corporation
Placer Dome Inc
PricewaterhouseCoopers
Rio Tinto plc
The Rockefeller Foundation
Sibal, Sibirsky Aluminium Group

Somincor
Sumitomo Metal Mining
Teck Cominco Ltd
United Nations Environment Programme
WMC Ltd
The World Bank

CHAPTER 4

MESO LEVEL: THE MINERALS COUNCIL OF AUSTRALIA

This chapter outlines the changing configuration of sector associations in the Australian mining industry at the national level. The key organisations are the Australian Mining Industry Council (AMIC) established in 1967, and its successor the Minerals Council of Australia (MCA), formed in 1995 with a broader rubric. AMIC was formed to deal directly with state and federal governments on issues affecting the mining and metallurgical industries in Australia and its territories. As this chapter will show, over time, the AMIC's narrow and aggressive approach, apparently motivated by short-term considerations, came to be seen as outmoded and inappropriate. AMIC's close links with the (centre-right) Liberal-Country Party Coalition government at the national level, and governments of similar complexion at the state-level, hampered its capacity to deal with the centre-left ALP government elected in March 1983. The hard-line approach of AMIC's public relations put the Council in direct conflict with the proponents of land rights for Aborigines, and environmental lobbyists, and relations with the ALP national government quickly deteriorated. This became a serious problem for the mining sector, as the ALP was elected for subsequent terms, and remained in office for over 13 years, until mid-1996.

The MCA's role in representing the exploration, mining and minerals processing industry was to become a 'leadership' one; with a strong emphasis on reputational factors, and the need to work simultaneously at both national and global levels, especially but not solely around the development, and implementation of environmental sustainability.

It is also important to note that the changing pattern of associability in the mining industry was part of a wider trend. For example, the manufacturing sector had already shifted from the Manufacturing Industry Advisory Council (MIAC), to the Australian Manufacturing Council by 1977. Then in 1996—around the time that the Minerals Council of Australia was formed—the Australian Manufacturing Council merged with the Metal Trades Industry Association to form the Australian Industry Group (AIG).

Given the historically high tariff wall supporting Australian manufacturing, one would expect manufacturing to be well embedded in the structure of governance. The tariff was a national-level instrument, hence manufacturing would be expected to be well-represented with national structures, and in the orbit of particular government departments, and statutory authorities. (The industry also operated through long-established state chambers of manufactures regarding regional level support and wages policy).

Mining had long been dependent on state governments for the provision of infrastructure, and had tended to lobby at that level—hence the continuing importance of the state-level chambers of mining in key mining regions of Queensland, Northern Territory and Western Australia—to be discussed in the next chapter. The timing of mining's shift to the national level can also be linked to the end of the 'long boom' (1949-66) and the beginning of the 'age of uncertainty'.[1] The national setting of economic levers was becoming contestable.

Origins of AMIC

The formation of AMIC came in response to state-centric factors, particularly a desire from policy-makers for a representative voice to speak for the industry.[2] The context was a meeting of the Export Development Council (EDC) in Brisbane in 1966. Sir Clarence Byrne (CEO of Comalco) was invited (as President of the Queensland Chamber of Mines) by Sir Alan Westerman, Secretary of the Commonwealth Department of Trade and Industry, to put the mining industry's view regarding export development. Sir Clarence replied that it would be 'presumptuous for any one state to enunciate a policy on behalf of the whole Australian Mining Industry. . . .' Sir Clarence suggested to Westerman and G. Paul Phillips—who at this time was Sir Alan's Deputy Secretary— that it would be preferable if they sought

---

[1] See Kelly 1992.

[2] The details of the formation of AMIC are set out in a letter dated 26 May 1976 from Sir Clarence Byrne (CEO of Comalco and President of the Queensland Chamber of Mines at the time of AMIC's creation) to G. Paul Phillips, Executive Director of AMIC, held in the files of the Minerals Council of Australia. Phillips, who had been foundation Executive Director, had written to Byrne on 22 April seeking his account of the founding of AMIC, because 'A couple of people have said to me recently that A.M.I.C. was established at the request of Sir Robert Menzies—a new slant as far as I am concerned.'

the view of one of their mining members on the EDC, to which they replied there was no such member on the EDC.[3]

This desire of the national government to have the view of the sector was therefore the stimulus for the formation of a national sector group. There had been earlier attempts to form an association, but these came to naught until the request for representation provided a strengthened basis of national association in a sector which at that time was organised only in the states of Queensland and Western Australia, and the latter was then mostly concerned with gold. (There was also a Northern Territory chamber). There had been discussion of a national association at a meeting in Melbourne in 1963, but it had not amounted to anything. Byrne called a meeting of the Queensland Chamber of Mines and proposed the formation of a 'Commonwealth Mining Council', and an invitation was subsequently issued on 1 September 1966 to a meeting held on 11 October at the rooms of the Australasian Institute of Mining and Metallurgy, at 399 Little Collins Street in Melbourne, at which AMIC was formed.

The meeting was private—by invitation only, and with no press. Not in attendance were Maurie Mawby (head of Conzinc Riotinto of Australia—CRA, the Australian Rio Tinto subsidiary) and George Fisher (head of Mount Isa Mines), who was elected the foundation president, and who had taken the initiative at the 1963 meeting. (Some 40 years earlier, Mawby and Fisher had been colleagues at Broken Hill). Mawby was taken ill, while Fisher's wife had been killed in a plane crash on her way to Mt Isa just before the meeting. Ian McLennan, Chairman of BHP, declined the presidency on the grounds that it was inappropriate for the largest company to be seen as controlling AMIC. The meeting decided that the constitution should be modelled on that of the American Mining Congress. Financial contributions would be scaled according to the number of employees each member company had. Significantly, its scope was limited to metals miners, to the exclusion of the coal industry. As Byrne was later to describe it, 'the meeting accepted my view that at that stage we "Metals" had enough problems of our own and in any event the Coal Industry had traditionally "paddled its own canoe".' The position of Executive Director was subsequently advertised but, Byrne's suggestion was that an offer should be

[3] Byrne responded that 'It's a disgrace that the industry which will be the greatest earner of export income is not represented on your Council.' As Sir Clarence recalled the exchange ten years later, 'Alan said "will you do something about it?" And I said with some heat and great sincerity, "I bloody well will".'

made to Phillips, Deputy Secretary of the Department of Trade and Industry (who had not applied).

By 1975 AMIC had grown to represent about 97 percent of companies involved in the mining, smelting, and refining of metallic minerals in Australia, with 145 members and income from subscriptions of $253,000. It worked cooperatively with the petroleum industry in the form of the Australian Petroleum Exploration Association (APEA), the employers' industrial organisation for the sector, the Australian Mines and Metals Association (AMMA) and the commodity group representing the mineral sands industry, the Rutile and Zircon Development Association.

It also worked cooperatively with the Chambers of Mines in Queensland, Western Australia and the Northern Territory, but there were no state chambers in New South Wales, Victoria, South Australia or Tasmania at this time. To overcome this limitation, state committees of AMIC were established in NSW, Victoria and South Australia to ensure matters of special concern to each were fed into AMIC. (The Victorian state committee also represented Tasmania). In addition, members of the Executive were requested to bring matters to the attention of the Executive Council to supplement the role of State Committees.

In 1975 AMIC had the following committees active, which indicate the issues with which it was dealing: Environmental Quality (with an Air Quality Sub-Committee); Mining Equipment; Mining Legislation; Mining Regulations; Public Relations; Tariff; Taxation; and Transport. The Australian coal industry at this time was expanding rapidly, with export markets emerging, first for coking coal and later for steaming coal. Among the new members joining AMIC in the mid-1970s were coal companies like Theiss Peabody, Mitsui Coal, and Kianga Coal, despite the fact that there was a separate Australian Coal Association to represent coal producers to the Commonwealth government.

One of the main issues AMIC was dealing with in 1975 was legislation proposed by the Whitlam ALP government to establish a Petroleum and Minerals Authority, which prompted consideration by AMIC, APEA and the Australian Coal Association of how these three bodies might cooperate on this agenda. This led to greater cooperation between the three but they stopped short merging or establishing any formal links. Instead, it was agreed that the presidents and CEOs would meet twice a year to develop common positions as needed.

Having established a Public Relations Committee (chaired by Western Mining's Hugh Morgan) in 1976, AMIC began monitoring public opinion in 1978. This research revealed that the public perception was that the mining industry made too much profit, paid insufficient tax, had levels of overseas investment that were too high, that there was insufficient government control, that it was not sufficiently concerned for the environment, that it did not respect Aboriginal land rights, and that there was uncertainty over uranium mining. These concerns saw the immediate response of the formation in 1979 of committees dealing with Aboriginal Affairs and Foreign Investment.

By 1980 significant developments were evident at both the state level and international levels. At the state level, 1980 saw the establishment of a state chamber in South Australia, although in New South Wales AMIC continued to interact with the state Department of Mineral Resources in NSW. Internationally, the negotiation of the UN Convention on the Law of the Sea was the most significant matter on the horizon for the industry. An appreciation of the need to develop an awareness of issues affecting the mining industry at the global level was beginning to emerge, and in April and May 1979 the Assistant Director of AMIC visited the United States, Canada, the United Kingdom and South Africa to discuss public relations with mining companies and AMIC's sister organizations.

The operation of the *Environmental Protection (Impact of Proposals) Act* and the *Heritage Commission Act* continued to concern the industry, as they both affected (via Commonwealth legislation) access to land for exploration and exploitation, extending Commonwealth jurisdiction into a previously state government preserve. Lobbying on this issue paid off in 1980 when a review was commenced of both acts. Aboriginal land rights had also emerged as an issue of concern and AMIC secured an undertaking for a review on this issue, and AMIC agreed with Minister Fred Chaney to remain silent on land rights while Barry Rowland QC conducted a review of the *Aboriginal Land Rights (Northern Territory) Act*. But Chaney was replaced during the review by Peter Baume and the resulting Rowland Report was subsequently described only as a 'Discussion Paper', much to the disappointment of AMIC.

The globalisation of the environment debate was noted in the 1990 annual report of AMIC, and by 1992 other concerns including waterfront inefficiency and protectionism, land rights, especially the High Court's decision in the *Mabo* case[4] to grant land rights, the Resource Assessment Commission (RAC) inquiry into Kakadu in 1989, and sustainable development (especially preparations for UNCED in Rio in 1992) were on AMIC's radar. AMIC was also involved in the Ecologically Sustainable Development process (a quasi-corporatist consultation aimed at resolving conflicts) participating in Working Groups on mining, energy and manufacturing and supporting past president Sir Bruce Watson in his role as a member of WBCSD which was to submit a business perspective at Rio.

AMIC's handling of the RAC inquiry into mining in parts of Kakadu was a public relations nightmare, as it was presented in the media as being out of touch with public opinion, and working closely with a minority, and neo-liberal section of the centre-right Liberal Party. Significantly, the RAC Inquiry had found no environmental objections to mining in certain parts of the Kakadu national park, but maintained that mining would be offensive to the spiritual life—the serpent god, Bula—of the local Jawoyn people. Liberal Party leader, Dr John Hewson argued that: 'If you know anything about Aboriginal heritage, Bula didn't exist ten years ago. He suddenly emerged as a device to block Coronation Hill.'[5]

Environmental concerns were growing in prominence, not just in absolute terms, but relatively, as some traditional concerns in areas like trade began to recede. For example, 1992 saw the removal of an export levy on coal, and rising hopes that greater access to the German coal market might result from the Uruguay Round of trade liberalisation. So while issues like transport continued to be significant, emerging issues like climate change and biodiversity presented new challenges to the industry and its association, and the international nature of many of these issues challenged its national orientation.

During the first half of 1992 AMIC agreed to participate in the Council for International Business Affairs (CIBA) a new peak business group focusing on foreign trade and foreign direct investment policy issues. CIBA's members were interest groups—both sector groups and peak associations: the Australian Chamber of Commerce and Industry; Australian Coal Association; Australian Coalition of Service Industries; Australian Mining Industry Council; Business Council of Australia; Metal

[4] The *Mabo decision* was a legal case decided in 1992: *Mabo and others v Queensland (No 2) (1992)*. The legal decision was given by the High Court on 3 June 1992.

[5] *Commonwealth Hansard* 17 May 1991

Trades Industry Association; and the National Farmers Federation. CIBA also had a number of Associate Members: the Australian Chamber of Manufactures; Australian Society of Certified Practising Accountants; Electricity Supply Association of Australia; Institute of Chartered Accountants in Australia; and the Law Council of Australia. CIBA started out as a division of the Australian Council of Commerce and Industry (until December 1992) and the growth of its membership reflected the emergence of various international issues—the joining of both the Australian Coal Association and the Electricity Supply Association, for example, clearly reflected emerging concern over the Framework Convention on Climate Change.

AMIC, under Executive Director Lachlan McIntosh, took a combative stance on most of these issues. He wrote in 1992 of 'a green lobby unable to compromise and find solutions' (AMIC 1992 Annual Report, p5). But if the loss of the proposed Coronation Hill mine in the Conservation Zone of (World Heritage listed) Kakadu National Park in the Northern Territory after the RAC inquiry was not enough, Aboriginal land rights soon made mining industry access to land for exploration and mining even more problematic, with the Mabo decision recognising that a system of native land title persisted on unalienated public land being handed down in June 1992. AMIC responded quickly to this development by establishing an Aboriginal Affairs Committee. This defensive strategy was accompanied by greater reliance on advertising in response to political parties' greater use of opinion polling and AMIC's own research which continued to reveal that the public doubted the industry's credibility (AMIC 1992 Annual Report, 7). This strategy (and AMIC) was to change.

The High Court decision in *Eddy Mabo and Others v the State of Queensland* handed down on 3 June 1992 established the concept of native title. Native title as defined by the High Court is a bundle of legal rights and interests held by Aboriginal and Torres Strait Islander peoples in land and waters. It can exist on vacant (or unallocated) Crown land, national parks and reserves, forests and beaches, some types of pastoral leases, land held for Aboriginal communities, bodies of water that are not privately owned, and land held by government agencies. Native title exists only where it has not been extinguished by some allocation of title by a government. Because native title does not remove the valid rights of others, where native title rights and the rights of another person conflict, the rights of the other person prevail.

In most cases where native title is successfully claimed, the land will be shared by the native title holders and other people with rights and interests in the same area. Native title rights can therefore coexist with other rights in the area. (Pastoral lease holders can run their pastoral business while native title holders can access the land to practice their culture). Exploration and mining companies need to consult with native title holders who may have a right to negotiate over development and exploration.

Indigenous people can apply to the courts to have their native title rights recognised, but the *Native Title Act 1993* established a system of National Native Title Tribunals to deal expeditiously with native title applications, provide mediation and help negotiate indigenous land use agreements. The Tribunal system recognises that court cases can be lengthy, expensive and stressful, and even where a court determines that native title exists, the parties will usually need to reach separate agreement on what it actually means 'on the ground'. An alternative method called an Indigenous Land Use Agreement or ILUA can be used. An ILUA is a legally binding agreement (registered with the National Native Title Tribunal) about how a body of land or water will be used or managed. ILUAs can be an alternative to court proceedings and determinations.

The Australian Mining Industry Council pursued a more confrontational approach to defending the industry than was to be the case with its successor, the Minerals Council of Australia. It was particularly concerned with the effect of the removal of land from exploration and mining. For example, in launching an AMIC paper entitled *Shrinking Australia* in 1990 (AMIC 1990), executive director, Lachlan McIntosh claimed that the 'area of land where mineral exploration or mining is either prohibited or restricted in Australia has grown by 11 per cent during the past two years to nearly a quarter of the entire country'. Moreover, 'the mining industry would be slowly choked to death if the trend was allowed to continue' (*Sydney Morning Herald*, 27 June, 1990). McIntosh, stated that if current demands by the green lobby for the reservation of a further 21.7 per cent of land in national parks, reserves or World Heritage areas were met, it would put almost half the country out of the reach of the mining industry and the mining industry would be slowly 'choked to death.'

The *Shrinking Australia* paper employed the latest information on land use compiled by the Australian Surveying and Land Information Group, part of the Federal Department of Administrative Services, for the Mining Council. This data showed that most of the total of 26 per cent of land locked away from the mining industry was under Aboriginal control

(15.3 per cent), while about 5.6 per cent was in national parks, reserves and other conservation areas. A further 5 per cent of land was made up of forestry reserves, urban areas, coastal zones and freehold land where the use was restricted. In addition, there was a large amount of land held by State and Commonwealth Governments used for various purposes such as defence. In NSW about 11 per cent of the area of the state was reserved from mining activities, compared with 34 per cent of land in Victoria, 7.2 per cent of Queensland, 39.1 per cent of South Australia and 30.3 per cent of Tasmania. In contrast, McIntosh pointed out, the total area occupied by mining operations in Australia was less than 0.02 per cent. He therefore claimed the industry was having 'an infinitesimal impact' on the land.

In addition to bringing these facts to the attention of the public, however, McIntosh made a demand which was rather extreme, especially when it is remembered that this was 1990, the year widely regarded as witnessing the 'greening of Australian politics', when the ALP retained power at the election that year largely thanks to preferences directed by the environment movement. It was reported that the AMIC believed that all of Australia ought to be open to mining exploration and that no land ought to be set aside for single uses such as national parks where mining and other activities were prohibited. 'The mining and rural industries built Australia and the mining and rural industries are today keeping Australia from going bankrupt,' Mr McIntosh said.

This was seen as a 'land grab' by the Australian Conservation Foundation which cited the concept of ecologically sustainable development in arguing the need for preservation of areas of high conservation value in addition to the sustainable use of natural resources. It argued that it was recognised worldwide that the best way to protect biological diversity was by dedicating areas as national parks. The ACF claimed that 'figures from overseas' indicated that the area of land tied up in national parks ought to be about 10 per cent if a country's biological diversity was to be protected. On AMIC's figures, the area in reserves in Australia was only about half that amount.

On another occasion AMIC claimed that in most cases mining was more environmentally sensitive than forestry or farming. McIntosh claimed Australian mining companies led the world in land rehabilitation and that the industry planted about two million trees a year. He said that to pay for environmental protection, Australia needed to earn export dollars from major industries like mining. 'If we do not have competitive industries we will go broke, we would not be able to have the protection we would like' (*Australian Financial Review*, August 23, 1990).

This confrontational approach was not well received in some quarters. In a speech to the NSW Fabian Society, Minister for the Environment Mrs Ros Kelly accused AMIC of thinking sustainability meant they should mine how, when and where they wanted *(Sydney Morning Herald*, August 30, 1990). Kelly claimed that AMIC's idea of a sustainable industry was

> one in which miners can mine where they like, for however long they want. It is about, for them, sustaining profits and increasing access to all parts of Australia they feel could be minerally [*sic*] profitable even if it is of environmental or cultural significance (*Australian Financial Review*, August 30, 1990).

The confrontation between AMIC and the environment minister extended to other issues, such as climate change. AMIC argued that Ms. Kelly's claim that a 20 per cent reduction in greenhouse gas emissions by 2005 would be 'readily achievable' was 'nonsense'. McIntosh claimed such a reduction would harm Australia's export competitiveness and would cost about $30 billion. He said the benefits of such a reduction had not been fully quantified and that support for such a target without full research was foolish. He stated: 'If you are already clean and very efficient, such targets might be impossible, or at the very least impose an enormous competitive impediment on export industries' (*Australian Financial Review*, September 7, 1990).

Giving evidence to the RAC inquiry on potential land uses of the Kakadu conservation zone, McIntosh, said wealth created by mining in the park would enable the park to be more adequately funded. In its submission to the RAC, AMIC stated the living standards of all Australians were being put at risk as a result of reduced investment because of an increasing tendency to protect large tracts of land from mining. AMIC estimated that the park contained $106.4 billion worth of mineral resources. This position generated a headline which was hardly flattering to the industry: 'Mining Lobby Wants All of Kakadu', stated the *Sydney Morning Herald* (September 28, 1990).

But it was not long before the industry commenced a more sophisticated strategy to engage more positively with environmental issues, announcing in November 1991 the establishment by AMIC of the Australian Minerals and Energy Environment Foundation to help the industry improve its environmental management, with the mission to promote excellence in environmental science and management (*Australian Financial Review*, November 1, 1991). AMEEF was, however, to operate independently of AMIC and had its own independent board of directors. It was intended to encourage the transfer of information on environmental management in the minerals and energy industries and with other industry and community sectors. It was anticipated that it would be able to provide practical advice and information on environmental science and management to the minerals industry and to other industries. It planned to publish a textbook on environmental management.

This positive approach, coincided with a softening within the Hawke Government towards the mining sector. The union movement had been instrumental in convincing Prime Minister Hawke that the federal government should help the mining and manufacturing sectors. Australia was headed for an economic downturn, and it was feared that the policing of foreign investment requirements, plus restrictions surrounding Aboriginal land rights and environmental considerations, were making employment prospects weaker.

AMIC continued its previous aggressive strategy, however. In 1992 it co-sponsored a report that found a 'unilateral decision to reduce Australian carbon dioxide emissions 20 per cent by 2005 would devastate the steel and aluminium industries and severely affect the coal, iron ore, oil and gas industries' (*Australian Financial Review*, February 6, 1992). But things were changing. From about 1994 CRA disengaged from the hardline AMIC approach, particularly on indigenous issues. After the loss of the Panguna copper mine on Bougainville as a result of the separatist movement there, it had adopted the position that it would not operate without the consent of the community. With the development of the Century Zinc mine in Queensland, Aboriginal activist Murandoo Yanner was threatening to block construction of the slurry pipeline that would carry concentrates to the export port, so—unable to meet its own standards—CRA abandoned the project, and sold its interest to Pasminco, for whom it was important. (Pasminco had a zinc smelter in the Netherlands which would have to close unless it could access low-iron ore from Century).

This signalled a new era in relations between mining companies and indigenous people in Australia. By walking away from Century, CRA showed that it was serious. Ironically, with hindsight, the dispute over Coronation Hill (located in Kakadu National Park) also represented the high point in the alliance between green and indigenous groups that had dominated for over two decades, and the campaign against the Jabiluka uranium mine in the Kakadu conservation zone was essentially the last front of the old battles involving an alliance between greens and Aborigines.[6] With Jabiluka, pre-existing arrangements dating back to the Ranger uranium mine days meant that companies could not negotiate directly with traditional owners, and the agreements were only about money, which had by now been recognised as having a pernicious effect on Aboriginal communities.

The revolution in land rights after *Mabo* meant that companies could negotiate directly with traditional owners and include a broad range of factors in agreements, including educational and employment opportunities. This enhanced the individual firm-traditional owner relationship, and reduced the need for traditional owners to build coalitions outside their communities, thus effectively dealing green groups out of the arena. At a time when AMIC was playing hardball on Coronation Hill and other policy negotiations, first Rio and then other companies such as BHP and WMC were negotiating long-term progressive agreements with traditional owners. Environmental groups were thus effectively locked out of most Australian mining issues relating to indigenous people; they still had some purchase on indigenous issues in other countries in the region, though this was refracted through an aid lens.

There was effectively no role being played by AMIC in these developments. There was no sharing of best practice—not surprising, since best practice on such issues was likely to bear fruit at the level of the individual company. But industry associations often earn their way by adopting hardline positions while their member companies pursue softer, more sophisticated public relations strategies. As we shall see, reform to the industrial relations system was to further weaken associability in the sector, and many of these issues were also being handled at the level of the individual firm. But there was dissonance between the individual positions of the leading companies and the industry association position with the emergence of a more positive engagement, and this began to be reflected in thinking within AMIC, especially after it appointed a new Executive Director in August 1994, not from within the industry, but from the federal bureaucracy, in the form of David Buckingham, who had been head of the Commonwealth Environment Protection Agency. Buckingham instituted a review of AMIC, which subsequently changed its name to the Minerals Council of Australia and adopted a structure which freed it from seeking

[6] According to Bob Hawke, ACF leader Philip Toyne was instrumental in persuading Hawke to initiate the RAC inquiry into Kakadu (Hawke 1996, 506).

consensus (and thus lowest common denominator) decisions. Intriguingly, Buckingham had worked in Prime Minister Hawke's office during his first two terms in office. He went on to head the Business Council of Australia (BCA) which had been created in 1984, in response to the neo-corporatist Economic Summit.

A New Beginning: The Minerals Council of Australia

It was not that the change from AMIC to MCA resulted in a more accommodative strategy in the industry's interactions with the government, but that transition from McIntosh to new Executive Director Buckingham both reflected and resulted in an immediate change of approach. Through Buckingham, AMIC criticised the Australian Government following its announcement that it would not meet its greenhouse gas emissions commitment. Environment Minister, Senator John Faulkner, claimed that if Australia continued with its then current level of greenhouse response, it would be 7 per cent above 1990 levels of gas emissions by the year 2000, whereas the non-binding target adopted in the Framework Convention on Climate Change was for stabilisation at 1990 levels by 2000.[7] Buckingham criticized the predilection of the Australian government to be 'caught short' in its appreciation of the potential impacts of new treaty instruments it had entered into. But rather than just oppose climate change policy, he tried to position the industry better in future negotiations. He argued that this was only likely to change with closer community and industry involvement in the development of Australia's negotiating position. He argued that 'Damage limitation assessment after the event is not a responsible, or effective, way in which to proceed' (*Australian Financial Review*, October 11, 1994).

This was the precursor to the greater involvement of both industry and environment NGOs in the formulation of negotiating positions and on delegations to negotiations which was central to Australia's tough negotiating strategy at Kyoto. Almost uniquely, Australia had industry representatives on its delegations to climate change negotiations. Australia secured a target at Kyoto many saw as generous, but it was a target which has proven more realistic than many, and one which it met while many other parties failed to meet theirs.

---

[7] In point of fact, the FCCC set a *shared* target for all Annex I Parties to collectively stabilise emissions at 1990 levels by 2000.

The Minerals Council, in developing a strategy of more positive engagement, was not averse to continuing to take a hard line to protect its interests, however. It lobbied successfully to continue to exempt the industry from diesel fuel excise, and had the *Hazardous Waste Bill* amended to deny standing to many groups and individuals (including those overseas) to challenge government decisions. It took advantage of the election of the Howard Liberal-National Coalition government in 1996 to lobby hard on climate change and applauded the Government's decision that 'it will not "sacrifice" tens of thousands of jobs by agreeing to inequitable international greenhouse gas reduction strategies', after Cabinet endorsed a tough negotiating position for second Conference of the Parties to FCCC in Geneva in July 1996. David Buckingham said the Government had quite properly shown it would be 'driven by protecting Australia's economic and trade interests' (*Sydney Morning Herald*, June 5, 1996).[8] A significant part of that negotiating position was a rejection of legally-binding targets in what was to become the Kyoto Protocol. The Minerals Council of Australia later co-signed a letter to Australian Prime Minister John Howard urging him not to abandon Australia's position on greenhouse gas emissions—a stance the US President, Bill Clinton, said should be abandoned in favour of legally binding targets (*Australian Financial Review*, November 25, 1996).

The Code for Environmental Management

Simultaneously, however, the Minerals Council was developing a voluntary Code for Environmental Management for its members, a key requirement of which was that participating companies prepare annual environmental reports which would be available to the public. The development of the MCA Code was driven by the experience of BHP at Ok Tedi and was essentially a defensive mechanism. The development and operation of the Ok Tedi mine exemplified the problems of operating in developing countries, especially when poor regulatory standards were applied because the appropriate government was compromised. Despite complying with regulatory requirements imposed by the government of Papua New Guinea, BHP came to considerable reputational harm.

BHP had originally preferred to exploit only the gold-rich ore that sat atop the larger copper-gold deposit. The PNG government had insisted as a condition of developing the mine that BHP develop the whole deposit,

[8] In a display of subeditorial confusion, the *Sydney Morning Herald* headlined this story 'Australia Places Jobs Before Ozone'.

giving rise to considerably more mine tailings than would have resulted from a gold-only operation. The area had very difficult terrain, peppered with limestone caves, and was subject to tropical rainfall. An attempt was made to construct a tailings dam under these difficult conditions, but a flood washed it away. The PNG government had taken equity in the project, and was thus doubly compromised: not only did it benefit from foreign exchange earnings, taxation and the purchase of labour and other services by the mine, but it had a direct interest in the profitability of the mine. When the question arose as to whether Ok Tedi should be permitted to continue to operate without a tailings dam, the PNG government not just permitted it, but actively encouraged this course.

The value of Ok Tedi to PNG became even greater when the war mounted by Bougainville separatists resulted in the closure of CRA's Panguna copper mine in that province. Operating Ok Tedi without a tailings dam had a devastating impact on a large section of the Fly River, and gave rise to a class action by landholders in the Australian courts, which BHP settled out of court, subsequently quitting its interest in the mine (which nevertheless continued to operate) and placing its compensation payment for landholders into an independently administered trust fund.

The Code was intended to ensure that Australian companies met standards of practice which would prevent a recurrence of the Ok Tedi case, both domestically and in developing countries. Australian-based companies were involved (in the immediate region) in Indonesia, PNG and the Philippines, but the increasingly transnational nature of the industry raised some interesting issues, especially given the activities of NGOs in raising issues about corporate conduct in the region. But not all the companies active in the area were Australian, and not therefore members of the MCA. This raised difficult issues. Would the Minerals Council take action to defend Freeport-McMoRan, a US-owned company that operated a controversial gold mine in Irian Jaya province of Indonesia? The Australian interests with equity in the mine were owned mainly by English companies, but the audience the NGOs were playing to was in Australia, so the MCA would be almost compelled to assist in the defence, unless an international body was formed to do so.

Signatories to the Code committed to:

- Integration of environmental, social and economic considerations into decision-making and management, consistent with the objectives of sustainable development.

- Openness, transparency and improved accountability through public environmental reporting and engagement with the community.
- Compliance with all statutory requirements, as a minimum.
- A continually-improving standard of environmental performance and, through leadership, the pursuit of environmental excellence throughout the Australian minerals industry.

The signatories had seven principles they had to uphold:

1. 'Accepting Environmental Responsibility for all our actions'.
2. 'Strengthening our Relationship with the Community'.
3. 'Integrating Environmental Management into the Way we Work'.
4. 'Minimising the Environmental Impact of our Activities'.
5. 'Encouraging Responsible Production and Use of our Products'.
6. 'Continuingly Improving Our Environmental Performance'.
7. 'Communicating our Environmental Performance'.

Commitment to the Code brought with it a number of obligations. Code signatories had to (p.2):

- Apply the Code wherever they operate, both domestically and overseas, including application to the relevant activities of contractors engaged by the signatories;
- Commit to continual improvement by progressively implementing the Code's principles;
- Produce an annual public environment report, with the first report produced within two years of signing;
- Complete an annual Code Implementation Survey to assess signatory progress against implementation of Code principles; and
- Have the results of the Code Implementation Survey verified at least every three years by an accredited internal or external auditor.

Minerals Council assistant director Ian Satchwell considered that the Code did not set entry standards but signatories would be required to demonstrate their commitment to environmental excellence. The Code was particularly addressed to the reputational issues confronting an industry increasingly wishing to conduct business globally. In announcing the pending launch of the Code, it was claimed that companies which adopted the new code could gain a competitive edge, particularly in the case of Australian companies looking to invest offshore where environmental credentials could be required (*Australian*, November 18, 1996). When the Code was launched in December 1996 it was well-received by the investment community. Industry analysts predicted that the voluntary environmental code would lift its international competitiveness and 'help solidify public support for mining' (*Dow Jones Commodities Service*, December 10, 1996). By the end of 1998, 41 companies had signed the Minerals Industry Code for Environmental Management. This grew to 44 signatories by the end of 1999.

Australian mining companies were active in about 80 countries, as explorers, miners and as providers of industry goods and services. At the time of launch, 18 large mining companies (including Broken Hill Proprietary Co., MIM Holdings Ltd., Normandy Mining Ltd., WMC Ltd. and CRA Ltd) had either adopted the Code or announced an intention to do so. Jerry Ellis, president of the Minerals Council, considered the Code would enhance both investment prospects for the minerals industry and sales by its related goods and services supply sector, including environmental services. Resources Minister Warwick Parer, speaking while launching the Code, said that as other countries opened their minerals sectors to foreign investment, sensitivity to environmental and other community issues was important in gaining land access and keeping community support. Praise also came from Environment Minister Robert Hill, who was also involved in the launch (*Australian*, December 10, 1996). There was, however, criticism of the Code by the Australian Conservation Foundation: 'It is so general and vague that it could mean many different things to many people,' according to ACF policy analyst Dr Helen Rosenbaum (*Australian*, December 10, 1996). Conservation groups generally dismissed the Code as an attempt to 'green-wash' the Australian community.

The voluntary code was part of a push by the mining industry to lift its green image and it began to bear immediate fruit, especially with the Coalition government in office from 1996. The launch of the Code came immediately after the Government announced a decision to rezone Australia's national parks, leaving the option open for mining in second-grade forest reserves (*Sydney Morning Herald*, December 7, 1996). New Minerals Council executive director Dick Wells (who had joined the MCA from APPEA in the petroleum sector) welcomed the Australian Government's decision to open up millions of hectares of forest around the country to mining and its consideration of a radical plan to remove the massive protected wilderness zone within Kakadu National Park.

The Commonwealth Government decided to open up native forests of 'lesser conservation value' to mining, committing itself to examining a forest's mineral prospects before reserving it, and to exclude from new reserves areas of high mineral potential where such exclusions did not significantly compromise nationally agreed reserve criteria. The Minerals Council was not entirely happy with the decision, claiming the dedicated reserves could be locking up mineral resources forever, but this was a substantial victory for mining interests (*Australian*, December 18, 1996).

The Minerals Council pushed for voluntary approaches to other regulation, both in terms of international policy and domestic approaches. It backed the Australian Government's resistance to US pressure for it to support legally binding targets in Kyoto, even in the face of US threats to impose trade sanctions on countries that rejected targets (*Australian*, February 25, 1997). At the domestic level, the Minerals Council signed a cooperative agreement with the Commonwealth Government to participate in its Greenhouse Challenge program, a voluntarily initiative to be undertaken by industry. The Council committed itself to work with its member companies to abate emissions of greenhouse gases (*International Market Insight Reports*, September 19, 1997). It also backed the Government's refusal to support a 15 per cent cut in global emissions between 1990 and 2010 in the face of pressure from Europe and the US (*Herald Sun*, October 13, 1997), congratulating the government particularly for withstanding pressure from Europe to accept its stand for uniform targets (*The West Australian*, October 14, 1997).

The Minerals Council was clearly enjoying a close relationship with the new government, but it was not averse to being more confrontational with the Opposition. Executive director Dick Wells expressed displeasure with the ALP's decision that it would not allow any more uranium mines in Australia. He stated: 'It's ridiculous. We had hoped the ALP had learned that those kinds of policies make no sense when you get into government' (*Australian Financial Review*, November 15, 1997).

The Minerals Council was less happy in 1999 with the Government's *Environment Protection and Biodiversity Conservation Bill*, claiming that the Bill 'will dramatically downgrade the role of economic issues in Commonwealth environmental assessments . . .' (*Australian Financial Review*, June 23, 1999). This legislation was the most comprehensive reform of environmental laws undertaken since the emergence of environmentalism. In many ways the *Environment Protection and Biodiversity Conservation Bill* marked the end-point of a process of redefinition of state and

Commonwealth powers in relation to the environment which had commenced in the late 1970s and early 1980s with cases involving sand mining on Fraser Island and the Franklin dam in Tasmanian. While the Commonwealth intervened decisively in these cases and others involving the Wesley Vale pulp mill proposal and the Wet Tropics, the 'New Federalism' of Prime Minister Bob Hawke in the early 1990s saw the emergence of a reluctance on the part of the Commonwealth to assert greater authority, perhaps reflecting a belief that it lacked the capacity to govern effectively a land mass the size of Australia. New Federalism produced an Intergovernmental Agreement on the Environment, the most significant result of which was perhaps the establishment of the National Environmental Protection Council, an intergovernmental body which was to develop harmonized national approaches to many environmental problems with the development of National Environmental Protection Measures (NEPMs) and a National Pollutant Inventory (NPI).

The adoption of the *Environment Protection and Biodiversity Conservation Act* fundamentally recast the responsibilities between Federal and State Governments for environmental protection, and (importantly) limited the possibilities for decisions at the state level to be 'appealed' subsequently to the Commonwealth (as had been the case with the Franklin Dam). The Bill offered a diminution of sovereign risk for the mining industry, and it might have been expected to support it. But the Coalition did not control the Senate, and in order to secure the necessary Australian Democrats support for the package, the Federal Government agreed to more than 400 amendments to the Bill, which had been first introduced in 1998.

The changes were finally agreed to by the Minister for Environment and Heritage, Senator Robert Hill, and the Democrats after weeks of secret negotiations. Under the legislation, the Commonwealth would have the primary role in assessing and approving individual projects in six areas of 'national environmental significance,' including world heritage properties, nationally endangered species, and management and protection of the marine and coastal environment. Environmental assessments for these projects could still be conducted by State governments, though only under nationally accredited environmental benchmarks and principles. Under the amendments agreed with the Democrats, key economic considerations, including 'the need to maintain international competitiveness and a strong national economy,' were removed from the objectives of the bill and replaced with the need to ensure that 'the conservation of biological and ecological integrity is a fundamental consideration in decision-making.'

Business groups were critical of these changes. The Australian Petroleum Production and Exploration Association held they would 'fundamentally unbalance' the legislation. Dick Wells, for the Minerals Council, and Karen Grady from the Business Council of Australia said the changes had completely overturned the basis on which industry groups had agreed to key provisions of the Bill. Wells said the changes would have a symbolic and practical effect, with the amendments providing a solid basis for a legal challenge to any approval that gave weight to economic factors (*Australian Financial Review*, June 23, 1999). Senator Hill defended the Bill, stating that it would not come into effect for 12 months 'to enable the negotiation of bilateral agreements, for getting industry comfortable and familiar with the new processes.'

Nevertheless, the legislation rationalized the way in which environmental matters could become issues for the Commonwealth, much to the chagrin of the Greens. Greens Senator Bob Brown lamented this point, noting: 'When you boil this deal down, the Commonwealth's list of national environmental significance triggers is unchanged. And the central issue of the Commonwealth handing its environmental power and responsibilities to the States is unchanged' (*Australian Financial Review*, June 23, 1999).

The greater sophistication of strategy by the Minerals Council continued, with a hard-nosed negotiating approach on both international and national policy development on issues central to its interests coupled with an approach of positive engagement on reputational issues where enhanced performance might translate in to benefits in the form of better access to land for exploration and mining or better stock prices. An example of the focus on the industry's 'licence to operate' came with the opening address of President David Stewart (of Pasminco) to the Minerals Council's annual seminar in 2000. Stewart recognized that 'Community disapproval was a greater threat to mining companies than business competition or technology' (*Australian Associated Press*, June 7, 2000). He said the industry had to engage with growing consumer activism about product safety and manufacture, the emergence of 'green' share portfolios and increased local and international regulation of environmental dangers, and called on mining companies to show some leadership and prove they were committed to socially and environmentally responsible mining. Pasminco was then facing legal action over lead emissions from two smelters in South Australia and New South Wales, and the industry's reputation had also taken a hit with the cyanide spill in Romania earlier that year from a mine operated by the small Western Australian company Esmeralda.

The adoption of self-regulatory approaches like voluntary codes of conduct can help forestall the introduction of formally imposed regulatory approaches, and NGOs often oppose them on these grounds. The Minerals Council's approach came in for some criticism on these grounds. Executive Director of Community Aid Abroad Oxfam Australia, Jeremy Hobbs, claimed that the Minerals Council's Dick Wells had opposed the introduction of legislation to govern industry standards offshore, suggesting reliance should instead be placed on voluntary codes of conduct and, in particular, the Mineral Council's own Code. Dick Wells argued that its strength lay in the flexibility it offered inasmuch as companies volunteered to commit within a framework of principles, and could choose to implement the Code in a way that was appropriate to their operations and their environments. Wells had argued, said Hobbs, that this was preferable to insisting that mining companies comply with the internationally accepted standards on the environment, human rights and the rights of women (*Australian Financial Review*, July 10, 2000).

Wells countered that he had made no such statement, and that Hobbs was misrepresenting what the Code was about (*Australian Financial Review*, July 11, 2000). He stated that he would never

> argue that the code replaces domestic or international law. It is an adjunct to legislation. It does not replace it, nor should it be misconstrued as a quasi-regulatory instrument. In fact, the code is explicit on this point when it asks its signatories as a core value to commit to 'compliance with all statutory requirements, as a minimum.'

Rather, the Code embodied 'the commitment of the Australian minerals industry to continually improve its environmental performance, and to being open and accountable to the community.' It had been praised by the UN Environment Program as being one of the most comprehensive voluntary codes yet devised for the mining industry, and the only code to require disclosure of environmental performance. Further, it sought to harness the competitive nature of business to improve performance relative to other companies in the sector, because investors would savage those companies which failed to match their rhetoric with performance. Wells flagged future improvements to the Code, which he stressed needed to be flexible and to evolve over time in tune with changing community expectations. This would necessarily include broader social and cultural issues, and he pointed to new initiative under the code—the formation of the Australian Minerals Industry External Environmental Advisory Group.

This exchange took place within the context of legislation introduced by the Democrats. The *Corporate Code of Conduct Bill*, introduced to the Commonwealth Parliament by the Australian Democrats during 2000 sought to impose environmental, health and safety, labour and human rights standards on the conduct of Australian corporations employing more than 100 persons in a foreign country. The Minerals Council cooperated with the Australian Industry Group and the Business Council of Australia in preparing a submission to the parliamentary inquiry into the Bill. In this submission, the Council noted that while it shared the concerns that the Bill sought to address regarding human rights, the environment, labour and occupational health and safety, it 'did not support extraterritorial legislation that proposes to regulate the activities of Australian companies in these areas' (Minerals Council, *Annual Report* 2001, 14).

The Council did use the voluntary Code as a foil to the demand for legislation, when it argued that a framework of local laws and voluntary industry measures, international covenants and agreements, together with negotiated agreements between companies and local communities, could be much more effective in bringing about real change and improvement in these areas (Minerals Council, *Annual Report* 2001, 15). Ultimately, the parliamentary inquiry found that the proposed legislation was both unworkable and inappropriate, and the Bill was withdrawn from Parliament.

The benefits seen as coming from the Code were spelled out in the second progress report on the Code, published in November 2001 (Minerals Council 2001, 4). The benefits claimed were:

- The Code provides an opportunity for the minerals industry to demonstrate application of a consistent approach to environmental management across State, Territory, and international boundaries.
- Information in annual environmental reports will help the industry establish benchmarks of excellence in environmental management and help the transfer of technology.
- Signatories and minerals industry associations can use information in annual reports to promote industry achievement and to foster community consultation. The disclosure of environmental performance provides an avenue for disseminating facts about company performance and helps communication with people and groups which are interested in a mineral company's activities.
- A track record of conformance with the Code will increase the confidence of regulatory agencies and the community in a company's ability to manage its environmental performance.

This could result in less intrusion by regulatory agencies and lower licence and permit fees. It could help expedite environmental approvals.

- Conformance with Code principles will help companies to demonstrate their diligence in managing the environmental aspects of their operations.
- Commitment to the Code has potential to help companies increase their standing with insurers and with ethical investment bodies, which could ultimately mean lower insurance costs, easier access to capital and lower capital servicing costs.
- The Code will help signatories build a company and community culture supporting constant improvement in the workplace and promoting better environmental results from company operations.

The success of a voluntary code would depend ultimately on the extent to which it covered the industry. By the end of 1997 there were 32 signatories to the Code applying it at some 235 sites world-wide (Minerals Council, *Annual Report*, 1997: 14). By the end of 1998, 41 companies had become signatories and it was being applied at more than 250 sites across the world and covering 85 per cent of production by the Australian minerals industry (Minerals Council, *Annual Report* 1998, 12). Coverage reached 44 companies and over 300 sites in 1999 (Minerals Council, *Annual Report* 1999, 12), but the number of companies which were signatories fell to 39 in 2000 (Minerals Council, *Annual Report* 2000, 13). Coverage remained at 85 percent of production, however, and the lesser number of companies involved simply reflected the consolidation of ownership that was occurring in the industry. At the end of 2001, coverage increased further to 43 companies, representing over 90 per cent of Australia's annual mineral production.

The Minerals Council established an independent External Environmental Advisory Group in July 2000 to provide advice to the Minerals Council's Environment Committee 'about those issues of interest and concern to the community regarding the environmental and related social performance of the Australian minerals industry' (Minerals Council, EEAG 2001, 2). Membership of the EEAG was Mike Archer (Director of the Australian Museum, Chair), Chris Burnup (Executive Director, AMEEF), Tricia Caswell (formerly ACF), Mick Dodson (an Aboriginal leader), Ros Kelly (former ALP Environment Minister), Michael Rae (WWF), Dr Fiona Solomon (CSIRO Minerals), and Anthea Tinney (Deputy Secretary, Environment Australia).

The External Environmental Advisory Group was briefed to:

- Comment on the industry-wide assessment of progress in implementing the Australian Minerals Industry Code for Environmental Management (undertaken annually by the Code Secretariat).
- Identify issues of interest and concern to the community about the environmental and related social performance of the minerals industry.
- Provide an annual report on its findings, which may include recommendations for improvement of the industry's environmental performance.

The EEAG made numerous critical observations about the 2000 Code Implementation Survey results. The Code Implementation Survey (CIS), which all signatories had to complete to determine the success or otherwise of their implementation of the code, had itself identified a number of improvements that could be made (Minerals Council, AMICEM 2001). The EEAG observed that the Code allowed signatories to decide themselves on how best to implement the Code for their particular circumstances, and the Code Implementation Survey sought to assess a signatory's progress in implementing Code principles. The results of the survey therefore contained a degree of subjectivity which might influence comparability between scores. Further, the monitoring system was confounded because each signatory performed its own assessment, so any differences between signatories could reflect either different performances or different assessment methodologies, and there was no way of distinguishing these from present data. The results therefore did not explicitly measure a signatory's environmental performance.

The EEAG also noted that under the Code, signatories were obliged to submit a completed CIS return at the corporate level only, which meant that CIS data gave equal weight to a signatory with only one site as to a signatory with multiple operations. The EEAG therefore considered that the data collected in the early years was more appropriately considered as setting a baseline against which future years' progress might be assessed.

The EEAG made numerous recommendations to the Minerals Council Environment Committee on the basis of its observations, the interests of greater transparency and increased stakeholder confidence in the CIS results. For example, the EEAG encouraged Code signatories to publish their CIS results, preferably on a site by site basis, in their public environmental reports as well as proposed actions for improvement, including progress to date. They suggested adding some sanctions. The EEAG felt that unless a company could provide proof that they were able, and intended, to comply with Code obligations that they should be withdrawn from the Code.

The first report by the EEAG attracted some negative press coverage for the Minerals Council and its Code (see, for example, 'Australian Mineral Cos Must do More for the Environment', *Asia Pulse*, December 9, 2001), but it was clear that the Group was playing an effective and independent role. The Code was one step towards meeting community expectations for transparency and accountability; the establishment of EEAG was a further step towards positive engagement. On issues such as climate change, however, the Minerals Council continued to play hardball, lobbying to ensure Australia did not ratify the Kyoto Protocol (see below).

The development of the Code by the Minerals Council had a wider impact. The International Marine Minerals Society adopted a Code for Environmental Management of Marine Mining in 2001, and explicitly acknowledged a debt to Minerals Council, using sections of text from the Code. The Code was also the forerunner of the *10 Principles for Sustainable Development* adopted in 2003 by ICMM and embodying the global industry's commitment to manage social, health, safety, environmental and economic issues. The Minerals Council in 2005 then adopted *Enduring Value — the Australian minerals industry framework for sustainable development*, a regional level initiative to extend the ICMM principles to a broader audience and facilitate site level implementation. Commitment to the *10 Principles* and *Enduring Value* was then required as a condition of membership of both organisations.

The MCA and Climate Change

In an effort to provide a rationale against ratification of the Kyoto Protocol, the Minerals Council commissioned and released in October 2000 a report by the Allen Consulting Group on the economic impact of the Kyoto Protocol on Australia. This report found that complying with the protocol would reduce Australia's gross domestic product by 1.9 percent, or more than A$11 billion pa at current prices. Some states would suffer more than others, it found, with the Gross State Product of Western Australia, the nation's leading minerals state, falling 3.3 percent. Some regions would suffer declines in employment of up to 11 percent, with Queensland losing more than 50,000 jobs outside its capital of Brisbane city (*Dow Jones International News*, October 11, 2000). Some industrial sectors would also suffer severe production declines, the study found, with aluminum production likely to contract by 24 percent and black coal output by 17 percent.

But both the Coalition and the ALP disagreed with the report's findings (*Australian Financial Review*, October 12, 2000). Environment Minister Senator Robert Hill stated that compared with modeling done by Australian Bureau of Agricultural and Resource Economics (ABARE), the impact on GDP predicted by the study was 'dramatically overly pessimistic.' Labor's environment spokesman Senator Nick Bolkus characterised the report as 'unhelpful scaremongering.' And the Government, Opposition and the Australian Conservation Foundation all said the Allen study was flawed because it did not consider the cost of Australia's failure to comply with the Kyoto Protocol.

The *Financial Review* reported that while both the Government and the Opposition nominally supported action to reduce emissions of greenhouse gases, both were wary of the electoral cost of doing so, and Labor was particularly vulnerable because it held seats in many of the areas in regional Australia likely to be affected. The ALP dilemma was underscored by Mr Christian Zahra, MP for the seat of McMillan in Victoria's Latrobe Valley which, according to the study, faced an 8 per cent cut in jobs. He was quoted as stating that 'We need to be sensitive to the employment implications of whatever policy is adopted.' Mr Zahra was skeptical of arguments that Australia could meet its Kyoto targets through adoption of renewable energy technology, and the brown coal on which the economy of the Latrobe Valley was based was the most carbon-intensive source of energy used in the country.

The Minerals Council report on the effects of implementing the Kyoto protocol also proposed delaying the deadline for Annex B countries to meet their Kyoto targets, and persuading developing countries like China and India to adopt emission targets, in part by a transfer of wealth and technology from developed countries. It argued that the Australian economy was particularly susceptible to Kyoto's effects because it was so dependent on cheap, coal-fired electricity, and that the Government should refuse to ratify the protocol unless Australia's particular interests were satisfied. These interests were seen as including a global trade regime for carbon and a substantial role for forest sinks in that carbon credit market (*Australian Financial Review*, October 13, 2000). Significantly, at this stage (on the eve of COP-6) the Clinton administration was still in office in the US and the

Australian government was under some considerable pressure from Washington to support its position and ratify.

The MCA pursued a slightly different line on Kyoto from the peak business group, the Australian Chamber of Commerce and Industry (ACCI), and this was apparent in their respective reactions to the failed outcome at COP-6. While the Minerals Council described the failure of the Kyoto Protocol implementation negotiations as 'a step in the right direction,' the Australian Chamber of Commerce and Industry said the failure to reach agreement on the greenhouse strategy meant continuing investment uncertainty. 'Business has not been given the certainty it wanted in terms of planning for the costs of carbon and the world has missed the opportunity to take real steps to reduce greenhouse emissions,' the ACCI chief executive, Mr Mark Paterson, said (*Australian Financial Review*, November 28, 2000).

The Minerals Council position on climate change was set out in its *Minerals Industry Survey Report 2001* (Minerals Council, 2001, 6-7):

> The Australian minerals industry advocates that international climate change policy should be based on sound principles that:
>
> - lead to an effective environmental outcome. Climate change is a global issue which must be addressed through enduring international solutions involving all countries;
> - recognise the economic growth and development aspirations of developing countries. Developing countries must be able to pursue economic growth and development opportunities to meet the needs of their peoples and should have an economic incentive to abate greenhouse gas emissions;
> - ensure that all countries face the same price signal for greenhouse emissions. Without this condition international trade and investment decisions are likely to be distorted and lead to emission 'leakage';
> - result in a least cost global outcome that is in the interests of all parties; and
> - lend themselves to streamlined and efficient administrative arrangements. Measuring, monitoring, reporting and verifying greenhouse gas emission abatement are essential elements for all participating countries. A simple and efficient approach here will enhance the capacity of developing countries to undertake this work and minimise costs.

Once the election of the Bush administration changed the atmospherics in Washington, the Minerals Council made it clear that it did not want the government to ratify the Kyoto protocol without US support (*Australian Financial Review*, September 3, 2001). But an election was looming in Australia; the Minerals Council faced the possibility that the ALP opposition might win that election, and the ALP adopted as a policy commitment the ratification of Kyoto by September 2002.

The Minerals Council locked horns with the ALP prior to the election, contesting especially the ALP's claim that the implementation of the Kyoto protocol would lead to an *increase* in jobs, pointing to its analysis showing the loss of more than 50,000 jobs in Queensland alone (*Australian Financial Review*, October 10, 2001). The Minerals Council argued that Australia should at least have before it the details of an agreed legal text before committing to ratify Kyoto. While he welcomed the Opposition's recognition that climate change policy must be 'driven by a realistic appraisal of Australia's unique situation, and a determination that measures taken will be overwhelmingly positive for the economy and the nation,' the Minerals Council's Dick Wells argued it was important for all policy makers to recognise that climate change demanded a comprehensive policy response. 'We do not want to compromise the long-term prospects for the Australian economy and industry by short term policies or hastily developed approaches that provide little benefit to the global environment,' he argued (*Australian Mining*, October 10, 2001).

The Minerals Council view was that the Opposition's proposed September 2002 deadline for ratification by Australia was premature given the absence of an agreed legal text, the ALP's undertaking to consult with industry, the need to undertake a National Interest Assessment and the time required to develop sensible legislation. The Minerals Council was also concerned at ALP proposals for national, state and sectoral emission reduction targets, a greenhouse trigger under the *Environment Protection and Biodiversity Conservation Act*, and early emissions trading in advance of a global scheme. The Minerals Council held that any agreement should ensure that all countries faced the same price signal for greenhouse emissions, lest international trade and investment decisions be distorted and lead to emissions leakage. The point of contention for the Minerals Council was that only about 25-30 percent of global greenhouse gas emissions were to be subjected to restraint by Kyoto, and therefore not all countries would face the same price signal, preventing an effective environmental outcome.

As it happened, the Coalition retained power at the 2001 election and the Minerals Council eventually found itself more in step with other industry groups when five industry organisations agreed in July 2002 to establish a business coalition to discuss the next stages for national greenhouse policies. The Australian Chamber of Commerce and Industry, the Business Council of Australia, Australian Industry Group, Electricity Supply Association of Australia Ltd and the Minerals Council chief executives formed the Business Coalition for Greenhouse Strategy, and committed it to involving other interested national organizations (*Australian Associated Press*, July 24, 2002). The principal objective of the Business Coalition was to 'progress the development of effective, equitable and efficient greenhouse policies and measures to address global climate change consistent with sustainable development and Australia's position in a highly-competitive and dynamic global economy,' the groups said in a statement.

The Coalition stated it accepted the merit of Australia working towards meeting its international greenhouse gas reduction commitments in a fair and equitable manner, but noted that industry was also committed to the identification of cost-effective options on greenhouse gas abatement which would maintain Australia's competitiveness. The group was formed just a month ahead of the start of the World Summit on Sustainable Development in Johannesburg, where the agenda was to include climate change issues.

The Business Coalition was able to present a united business front to the Government and it also pressed for technological approaches to the problems which held the promise of permitting continued coal consumption with lowered emissions. On the eve of a meeting of what was known as the Government-Business Climate Change dialogue, the Minerals Council raised the possibility of zero emission coal-fired power generation, holding that Australia's coal-fired power stations could operate without emitting greenhouse gas emissions within a decade (*Australian Associated Press Financial News Wire*, August 21, 2002).

Following the meeting of the Government-Business Climate Change dialogue, the Minerals Council applauded the Australian Government's decision not to ratify the Kyoto protocol. Minerals Council policy director Brian Horwood described the meeting as 'fantastic' because it allowed the minerals industry to plan investment over a 40-year time frame. 'It gives us a chance to meet our targets and commitments without destroying Australia's industry and without letting industry transfer offshore,' Mr Horwood said' (*Australian Financial Review*, August 22, 2002).

It should be noted that despite the Australian Government refusal to ratify the Kyoto protocol, Australia claimed to be largely on track to meet its Kyoto target. The Minerals Council said in a statement just after the decision not to ratify that Environment and Heritage Minister David Kemp had recently released data that indicated Australia was within striking distance of its target of a net 108 percent of 1990 emissions over the commitment period 2008-2012 (*Platts International Coal Report*, August 26, 2002). As the world's leading exporter of coal, and with high domestic coal consumption in the export metals trade, Australia was a leading *per capita* producer of greenhouse gases and the Minerals Council was able to convince the government that it clearly was in Australia's national interest to meet its international commitments on greenhouse gas abatement without (as the Council's new chief executive Mitchell Hooke put it) 'surrendering its sovereignty to an inadequate and indeterminate international instrument' (*Platts International Coal Report*, August 26, 2002). He said, however, that the Council strongly supported Australia's commitment to meet the Kyoto target. (Hooke joined Minerals Council from the Food and Grocery Council in May 2002).

The Minerals Council then on numerous occasions praised the government, both on its Kyoto decision and on its performance at WSSD in Johannesburg. It had also lobbied successfully for government investment in research into clean coal technology, and defended the decision to cut renewable energy research funding at the expense of an injection of $68.5 million into coal research (*Australian Associated Press General News*, December 11, 2002). Minerals Council chief executive Mitchell Hooke dismissed suggestions that renewable energy research was suffering at the expense of the mining industry. 'This is about energy efficiency, it's not about a public, populist mantra that windmills are going to supply the sort of energy requirements of this country or the world,' Hooke told reporters. While not wishing to deny renewables a place, Hooke said the bottom line was Australia needed to make the best use of its available resources, including 260 years of coal reserves and 70 to 80 years of natural gas reserves.

By the end of the 1990s, therefore, environment was a major concern for the Minerals Council, with issues like climate change, National Environment Pollution Measures, the National Pollutant Inventory, the *Environmental Protection and Biodiversity Conservation Act 1999*, and the negotiation of a convention on persistent organic pollutants featuring on its policy agenda—along with traditional concerns like taxation reform, trade, transport, and competitiveness. The emphasis under Hooke was on policies for sustainable growth, and in contrast to its defensive strategies at the beginning of the 1990s, its strategy was one of proactive engagement. It had established a Public Affairs Network in 1998 to communicate across companies and industry organizations, and External Environmental Advisory Group, and a Community and Environmental Health Advisory Committee. Rather than seeking to change public opinion, as it had in the early 1990s, the emphasis was now on engaging with it.

Discussion

Throughout the 1990s, therefore, the minerals industry developed a much more sophisticated approach to the 'licence to operate' issues related to reputation and access to land. Ironically, the provision of land rights to indigenous people split the indigenous political movement from the green movement (at least domestically) and the *Environmental Protection and Biodiversity Conservation Act* completed at the end of the decade what had commenced in 1992 with the Intergovernmental Agreement on the Environment: a formalisation of federal responsibilities on environmental matters which provided a reduction in sovereign risk. But on the climate change issue the Minerals Council continued to push hard, with the success of its lobbying enhanced by both its improved reputational standing (thanks to its positive response to land rights and the defensive move in developing the Minerals Code) and the election of a more sympathetic Coalition Howard government in 1996.

The changes in the industrial relations system in Australia (see Chapter 6) did not impact greatly upon the Minerals Council, because there was a separate industrial bargaining association, the Australian Mining and Metals Industrial Association (AMMIA), which was not linked to the Minerals Council. But all industry associations found it more difficult to recruit members and the view of one insider was that they would never recover their previous position, and the Minerals Council has also had to face these challenges.

These factors did not work in a consistent direction for the Minerals Council. The settlement of indigenous issues by positive actions at the company level undermined associability, while the development of the Minerals Code as an industry-wide response to the reputational issues, the *Environment Protection and Biodiversity Conservation Act* and the climate change issue enhanced it. Industrial relations reform affected the associability of business (and unions) more generally rather than the Minerals Council specifically. These new roles required different skills, and they recruited specialist lobbyists rather than people from within the industry—not always without arousing the suspicion on industry insiders, who feared that damage might be done by 'former bureaucrats' yielding ground on agendas developed outside the industry.

But changes within the industry also changed the nature of the Minerals Council. Especially significant was the consolidation of ownership and the greater transnational character of the industry which came with globalisation. In 1975 AMIC had 145 members and represented about 97 percent of the mining, smelting, and refining of minerals in Australia (AMIC 1975, 4, 7). Membership declined marginally to 134 by 1979 (AMIC 1979, 3), but by 1994 AMIC had only 42 members, and after AMIC became the Minerals Council it had only 38 members in 1997, 33 in 1999, 30 in 2000, and bottomed out at only 26 members in 2001. Membership by mining companies was even lower than this figure suggested, because the 26 members included companies which were essentially suppliers to the industry, supplying explosives and other goods and services. The 2001 membership included six suppliers (Accenture, Orica, Allens Arthur Robinson, Dyno Nobel, P&H MinePro Services, and PriceWaterhouseCoopers). Membership increased marginally to 27 in 2002, but this was thanks to the accountancy and consulting company KPMG joining.

This decline in membership reflected both consolidation of ownership and lower associability at the national level. While it is true that consolidation of ownership had reduced the number of potential members, there were still plenty of companies prepared to join an appropriate sector group at the state level, as we shall see in the next chapter. The Chamber of Minerals and Energy of Western Australia, for example, in 2004 had 50 'production' members, plus five contractor members, seven exploration members, one business development member, and 58 associate members—categories which covered all the members of the Minerals Council. CMEWA therefore had 121 members as against the Minerals Council's 27. The MCA had become much more a large-firm club, playing much more a leadership role nationally in the industry.

A very powerful illustration of our point that associability reflects institutions (including policies as institutions) was provided by the (bungled) introduction in 2010 of a resources rent tax (Kellow 2016), which galvanised the sector so that it could contest the issue. By 2013, the Minerals

Council had 52 full members and 44 Associate Members—more than double the membership at its lowest point.

AMIC was established to talk to the federal government. It had some state offices, but it was not formally a federation. Each state has its own mining act. The coal industry was regulated at the federal level and had its own Superannuation Board, research agency, a Joint Coal Board and an industrial relations system with a separate Coal Industry Tribunal. This industrial relations system was the template upon which coal industry organization formed at the national level. The Australian Coal Association had only two members: the Queensland and NSW mining councils. The ACA provided a vehicle so that they could go to the Commonwealth if needed; it provided a vehicle to be recognised before the Coal Industry Tribunal, which consisted of a bench of one, administering one industrial award and from which there was no appeal. Industrial Relations was thus the reason for the existence of the ACA.

Reforms in the early 1990s moved coal into the mainstream IR system for the first time, and because it provided for industrial agreements at the enterprise level, this removed one factor affecting associability. The *Workplace Relations Act 1996* further emphasised individual firms rather than the sector as a whole, so that companies then managed their own industrial relations on-site at the company level. (As a result, the Queensland Mining Council shed all of its industrial relations staff in 1999).

Individual companies were emboldened to change industrial relations by the *Workplace Relations Act*, particularly by its secondary boycotts provisions. Previously, any strike at a single mine, especially a coal mine, would spread throughout the industry and secondary boycotts imposed by the maritime unions would close the waterfront—especially costly for an export-oriented industry. Their resolve was stiffened also by the prevailing economic climate. A steep decline in coal prices, with lower cost producers in South America, Canada, Indonesia, and the US gave them the reason to find the courage to improve productivity through workplace reform. Since the reform to industrial relations there has been a claimed 35 percent rise in productivity. The last vestiges of federal regulation (the tribunal, export controls, Superannuation Board, Joint Coal Board) have gone, and this has impacted on the associability of the coal industry.

This suggests that the concentration of ownership internationally might have reduced membership of mining associations marginally, but membership numbers were still the same order of magnitude. What happened, however, is that most memberships shifted to *state* level mining associations. In some states, it should be remembered, state mining associations did not exist at the time AMIC was formed. Ironically, some of them struggled for existence, and there was consideration of an amalgamation between the Victorian Minerals and Energy Council and the Tasmanian Minerals Council, and the Victorian government assisted VMEC in its quest to continue in existence because it preferred to speak to an association, rather than having to deal with individual firms. But by about 2005 there were only 20 mining company members of the national level MCA, while there were something around the same number in state associations as there were at the AMIC/MCA peak. The trajectories of state mining associations are described in the next chapter.

The Minerals Council therefore became much more of a ‘leadership’ association, advancing ideas and standards rather than representing the industry as a whole. The key development was the recruitment of David Buckingham from CEPA to the Minerals Council, because Buckingham changed the nature of the association. Prior to 1996 the Minerals Council had to please its members; after 1996 the Minerals Council could act independently of its membership. Prior to this, its staff largely came from within the mining industry; then they were predominantly former government officials and public affairs specialists. Policies were now decided by committees, not the membership (which is closer to the German way). The Business Council of Australia had the same approach to policy-making, but (unlike the Minerals Council), the BCA was originally created solely to be a kind of think tank, not as a vehicle for representation. The state chambers were still as they were, and would tend not move if there was an unhappy member, so were restricted to what are essentially lowest common denominator positions.

In the Minerals Council there was a movement away from analysis and data collection to a greater reliance on principled arguments, but there was less capacity to engage in this activity at the company level. The industry no longer employed as many staff as it once did. Competitive pressures reduced staff to those needed to do the job, and the industry was notorious for cutting costs (and staff) periodically as price reductions impacted upon profitability. (The industry is a classic price-taker). Company staff engaged in public policy were decimated in the late 1990s. Industry staff were considered to be more ambitious than they once were and there was no career progression in the industry in influencing government policy, especially compared with working in production divisions. Secondment into industry associations increasingly came to be regarded as a dead end. (The WBCSD uses secondments, but this is not sustainable for corporations unless they are the size of Shell or BP). There was therefore pressure on the Minerals Council to hire technical specialists, but with technical and commercial issues it was considered that there is no substitute for the knowledge possessed by company people, and the companies were seen as vulnerable because there was a danger that if they depended on the Minerals Council they would not be able to understand the issues for themselves.

There was also a leadership issue in the representation of the sector which was of fundamental significance, and it had come about by a combination of globalisation and other changes in the conduct of business. Global ownership of the larger players meant that CEOs were less willing to engage at the national level, since that now meant engaging at *several* national levels. What suffered was the maintenance of political relationships at the personal level which could be mobilised when needed. In 1996, when Dick Wells started as the Director of the Minerals Council, at the time when the industry was arguing strongly for exemption from diesel excise for fuel consumed off-road in mines, there were five or six people in the industry who could pick up the phone and talk to the prime minister. By October 2000 only Hugh Morgan (WMC Resources) and Robert Champion de Crespigny (Normandy Mining) could do so. There had been no crisis for a couple of years and CEOs had not maintained relationships. This was exacerbated by a rapid rotation of CEOs, many of whom were rotating on a cycle (not uncommon in other sectors of business) of three or four years—too short to develop personal networks. Many were now recruited from outside Australia, as part of a global managerial elite.

The nature of interaction with government also changed and evolved. The Hawke government was consultative in style and had considerable policy capacity independent of that the resources industry could provide. After then, the public service was downsized and lost much policy capacity, and the Minerals Council often found itself ahead of the bureaucracy, and was able to achieve impact with well-argued policy research, much in the model of set by the Business Council. And the Minerals Council followed the lead of the BCA (set in the early 1990s) in engaging in 'alliancing': looking around on any issue and seeing who else might be interested, who might have more exposure to an issue and therefore be able to take a leadership role on it. It then assisted to convene working groups involving industry associations (PACIA, APPEA, Minerals Council, and so on) sufficiently interested to participate. One example of this was the Australian Industry Greenhouse Network (see above), which fluctuated between about five and twelve organisations and responded flexibly on an issue beyond the capacities of individual groups to manage. So while Australia lacked a single peak business lobby group, there was—through 'alliancing' considerable tactical, *ad hoc* cooperation to secure common objectives or deal with threats common to more than one sector.

But if there was greater coordination than meets the eye at the national peak level above the Minerals Council, the development of the Minerals Council as more of a leadership, large-firm club also created tensions beneath it. The Minerals Code was a national initiative which was more likely to appeal to those with national (or international) reputations to defend—members of the Minerals Council—than the smaller firms more likely to be active members of state level associations, and some tensions were noted between large and small firms over the Code, which was seen by some small players as a 'large firm plot.' If anything, this was exacerbated by the Global Mining Initiative, which (as discussed in the previous chapter) was led by a select group of the transnationals and involved a review of organizations globally, with the MMSD process of engaging with stakeholders and leading eventually to the creation of ICMM and the development of a similar international code of practice to that developed by the Minerals Council.

Concerns and suspicions arose among both smaller companies and the state chambers who were their primary representatives in the associational architecture. There were suspicions of multinationals among the 'dirt diggers' and 'rock kickers' in Western Australia, though there were also the beginnings of a realisation that they needed to take the emerging global agenda seriously. Fears emerged among the state chambers, such as Victoria (which apparently made some intemperate comments), over what the GMI review of associations in particular might mean for them. The smaller players, especially the smaller gold miners in Western Australia, lacked the longer-term investments and perspectives of the larger players: they had a three-year time horizon—why would they invest in strategic issues? The impetus to bring them more on-side came from an unlikely source: the European Union.

The EU began a push for the heavy regulation of cyanide, and without industry involvement in this policy development process this could have been a disaster for the gold sector (which has a very long tail of smaller companies, the worst performed of which could make or break the reputation of the sector). This helped focus the smaller miners in state chambers, especially in Western Australia, and the recruitment of the chairmen of state chambers onto the Minerals Council Board helped integrate the smaller players and state chambers at the national level, and with the establishment of ICMM national mining associations were given participation rights into that structure, which was otherwise a large-firm club.

Postscript: Reassertion of the Transnationals

The Minerals Council came under attack from its own member companies in 2017. BHP and Rio Tinto came under pressure from shareholder activism in the form of proxy fights organised by the Australian Centre for Corporate Responsibility (ACCR). On ACCR's board of four sat three individuals with interests in 'ethical' investing (John McKinnon, Howard Pender and Adam Verwey), so while it was a registered charity, its campaigns against fossil fuel miners would certainly not harm the interests of its board members. ACCR is only part of a global network targeting coal. While it seems to buy shares in companies solely to engage in proxy battles at annual meetings, Climate Action 100+ coordinates shareholder activism by investment funds—not all of them solely dealing with 'ethical' investments. Climate Action 100+ is coordinated by five partner organisations: Asia Investor Group on Climate Change (AIGCC); Ceres (US, formerly the Coalition for Environmentally Responsible Economies); Investor Group on Climate Change (IGCC, Australia); Institutional Investor Group on Climate Change (IIGCC, Europe); and United Nations Principles for Responsible Investing (UNPRI, an initiative established in 2005).

Minerals Council CEO, Brendan Pearson had warned in 2016 about the covert funding of anti-coal groups such as the Sunrise Project opposing the proposed Adani coal mine by the Sandler Foundation, the Sea Change Foundation, the Tilia Fund, the Growald Family Fund and the Flora Family Foundation revealed by the 'Podesta emails' leaked by Wikileaks before the 2016 US presidential election (*Australian*, 23 October 2016). Under his leadership the Minerals Council had advocated strongly that coal could play a role in a world responding to climate change, especially in High Efficiency, Low Emissions (HELE) plant and with Carbon Capture and Storage (CCS). Pearson had also pointed out publicly that renewable energy such as wind turbines required large amounts of coal in their manufacture—to make the cement in their foundations and steel for reinforcing there and in the towers.

ACCR launched proxy fights at the annual general meetings of BHP and Rio Tinto, seeking to pressure both to withdraw from membership of the

Minerals Council. Both companies had also been targeted by IIGCC and IGCC, and BHP (and Anglo American) by the Norwegian sovereign wealth fund (ironically, built up from its fossil fuel endowment). Pearson resigned in September 2017, just as ACCR lodged motions it wanted raised at the AGM in November. At an MCA board meeting in early September 2017, the head of BHP's Australian operations, Mike Henry, reportedly asked Minerals Council staff to leave the meeting. With only representatives of members present, Henry then expressed to the other members that BHP had lost confidence in Pearson's leadership (*Australian,* 22 September 2017).

BHP undertook a review of its membership of industry associations (BHP 2017), but continued to hold coal investments, although it was also a producer of uranium and oil and gas and these interests would be advantaged by restrictions on the use of coal. (High levels of intermittent wind and solar capacity in electricity systems require back-up, usually from gas turbines that can be started quickly). Rio Tinto sold all its coal assets by August 2018, but stayed with the Minerals Council. Both companies are significant producers of copper, which is hugely advantaged by regulatory policies restricting fossil fuel electricity generation and encouraging renewables—especially because renewables are of very low density and require considerable expansion of transmission networks in addition to the copper contained in generation equipment.

So, too, did BHP remain—ultimately. But by having Pearson removed as CEO, it brought to a rather abrupt end the era of having the Council act independently of its members, able to rise above lowest common denominator positions—a central aim at its establishment (and that of ICMM). Rather than being an internal document, the BHP review was publicly available, a fact that sent clear messages to the Minerals Council and its other members *and* to ACCR.

While Pearson's advocacy of coal was a major point of difference, BHP also sought to appease its critics by silencing the MCA on the criticisms Pearson had raised about murky donations and questionable advocacy activities by charitable organisations, noting

> that the MCA has on occasion adopted an approach to advocacy and communications at variance to BHP's preferred approach. An example was the MCA's recommendation that, as one element in broader reform options for Australia's charitable sector, policymakers consider imposing a cap on the advocacy activities of charities (BHP 2017, 12).

BHP noted ‘identified material differences’ between its position and the MCA and stated that it

> will formally communicate the identified material differences to the board of the MCA;
>
> BHP will request that the MCA refrain from policy activity or advocacy in these areas;
>
> BHP will maintain a register of material differences; and
>
> BHP will review its membership of the MCA if it has not refrained from such activity or advocacy within a reasonable period (being not more than 12 months) (BHP 2017, 17).

Ultimately, it remained in the MCA, though it quit the World Coal Association.

Pushed by activist investors and those using shareholdings to exert influence at the AGM, BHP undermined the ability of the MCA to take positions at odds with its larger members, and in so doing both returned the Minerals Council closer to the position of the mining industry association under AMIC and widened the gap between the large transnational companies and the smaller members which must now (especially those operating only in Australia) question the value the MCA delivers for them.

CHAPTER 5

MICRO LEVEL: STATE CHAMBERS DEVELOPMENT

The emergence of the Minerals Council of Australia as a national and, increasingly, global player, was to prove problematic for smaller firms—traditionally active at the level of state or territory associations, usually called chambers of mines. From this perspective the MCA and ICMM could be perceived as 'large firm plots'. Chambers of mines had a relatively long, unbroken history in three sub-national parts of Australia – Western Australia, Queensland, and the Northern Territory, where they drew upon regions with significant areas of exploration, mining and processing. These chambers engaged with national level politics, largely, but not solely through the MCA and its predecessor body, the Australian Mining Industry Council (AIMC). To strengthen its national level lobbying, the AIMC established committees, or branches, in those states without chambers of mines, South Australia, New South Wales, Victoria and Tasmania (largely represented through Victoria). The AIMC's relations with the state chambers, old and new, were largely—if not entirely—cooperative.

The subsequent development of the MCA as more of a leadership, large-firm club also created tensions beneath it. The Minerals Code—discussed in Chapter 4—was a national initiative more likely to appeal to those with national (or international) reputations to defend than those smaller firms more likely to be active members of state level associations, and some tensions between large and small firms emerged over the Code. Concerns and suspicions arose among both smaller companies and the state chambers which were their primary representatives in the associational architecture. There were suspicions of multinationals among the 'dirt diggers' and 'rock kickers' in Western Australia, though there were also the beginnings of a realisation that they needed to take the emerging global agenda seriously. Fears emerged among the state chambers, such as Victoria, over what the GMI review of associations in particular might mean for them. The smaller players, especially the smaller gold miners in Western Australia, lacked the longer-term investments and perspectives of the larger players: they had a three-year time horizon — why would they invest in strategic issues?

The global concentration of ownership of mining companies reduced membership of mining associations marginally, but membership numbers across both national and sub-national levels remained at the same order of magnitude. What happened, however, was that most memberships shifted from national to *state* level mining associations. In some states, state mining associations did not exist at the time AMIC was formed, though there had been chambers in many of the colonies that essentially aimed to attract capital. Ironically, despite the shift of membership to the state level, some state mining associations began to struggle for existence. There was talk of amalgamation between the Victorian and Tasmanian associations, and the Victorian government assisted the Victorian Minerals and Energy Council in its (ultimately futile) quest for survival because it preferred to speak to an association, rather than having to deal with individual firms. But there were at one point in 2004 only about 20 mining company members of the national level MCA, while there were around the same numbers in state associations as there were at the time of peak membership in AMIC/MCA.

State mining associations have undergone significant changes in their relationships with the national mining association. Most of the state chambers, with the exception of the Northern Territory—that is, the Western Australian, the New South Wales, the Queensland, South Australia, and the Tasmanian mining associations—opted to become Associate Members of the Minerals Council of Australia. The two largest and longest established chambers—Western Australia and Queensland—rejected outright the option of divisional status, thus effectively vetoing the possibility of a federal structure for the Minerals Council, although Victoria accepted that option as a means of survival. Each of the state mining associations followed trajectories that were shaped primarily by the policy developments of the state governments with which they interacted, and by the changing *compétences* of national and state governments in Australia, in three policy areas in particular: environment; industrial relations and land rights relating to the indigenous Australians, the Aborigines.

In this chapter we track the trajectories of the mining chambers in the Australian states and the Northern Territory as ICMM formed and MCA formed and developed. While each case history shows the influence of individuals and events, the key factors behind the changes described are institutional in nature. Each case study is based upon available documents (themselves patchy) and interviews with key informants (usually the CEO of each organization as they were undergoing change). While we have attempted to be comprehensive and to capture the key changes, they should therefore be regarded as limited by the information that was available to us—a constraint that varied from case-to-case. We commence with the more venerable organizations in Western Australia, Queensland and the Northern Territory, before moving on to describe those associations in New South Wales, South Australia, Victoria and Tasmania.

Part One: The Old Chambers of Mining

Western Australia

Perhaps the strongest state-based mining organization is the Chamber of Minerals and Energy of Western Australia (CMEWA), which dates back to 1901, when 37 members attended a meeting and decided upon a structure and constitution for a chamber of mines. Concerns in the sector in those days are indicated by the matters on the agenda for the first meeting a week after formation: opposition to the granting of a sluicing and dredging area recommended by the Mining Warden; methods of mine timbering; and a recommendation that the government provide additional railway rolling stock to convey fuel and fresh water to the mines. The Chamber grew with the industry, particularly through a 1960s mining boom, with the development of iron ore, bauxite and nickel mines and then oil, petroleum and natural gas, resulting in the formal renaming as a Chamber of Minerals and *Energy*. By the end of the 20th century, the mining and energy sector covered exploration, processing, downstream value adding and refining of over 40 different types of mineral and energy resources in Western Australia.

The Chamber was originally formed as the result of a merger of the Coolgardie Chamber of Mines and Commerce (established 1895) and the Kalgoorlie Chamber of Mines (established 1896), and its Head Office was located in Kalgoorlie until 1969. Later developments were to make Western Australia a mining powerhouse, as significant mineral resources were discovered: bauxite, iron ore, mineral sands, nickel, oil, natural gas, copper, diamonds and uranium. These made the Kalgoorlie location an anachronism.

By the time of what became known as the 'resources boom' at the time of the 1981 federal election, Western Australia was a diverse mineral province with a strong chamber of mines: 57 full members, eight staff, and a budget of a little under half a million dollars (CMWA 1981). It had Regional Councils in the East (Kalgoorlie), North West, South West and Metropolitan regions. It dealt with various taxation issues, workers' compensation, manpower and training, and safety, but it was also engaged with the emerging environmental agenda on issues including coastal zone management, and national parks.

It enjoyed a close relationship with the state government, led at that time by the pro-development Sir Charles Court, who (together with the Governor, Rear Admiral Sir Richard Trowbridge) addressed the annual general meeting. The premier's speech was classic Charlie Court, upbraiding the Commonwealth for seeing the state's mineral wealth as a reason for distributing to it a smaller share of revenue, but also encouraging the Chamber to use its voice to support development, especially against those he said 'masquerade as conservationists' (CMWA 1981, 22). Concerned particularly over opposition to bauxite mining in the Darling Ranges, Court urged those assembled to 'speak out not simply as a common interest group or even as a Chamber of Mines, but as the *mining industry of Western Australia*' (original emphasis). He reminded the members of the Chamber of his urging them (when he had addressed the 1978 conference) to 'use their great combined power to achieve changes in Government policies on mining which they perceived to be worthwhile' (CMWA 1981, 22-23).

The Chamber clearly enjoyed a 'privileged position' in the political architecture of Western Australia, with the Minister for Mines at the 1982 meeting, not only supporting the industry on the issues of environment and Aboriginal land rights, but encouraging the industry to support the government's attempts to resist calls for action on these emerging issues. Specifically mentioning environmentalists and 'activist groups associated with Aborigines', he asked:

> Where is the voice of industry? I am talking about a united voice, not a sectional one, not one part of the industry that pushes its own line for whatever purpose it might have, however valid, however responsible it might happen to be (CMWA 1982, 10).

The government was clearly encouraging a strong, united mining industry association because it saw that as essential to its developmentalist approach to governing the state. Indeed, the minister expressed regret that the Chamber had not been more supportive of the government's position in its reform of the *Mining Act* concluded in 1981, which failed to end the effective power to delay landowners held over the granting of mining rights (the so-called Agricultural Land Protection Provisions), thanks to the dominance of farming interests in the upper house, the Legislative Council. (This review of the 1904 Act had taken 12 years, and the new Act entered into force on 1 January 1982). While the strongly developmentalist government was likely to accommodate any mining project seeking development approval, the emerging regulatory issues demanded sectoral representation and the granting or mining rights to individual firms undermined sectoral organization; the government was trying to encourage it.

This began to change with the defeat of the Court government, as the incoming ALP government was more favourably disposed to both environmental protection and Aboriginal land rights. The Chamber already had an Environmental Review Committee, and established an Aboriginal Affairs Committee in 1982, but the latter issue in particular grew substantially in salience with the change of government. The new Minister of Mines, Fuel and Energy, Peter Dowding, addressed the 1983 meeting of the Chamber and promised to review the Agricultural Land Protection Provisions of the *Mining Act*. But he also brought a blunt message on land rights: 'There will be land rights in this state' (CMWA 1983, 30). The government established an Aboriginal Land Inquiry (the Seaman Inquiry) in 1984 which preoccupied the Chamber in its public affairs role (CMWA 1984, 13). Recognising that the Western Australian approach to land rights had national implications, CMWA acted in concert with both AMIC and the Australian Petroleum Exploration Association (APEA), and established a planned policy promotion program in September 1983 to promote its stance, which was essentially to deny Aborigines either ownership of minerals or the right of veto over mining developments on land to which they were granted rights under the Act. The Agricultural Land Protection Provisions of the *Mining Act*—which protected the farming industry—set a difficult precedent for land rights legislation, because the mining industry could not argue (as it did in other jursidictions) that to grant ownership of minerals or a right of veto would give Aborigines rights not held by others.

CMWA, AMIC and APEA also organised an Aboriginal Land Legislation Conference in Perth in February 1984 and was represented by its legal counsel at the public hearing of the Seaman Inquiry. CMWA argued against the granting of a power of veto, pointing to the negative effect on development they saw such a provision had had in the Northern Territory and in South Australia. As other landholders did not own the minerals beneath their land, the Chamber took the position that it neither advocated nor opposed the granting of land rights as such, but opposed their granting on terms substantially different to those enjoyed by other Australians. The Seaman Inquiry recommended that control be given to Aborigines. The Chamber resented what it saw as an implied threat that if the state approach did not go as far as the wishes of the federal government, Commonwealth legislation would be introduced to impose an outcome (including power of veto) on the state (CMWA 1984, 26).

The draft legislation was reviewed by a committee on which the Chamber and other interested parties were invited to sit, and the Chamber President saw the Bill as 'one that we felt would allow resource development to proceed with the minimum of disruption, and one which could become the model if Federal uniform land rights legislation was to be introduced' (CMWA 1985, 2). The legislation, however was rejected by the Legislative Council in April 1985, and so the future of the issue effectively passed to the Commonwealth. Both the Chamber and the Minister regretted this passing from state to Commonwealth control. As it happened, in March 1986 the Commonwealth government abandoned efforts to introduce uniform national land rights legislation and indicated it was prepared to accept a set of proposals suggested by the Western Australian government to provide secure title to land for Aborigines living on reserves in Western Australia. It was widely considered that this outcome resulted from the influence of the mining industry on the ALP within Western Australia and a shortage of funds on the part of the Federal Party.

This left it to the High Court,[1] in the *Mabo* Decision to discover the concept of native title and necessitate the development of the *Native Title Act* to resolve uncertainties. This was to enhance temporarily the importance of the Commonwealth level, before ultimately (through the establishment of a legislated right to negotiate) returning the issue not just to the state level, but to essentially a process of negotiation between traditional owners and individual firms. The Commonwealth later, however, amended the *Aboriginal and Torres Strait Island Heritage (Interim Protection) Act* to provide the Commonwealth with heritage legislation that could override state legislation. Ironically, the aftermath of the *Mabo* case resulted in one feature the Chamber sought: the ability to negotiate directly with traditional owners, which had been prevented by the previous procedures (CMEWA 1992, 7).

[1] Interestingly, one of the High Court justices bringing down the Mabo decision was Justice John Toohey, a long-time advocate of land rights in Western Australia. His role in arguing for land rights in Western Australia was publicly acknowledged by Minister Peter Dowding in his address to CMWA at the 1983 Annual Meeting. Toohey, then a Federal Court Judge, had been an Aboriginal Land Commissioner in the Northern Territory and in 1974 was with the Aboriginal Legal Service of North Western Australia. (CMWA 1983. 31).

Mabo was an enormous issue for the Chamber after the decision in June 1992. The main problem was uncertainty, since it recognised native title where it had not been extinguished by government grants such as freehold title. This meant 38 percent of the land area of the state of Western Australia, and while the judgment did not appear to threaten the concept of Crown ownership of minerals beneath the surface, two claims were made by traditional owners that sought mineral rights. Further, the uncertainty affected not just future access to land for mineral exploration, but potentially affected the validity of titles issued after 1975 (CMEWA 1993, 5). For these reasons, the WA Chamber was especially active on *Mabo*, acting in concert with AMIC to make strong representations to both the state and Commonwealth governments urging they make legislative responses to *Mabo* confirming existing property rights and the principle of Crown ownership. A new Liberal government at state level from February 1993 immediately established a Cabinet Sub-Committee chaired by the Premier to deal with the issue (CMEWA 1993, 9). The state government also attempted unsuccessfully to repeal the veto powers in the Agricultural Land Protection Provisions of the *Mining Act*. This was a continuing issue for the Chamber from the mid-1980s and, together with the land rights issue, heritage legislation and the closure of national parks and many reserves to exploration in February 1988 caused the Chamber concern over access to land for exploration and mining.

The saliency of these issues worked to increase associability for the Chamber, with a determined membership drive in 1987-88 increasing membership from 84 to 101 (CMWA 1988, 7). (This number included 56 production members, 31 exploration members and 14 associate members). The Chamber also sought members among the petroleum industry which had developed in the north of the state and in 1989 changed its name to the Chamber of Minerals and Energy and began to gain members from this area. By April 1990 it had 122 members (69 production, 32 exploration, 21 associate) and it was becoming more an organization run by professionals than it had been—as might be expected with an organization with an annual budget of $1.7m. One indication of this was the cessation of the inclusion of the past practice of including the President's report in the Annual Report from 1990, when a printed report was included instead from the Chamber CEO.

The WA Chamber also became more active at the national level on environmental issues, including the National Strategy for Ecologically Sustainable Development, Greenhouse Response Strategy, the Commonwealth *Endangered Species Bill*, the Intergovernmental Agreement on the

Environment and the establishment of a Commonwealth Environmental Protection Agency (CMEWA 1993, 9-10). CMEWA was spurred by 'a politicisation of many environmental issues' and these moves towards 'centralisation' to become 'more directly involved' in Commonwealth actions affecting mining developments in the state.

A high level of activity continued on *Mabo* and native title until 1995. The Chamber gave more than 110 briefings, made more than 90 public presentations, and developed and distributed more than 35 different information documents (CMEWA 1994, 7). It worked closely with AMIC, the Association of Mining Exploration Companies, APEA and numerous other interest groups, including the Australian Tourism Industry Association, the Western Australian Chamber of Commerce and Industry, Forest Industries Federation, Pastoralists and Graziers Association, WA Farmers Federation, and the WA Fishing Industry Council. It maintained a strong media presence and initiated eight full-page advertisements in association with other industry groups. Less publicly, it made numerous submissions to state and commonwealth governments and conducted two national opinion surveys in association with AMIC.

One problem for it, ironically, was the sympathetic hearing it received from the state government, which adopted the *Land (Titles and Traditional Usage) Act (Western Australia) 1993*. The Chamber supported the state legislative response and strongly opposed the *Native Title Act (C'wealth).* This prolonged the uncertainty, though there was really little doubt that the Commonwealth Act would prevail, and so it did when the High Court ruled on 16 March 1995 that the Western Australian Act was invalid and the *Native Title Act* valid. This ruling prompted a review of the Chamber's management of the issue (CMEWA 1995, 10). The new strategy endorsed by the Council was:

- to encourage cooperative state/commonwealth approach to minimise practical difficulties created by the workings of the *Native Title Act*;
- to urge governments to attend urgently to the practicalities of administering mining titles;
- to encourage state government 'to exert the maximum amount of control available to it' over the procedural aspects of native title through the introduction of legislation to mirror the salient features of the *Native Title Act*;
- to identify the specific amendments to the *Native Title Act* needed to make it workable in Western Australia;

- ° to continue to develop and publicise initiatives to improve the understanding between the mining industry and the Aboriginal people.

Following this last point, an historic meeting was held between the Chamber and the Aboriginal and Torres Strait Islander Commission (ATSIC), and the industry began to work on developing employment opportunities for indigenous people. The Chamber was more focused on pragmatic outcomes once the possibility of a state haven from the provisions of Commonwealth legislation was dashed.

But the acceptance of the new reality was grudging, and the implications were serious, especially for WA. A study by Allen Consulting Group suggested that the *Native Title Act* had lengthened and constricted mining tenement approval (CMEWA 1996, 8, 14). The rate of issuing mining titles decreased (from 76 pw to 21 pw) as a result of the introduction of native title, reflecting increased caution and lower exploration activity. This was an especially Western Australian problem. By the end of March 1996, 205 native title applications had been lodged with the Native Title Tribunal; 117 of these were in WA, covering 30 percent of the state. Not a single title had been issued two years after the commencement of Act. Continuing uncertainty over land access that was the major concern for the industry, but once the native title process became routinised, the salience of the native title issue subsided, as indigenous issues became matters between individual firms and those with a right to negotiate.

Environmental issues continued to be salient, however, and the Chamber was active in both state politics and national and even international politics. State issues included: contaminated sites; marine management; noise regulations; planning and environmental processes; a review of gold and mineral sands industry. Federal and international issues included: climate change and greenhouse gas reduction measures; Commonwealth Environmental Impact Assessment; the MCA Environmental Code of practice; Forest Assessment; gold tailings management; and the National Pollutant Inventory (CMEWA 1996, 16).

While land access, particularly in relation to land rights and national parks and reserves, continued to be a significant issue, more traditional concerns continued to exercise it, sometimes (because of their disproportionate impact on the Western Australian industry) leading to CMEWA action at the national level. One such instance was the proposal by the Commonwealth government to end the Diesel Fuel Rebate Scheme which effectively refunded excise paid by the mining sector and others who consumed diesel off public highways.[2] The Minerals Council was very active on this measure, proposed for the August 1996 budget, but about half the $800m it would have cost the industry would have been borne by mining companies operating in Western Australia, and CMEWA acted in concert with the Minerals Council and 'continued its practice of routine meetings and close consultation with the Coalition Government on the wide range of political issues which inevitably involve such a large industry group' (CMEWA 1997, 7).

The Chamber was less successful in resisting another state government levy—a royalty on gold, which had (for more than a century) had been exempted from royalties in order to stimulate development. Despite determined lobbying by the Chamber's Gold Industry Forum created in response to the proposal, the government introduced a 2.5% royalty, with the only concessions extracted being a phasing in of the measure with a royalty of 1.25% from 1 January 1998 and future increases to be subject to the price of gold. This issue stimulated the formation of a sub-sectoral (commodity) group. The Australian Gold Council was formed in October 1998, from the CMEWA Gold Industry Forum. Again, associability followed policy. Chamber staff provided the secretariat for the AGC for the first 18 months of its existence.

CMEWA formalised a 'close working agreement' with the employers' industrial group Australian Mines and Metals Association in 1997 by concluding a memorandum of agreement with it setting out principles of communication on human resource matters after AMMA relocated into office premises shared with CMEWA (CMEWA 1997, 12). Industrial relations reforms by the (Richard) Court state government had allowed the introduction of individual employment contracts into the mining sector in the state, diminishing associability for AMMA.

Native title concerns continued to be prominent, however. The Commonwealth government introduced a package of amendments to the *Native Title Act* in 1996. These were agreed to by the Coalition government, but largely based on amendments proposed by the previous ALP government (CMEWA 1997, 15-17). Further amendments were announced in April 1996 and debate was deferred, but after a meeting of the Council

---

[2] The excise was used to fund road construction and maintenance, so the industry (along with the agricultural sector) had a case that they used fuel off roads and should be exempt.

for Aboriginal Reconciliation in June a task force comprising Aboriginal organizations and industry bodies was established to try to find common ground on the amendments. This process was interrupted by the handing down by the High Court of another decision in the *Wik* case in December 1996 (*Wik Peoples v The State of Queensland*). The Court overturned the common belief that the grant of a pastoral lease extinguished native title, and this had a significant impact on the mining industry, but mostly outside Western Australia, in those states where titles had been granted without reference to the *Native Title Act*. Within Western Australia, there were 223 native title claims registered covering 70 percent of the state, and about 80 percent of mining lease applications were subject to negotiation. Little wonder that the president reported in 1999 that 'Land Access and, in particular the unworkable processes of the Native Title Act, is the most serious long-term issue facing the industry' (CMEWA 1999, 9).

The Chamber considered the right to negotiate processes unworkable, thanks especially to multiple and overlapping claims. Together with the MCA, the Chamber lobbied the Commonwealth government in support of amendments to the Act, which were passed in July 1998. The amendments provided for alternative state-based native title legislative arrangements, subject to approval by the Commonwealth Attorney-General. The industry then lobbied the state government to secure state regimes that were complementary to the Commonwealth legislation, and these efforts were coordinated through the Minerals Council of Australia to try to secure uniform state approaches where possible. In Western Australia, the government's Validation Bill could only be passed with significant amendments forced by the ALP opposition.

In its annual report for 2000, the Chamber listed its priorities in rank order. These were: safety; land access; environmental management; industry competitiveness (including taxation); greenhouse response; human resources; mining education; and external relations (CMEWA 2000, 3). Safety had been made a priority after a trend of increasing incidence of fatal accidents throughout the 1990s, peaking with 11 deaths in 1997-98.

The prioritising of issues reflected a rationalisation throughout the industry at a time of low commodity prices and falling returns. The industry has traditionally reacted in these circumstances by cutting costs, and public affairs staff have often been seen as dispensable in a heavily production-oriented industry. The CEO, Ian Satchwell, indicated in his 2000 report that despite rationalisation and downsizing in the industry, the membership base and fee structure had been maintained, and 350 member representatives had participated in Chamber committees (CMEWA 2000, 11), but this number was down from 400 the year before and 500 just three years earlier.

The land rights issue slowly began to be resolved. The WA *Native Title (State Provisions)* and *Native Title (Validation) Bill* were finally adopted in December 1999, with the support of a Legislative Council independent. Then, on 2 March 2000 the full bench of the Federal Court overturned on appeal the decision of Justice Lee in *Ward v State of Western Australia* (known as the *Mirluwung Gajerrong* case), holding that the granting of mining leases extinguished native title and that mineral ownership rested with the Crown (CMEWA 2000, 17). The Chamber adopted a much more engaged approach to indigenous issues, continuing its support for Aboriginal education, training and employment, proactively building relationships with Aboriginal communities to develop alternative approaches to land access, and developing its own statement on reconciliation. It began a Mining Industry and Aboriginal Business Network to integrate the development of business relationships between the two. Then in 2000 the Yamatji Land and Sea Council became a member of CMEWA and was represented on the Chamber's Aboriginal Affairs Committee, the first instance of an industry group in Australia accepting an Aboriginal representative body as a member.

This did not translate into legislative success, however, and on 9 November 2000 the ALP and Australian Democrats used their control of the Commonwealth Senate to disallow the Western Australian native title legislation, despite concerted lobbying in conjunction with other professional associations and industry groups.

The Chamber also recognised the challenge posed to it by the associations review component of the GMI. President Peter Johnston noted that 'While such a review is welcomed, it has sent a warning signal to all industry associations across the globe, including our own Chamber, that resources companies are looking to consolidate the market' (CMEWA 2000, 17).

The Western Australian chamber became more professionalised, appointing more staff (including the CEO) from outside the sector. Previous CEO Ian Satchwell, while more of a public affairs professional rather than a miner, was recruited from MCA and had previously worked for the Electricity Supply Association and the Tasmanian chamber. Tim Shanahan, who commenced as CEO in June 2001, was formerly CEO of the WA Local Government Association. He focused on 'rolling out a public affairs role', for which he did not see need for technical industry expertise, rather a need for 'influence and analysis' expertise and a role in educating the public.

The Chamber by now worked on a 'pre-competitive' basis, primarily on issues such as safety, environment, and community relations. By 'pre-competitive', is meant those issues which were fundamental to all companies, with which they had to deal before they reached the 'starting line' of competition between companies. Previously, the approach in CMEWA was more technical. There were 'silos' of specialists in areas such as economics, Aboriginal affairs, environment, and so on. Many of the staff were formerly former or present company staffers, and the quality was not always high because sometimes they were supernumeraries, offered by member companies on an 'in-kind' basis. By the turn of the century, many had gone on from the chamber to fill public affairs roles in companies. (In the three years to 2003, CMEWA saw staff turnover of 80-90 percent). The Chamber itself was now run much more along business lines, reporting against budget and against key performance indicators.

The CMEWA business model now became one of advocacy and influence which was not confrontational, but engaged. This created visibility problems, since confrontational approaches convey the impression to members that something was being done, even if that activity was unproductive (or even counterproductive). The problem for the Chamber was to demonstrate its value to the members, more difficult because of the global nature of the industry. Many of the key people in member companies were not based in Western Australia, so CMEWA had 'to work the system' to convince members of its value. There was a need to be clear and focused, but they were looking at competitors and potential allies all the time to maximise their 'market share.'

CMEWA began to actively recruit more members in the energy sector, to increase size and coverage of the sector, and thus increase leverage with the state government. (As CMEWA already covered about 95 percent of the state's mining by volume, there were few 'greenfield' opportunities for expansion). The other area of recruitment was associate and contractor members, which comprised only around 15 percent of members in 1990, but more than half in 2004. (While production membership shrank by a third and exploration membership by two-thirds over this period, associate and contractor membership increased threefold).

Outside the peak state business association, the Chamber of Commerce and Industry, the CMEWA is one of the largest and best resourced industry associations in the state. It is the largest state chamber in Australia and is large even when compared with the MCA. BHP had a third of its global assets in Western Australia, and so the political representation of the sector in this state was of considerable significance. A great deal of the operations of a company like BHP were potentially affected by the State Government, so the priority for members and the Chamber was jurisdictionally based issues. This provided both risks and opportunities. As we have seen, some national issues were of such importance to Western Australia that CMEWA became active at the national level. (It also worked on greenhouse policy at the state level with the MCA and the Greenhouse Industry Network). This reinvention of the chamber raises questions about the relationship between the state chamber and the MCA, both vertically and horizontally.

Horizontally, the recruitment of energy sector members at the state level (in both WA and Queensland) threw up questions further up the vertical dimension about the relationship between the MCA and Australian Petroleum Production and Exploration Association (APEA had added production). In addition, companies were increasingly global, but they were not always members of state chambers, or any industry association and this could cause difficulties. For example, Esmeralda which caused the Romanian cyanide spill was based in Perth, but was not a member of CMEWA or MCA. But reputational damage is not confined to small players: after it took over MIM Holdings, Xstrata (not a CMEWA member) closed an MIM vanadium and platinum mine in western Australia, helping the economics of its South African operation by limiting production, but harming its reputation and that of the industry in WA, because the state government had spent $30m on the Mid-West gas pipeline for the mine in 1997. (Xstrata, now Glencore, was an MCA member).

There was some overlap between the memberships of CMEWA and the MCA. The CMEWA brought a direct connection with member companies, whereas the MCA was more concentrated, with its members being the large national players—or (perhaps more accurately) the global players with business interests in Australia. Some of the CMEWA members such as Hamersley Iron were operating subsidiaries of the global giants (Rio Tinto in the case of Hamersley and Robe River Iron), but CMEWA had more members than the MCA. These issues raised difficult questions within the sector about the relationship between the MCA and state chambers. Farmers groups and the Local Government Association in Australia had a federal structure, for example, and this model had been considered for the minerals sector. Some form of federal association was suggested by the

MCA in May 2004, but quickly rejected by most state chambers, with the exception of the struggling Victorian Minerals and Energy Council, which elected to become an associate member of the MCA by invitation.

Queensland

In 1991 the Queensland Chamber of Mines and the Queensland Coal Association merged to form the Queensland Mining Council. A Joint Coal Board (Commonwealth and state) had existed in NSW since 1948, and coal had also been separately organised in Queensland. From the 1960s, the importance of coal in Queensland rose substantially, so that (by value) mining output came to comprise about 80 percent coal and 20 percent metals. Coal had initially been mined in Queensland at Ipswich, largely by family-owned companies, but in the 1960s the coal sector expanded with the development of the Bowen Basin for export, first with coking coal and subsequently with steaming coal (Galligan 1989).

The key factor driving industry association in Queensland was industrial relations. In coal mining, the union sector was a centralised, closed shop system on the British model, with a branch structure. Historically, coal was mined mostly in NSW and the many Welsh miners brought their union system with them. The Joint Coal Board was established in recognition of the national significance of the NSW industry. In Queensland, from the 1920s, the only mining industry association was the Queensland Coal Association, a purely industrial group with a central industrial award under the arbitration system, so by the 1980s what is now the second largest resources state in Australia had no incorporated mining association. In the metals mining sector, industrial relations had always been conducted by firms alone, with no centralised bargaining. The oil, gas, and metals industries were represented by the Australian Mines and Metals Association, a Melbourne-based national body to provide industrial relations support. Development approvals were granted on a firm-by-firm basis by a strongly developmentalist state government, where even environmental regulation of mining was (helpfully) conducted by the Mines Department. MIM Holdings dominated the non-ferrous sector for many years, later joined by aluminium producers such as Comalco, mining bauxite at Weipa and refining alumina and smelting aluminium at Gladstone.

So in 1991 the Queensland Chamber of Mines with 19 commodity groups and the Queensland Coal Association merged to form the Queensland Mining Council, with its brief being essentially to stop coal being seen as a separate sector from non-ferrous metals. (There had been a separate mineral sands association with seven member companies). In the 1980s David Buchanan, General Manager at Mount Isa Mines (MIM) was the moving force in establishing a state mining body. The Queensland Chamber of Mines name had been registered in 1948, but until 1980 it had never been an incorporated body. Between 1948 and 1980 there were loose informal meetings of company CEOs, but in the 1970s MIM provided coordination and MIM staff serviced this informal Queensland chamber. The industry did not lobby collectively at this time, with all interaction with government conducted at the level of the individual firm. From the mid-70s, the Queensland Chamber of Mines increasingly started talking to government on behalf of the industry as a whole, on issues such as royalties, infrastructure, environment, economics, and social matters (essentially the concerns of farmers whose land might be affected by mining). From 1991 the QMC was able set its own agenda.

The coal industry was regulated at the federal level and had its own Superannuation Board, research agency, and industrial relations system with a separate Coal Tribunal handling industrial relations. One rationale for establishing the QMC was to send a message that there was a single mining industry, rather than separate coal and metals sectors. QMC formed without commodity groups, butq it initially had a coal group in the form of a Coal Committee within the QMC. The Australian Coal Association had only two members: the Queensland and NSW mining councils. The ACA provided a vehicle so that they could go to the Commonwealth if needed; it provided a vehicle to be recognised before the Coal Industry Tribunal, which consisted of a bench of one, administering one industrial award and from which there was no appeal. Industrial Relations was thus the reason for the existence of the ACA.

The formation of the Queensland Mining Council on 1 April 1991 came after a national review had proposed merging the Queensland Coal Association and the Queensland Chamber of Mines. The Queensland coal industry accounted for 48 percent of national production, but Queensland was also significant in terms of other commodities, such as copper (70 percent), silver (45 percent), lead (40 percent), zinc (30 percent), bauxite (25 percent), and rutile (42 percent). The Queensland gold industry was of much less significance than the Western Australian industry, accounting for only 16 percent of national production (QMC Annual Report 1991-2, 6). It was agreed that the board of the QMC would maintain a balance between the coal sector and the non-ferrous metals sector, with 20 directors to be split evenly between each.

One problem for the merger was the requirement for some entity to represent Queensland coal producers in the Australian Coal Association, which had to continue because of the separate Coal Industry Tribunal. So while the QMC had a specialised Coal Committee to represent Queensland coal operators, it also formed an industrial relations company, the Coal Operators Industrial Organisation of Employers, Queensland, to represent it before the Coal Industry Tribunal. QMC also had a close relationship with AMMA, sharing the same office floor through a sub-tenancy and sharing reception services and a library.

In 1992 QMC had 13 staff and 123 members, with the merged entity soon attracting an additional 20 members, providing separate categories of membership for organizations holding mining tenements, service industries and individuals. It also formed a close association with two organizations representing small or individual miners, the Far North Queensland Small Miners Association and the Central Queensland Mining Association. It chose to work through AMIC on all matters which required a multi-state input, such as Commonwealth taxation and legislation, shipping, transportation, tariffs, and international treaty obligations, of which the conventions on climate change and biodiversity being negotiated for signature at UNCED at Rio that year were the most significant (QMC Annual Report 1991-2, 9). But the QMC pointed out that AMIC did not cover the coal sector, and so it needed to continue with the Australian Coal Association. In fact, AMIC could cover the coal industry on all matters except the industrial matters before the Coal Industry Tribunal.

It seemed the separate organization of the coal industry would endure for the foreseeable future, because it had received additional recognition by the Commonwealth government, with the minister accepting after extensive lobbying over two years that responsibility for administration of the coal research levy should pass from the National Energy Research and Development Research Program to the Australian Coal Association. Then there was the formation in December 1990 of the Australian Coal Industry Council (ACIC), bringing together federal and state ministers, the chairs of the New South Wales and Queensland Coal Associations and the national presidents of the two unions with coverage in the industry—the United Mineworkers and the Federated Engine Drivers and Firemen's Association. Significantly, industry representation was through the state coal associations rather than through the ACA, but the rather quaint names of the unions perhaps indicated the fact that industrial reform was overdue, and a move to a system based on bargaining at the level of the individual enterprise rather than the industry as a whole was to change the basis for association for both unions and employers.

The formation of ACIC reflected the penchant of the Hawke ALP government for quasi-corporatist arrangements to address issues affecting both business and labour in a sector by concertation rather than confrontation. ACIC commissioned reports on coal demand and supply, safety issues, response to the greenhouse issue and future prospects for the coal industry. Other issues at this time included the Ecologically Sustainable Development process (itself quasi-corporatist in nature), maritime issues and a Senate inquiry into the generation, transmission, distribution and use of electricity.

One point of interest was that the ACA at this time was funding the Australian membership of the International Energy Agency, and only in March 1992—after intense lobbying—did the Minister of Primary Industry and Energy, Simon Crean, agree to resume the costs of Australia's membership with effect from June 1992. The ACA, IEA and the Department of Primary Industry and Energy then jointly sponsored an international conference on 'Coal, the Environment and Development' in Sydney in November 1992 (QMC Annual Report 1992: 9). ACA was also active on committees of the UN Economic Commission for Europe and International Standards Association work on international classification systems for coal.

The QMC worked cooperatively with the Queensland government on some environmental issues, jointly developing an Environmental Management Overview Strategy (covering mine rehabilitation, water quality, planning and environmental auditing), but it differed with the government on some issues, including their (unsuccessful) objection to the inclusion of Interim Protection Orders over any existing mining area as part of a new *Nature Conservation Act.* They met with more success in opposing (with most business groups) inclusion of provisions to allow third party actions. An *Environmental Protection Act* also established an Environmental Protection Authority outside the existing department, but regulation of mining continued to be covered under the *Mineral Resources Act*, and the QMC succeeded in having mining tenements excluded from the *Contaminated Land Act* and covered by the *Mineral Resources Act.*

The relationship between the industry and the Department of Resource Industries at this time could probably be described as one of agency capture, so it was perhaps little wonder that the QMC should constantly lobby for regulation pertaining to it to be covered by the *Mineral Resources Act.* The minister at this time (Tony McGrady) came from a constituency at Mt Isa, a mining town dominated by MIM, and the QMC repaid the department by lobbying to strengthening the agency during a review by the Public Sector Management Commission, arguing it had lost stature and authority. McGrady was reappointed minister after the September 1992 election, and he renamed the department 'Minerals and Energy', 'which was warmly received by the industry' (QMC AR 1992-93, 11).

The ACA and QMC continued their efforts to dissuade the Commonwealth government from treating coal as a separate industry 'and in particular sought to change the archaic industrial relations arrangements whereby coal has a special Industry Tribunal outside the arbitration system.' A major objective for the industry was to bring coal industrial relations into the mainstream as quickly as possible. In December 1989 employers and employees had agreed to improve cost efficiency and cost effectiveness of the coal industry consistent with the aims of the Structural Efficiency Principles contained in a National Restructuring Agreement (QMC Annual Report 1991-92, 21-22).

The QMC followed the AMIC line on the response to *Mabo,* the *Endangered Species Act (C'wealth)*, maritime issues, coal classification standards, energy taxation, and foreign investment. State issues at this time were primarily occupational health and safety, environment, and, for the coal sector especially, coal rail freights, the insistence of the government in continuing a Queensland Coal Board (regulating miners' health, formed in 1949, abolished in 1997), long service leave provisions and mine rescue. Prior to the High Court decision in the *Mabo* case, handed down on 3 June 1992, the QMC had supported the provision in the *Aboriginal Lands Act (Qld)* for vacant Crown land to be open to claim by Aborigines. After *Mabo* it took some time before the QMC recognised that there was now a threat to existing titles.

The industry was searching for a new image at this time, as were other chambers seeking to move on from logos and other symbols involving picks, shovels and bearded miners. One experiment that seems not to have endured, perhaps thankfully, was captured in a photograph in the 1993-94 Annual Report (1993-4, 10), captioned: 'Benny Bauxite takes to the catwalk in the Magical Minerals Spectacular at the Annual Dinner.' Comalco-branded and looking somewhat like Mr Potatohead, Benny paraded, flanked by two attractive models.

The environment was growing in significance for the industry, with a range of issues including environmental impact assessment, the *Contaminated Land Act, Coastal Protection Bill*, *Water Resources Audit Act*, heritage legislation, waste management, nature conservation, environmental management systems, and environmental planning. Many of these issues were taking on an increasingly international dimension, especially climate change (UNFCCC), trade in hazardous waste (Basel Convention), World Heritage, Biodiversity (UNCB), Law of the Sea, and wetlands (Ramsar Convention). Safety and land rights issues continued to be prominent, but it was the industrial relations issue that was to transform the sector, as the *Industrial Relations Reform Bill (C'wealth) 1993* moved the basis of industrial relations from centralised wage fixing to an enterprise basis.

After years of lobbying for such an outcome, and in the face of strong union resistance, the Commonwealth government finally agreed to transfer industrial relations from the Coal Industry Tribunal into the industrial relations mainstream from 3 July 1995. Former chair of the CIT, David Duncan, was appointed a Deputy President of the Australian Industrial Relations Commission and the coal industry was to be covered by a special four-person panel headed by the president of the AIRC, a marked change from the old CIT system, with a one-man bench from which there was no appeal. The coal companies then voted to close down the Coal Operators Industrial Organisation of Employers, Queensland, which was formally deregistered as an industrial organization and dissolved on 1 July 1995. Again, institutions determining association.

AMIC also underwent changes in structure as a result of the review of the mining industry bodies that gave rise to the formation of the QMC, with the granting of representation to QMC and CMWA on the AMIC board. Another innovation was the establishment of a routine of holding two meetings each year—one in Canberra, the other rotating between states—at which the presidents and CEOs of all the state chambers, AMMA, the Australian Institute of Mining and Metallurgy and other kindred associations could discuss issues common to the whole industry.

The QMC continued to offer industrial advocacy services on a fee-for-service basis, and there was initially a high demand with the shift to enterprise bargaining before the AIRC. QMC membership continued to increase—to 147 by 1995 and 159 in 1996—and its staff increased from 13 (of which 3 were engaged in IR) to 15, but by 1997 IR staff were not being replaced as they resigned. Then, after the election of a Liberal-National

Coalition government in Canberra in March 1996, the QMC 'cooperated closely' with the government over the adoption of the new *Workplace Relations Act* that was to also contain the amendments to the *Trade Practices Act* outlawing secondary boycotts that the sector had sought during the 1993 reforms under the ALP government. In addition to removing these provisions, the legislation introduced provision for individual contracts known as Australian Workplace Agreements, stripped back the items that could be included in industrial awards to 20 basic matters, and removed monopoly coverage rights for unions. With this, the QMC was able to vacate industrial relations issues completely and become more focused on issues such as environment (especially climate change), native title, rail freight charges, and electricity reforms.

The reforms led not to widespread adoption of AWAs in the sector, but to the negotiation of a new industrial award, which was applied from December 1997. Negotiations and arbitration then proceeded over what matters were allowable in the coal awards under the new legislation, and in May 1998 Justice Boulton ruled four matters were not allowable: the traditional 'last on, first off' basis for the reduction of hands; preference for union members; preference for retrenched workers in new hiring; and the right of entry to mines for union officials (QMC, Annual Report 1997-98: 26). Thus, the new award not only allowed productivity gains by companies by overturning long-standing restrictive work practices, but reduced substantially the role of trade unions.

Land access became a major issue for the QMC after the *Mabo* decision and the subsequent adoption of the *Native Title Act,* with the QMC claiming the issuing of mining titles and exploration permits had come to a virtual halt, with delays of up to four years reported. Certainly, exploration expenditure in Queensland had halved from $181m in 1995 to $90m in 1999 (Annual Report 1999, 24), but part of this reflected low commodity prices. After the *Wik* ruling, the Commonwealth government introduced a *Native Title Amendment Bill* in 1998, allowing that alternative state regimes in the form of their own native title tribunals and land management processes could replace the much-criticised 'right to negotiate'. The QMC worked unsuccessfully with Peter Beattie, then ALP state opposition leader (and later premier), to try to get the federal ALP to support the legislation in the Senate, but it did not pass the Senate until it was supported by the independent Tasmanian Senator Brian Harradine, somewhat alarmed by a backlash in Queensland that saw the reactionary One Nation Party win 11 seats in the state election.

Having won the state election, however, the Beattie government was somewhat less helpful on the issue. Despite the QMC's 'strongest representations', the Beattie government resolved only to exclude 'low impact' exploration from the right to negotiate process and to impose an 'only slightly less restrictive' RTN regime on mining leases. Despite these disappointments to the industry, the QMC worked closely with the Queensland government, and a Bill was passed in November 1998, but it had to be ratified by the Commonwealth Parliament and signed off by the Commonwealth Attorney-General, a hurdle which was passed only in June 1999, which meant that the Queensland regime could not operate until at least January 2000. This delay was attributed by the QMC to a lack of leadership on the part of federal ALP leader Kim Beasley, who allowed the Left of the ALP and the Democrats to ensure the WA, Northern Territory and even the 'minimalist' Queensland laws could not be fully implemented. Finally, in September 2000 the new Queensland procedures—providing for a common Land and Resources Tribunal to replace the Warden's Court and consider environmental, native title and other landholder objections at the one time—came into effect.

The priority issue in 2001-02 continued to be access, with other important issues being safety, environment, indigenous relationships, infrastructure, and education. There were also concerns over the sustainability of the industry. A survey of members revealed that unless exploration levels could be restored quickly there would be no metalliferous mines other than Mt Isa operating in the state by 2015. Whereas in 1993-95 over 400 exploration licences were issued annually, this reduced to a little over 200 in 1996-97 and to less than 100 annually in the period 1997-2001 (QMC AR 2000-2001, 23).

The reforms under the *Workplace Relations Act 1996* provided for industrial agreements at the enterprise level, removing one factor affecting associability. Companies now managed their own industrial relations on-site at the company level. As a result, the QMC shed all five of its IR staff in 1999. Individual companies were emboldened by the *Workplace Relations Act*, particularly by its secondary boycotts provisions. Previously, any strike at a single mine, especially a coal mine, would spread throughout the industry and secondary boycotts imposed by the maritime unions would close the waterfront—especially costly for an export-oriented industry. Their resolve was stiffened also by the prevailing economic climate. A steep decline in coal prices, with lower cost producers in South America, Canada, Indonesia, US, gave them the reason to find the courage to improve productivity through workplace reform. After the reforms to industrial relations there was a claimed 35 percent rise in productivity. The last vestiges of federal regulation (the tribunal, export controls, Superannuation Board, CSL Board) had gone, and this also impacted on the associability of the industry.

If changes in the industrial relations system weakened the associational rationale for the QMC, reform of environmental policy therefore provided something of a counterbalance. For the industry in Queensland, the environment became more important, primarily in three areas: the site-related issues of air, noise, and water pollution; access to land for minerals and rehabilitation, especially after mine closure; and the range of international issues relating to climate change, toxics regulation and the possibility for hazardous waste regulation to impact on trade involving the numerous ashes, drosses, concentrates and other intermediate or waste products traded between processing plants internationally. As noted earlier. until 2000, environmental regulation of the mining industry in Queensland was, uniquely, undertaken by the Department of Mines and Energy. This was fundamentally a classic distributive agency, with its overwhelming mission being to support and foster the development of the industry. There was, therefore, a classic poacher-gamekeeper problem. The Department of Mines and Energy was an anachronism as a regulator in the environmental age, and it was seen as a protector by old lags in the industry.

The Goss ALP government adopted an *Environment Protection Act* in 1994 establishing an EPA, but this exempted the mining industry, which continued to be regulated by the Department of Mines and Energy. The proposed establishment of an EPA produced risk of double jeopardy for industry, since it felt it could be licensed under two acts. All polirical parties stated in discussions that they would prefer to operate under the *Environment Protection Act* for licensing, but it took seven years to achieve this outcome, with reform stalled under the Coalition Borbidge government. ALP Premier Beattie announced in May 1999 that the environmental regulation of mining would be transferred from the Department of Minerals and Energy to the EPA (Annual Report 1998-99, 13). The *Environmental Protection Act* was amended and this change occurred from November 2000.

The regulation of land management was also reformed. A Land and Resources Tribunal replaced the Wardens Court which previously had jurisdiction over mining, and this tribunal also absorbed the Native Title tribunal and Environment Tribunal. The QMC played a proactive role in the change, engaging with farmer, green and Aboriginal groups, having decided it was better to drive the process than have it imposed upon it. The

(Commonwealth) *EP&BC Act 1999* allowed states to gain accreditation for their environmental systems and the QMC wanted an end to fights between state and Commonwealth, and therefore favoured the development of environmental policy at the state level (where structural power was greater) which would minimise the chances of federal intervention.

There was a limited role for the QMC in structuring participation on international issues, though QMC played a role in organising industry representation on climate change. Australia's was the only national delegation in meetings of the Conference of the Parties to the Framework Convention on Climate Change containing industry representatives, and the QMC played a role there. It had feeder groups on climate change which provided a means of participating in the Australian Industry Greenhouse Network. The QMC was not involved in trade issues, but was active on: access; social issues; environment; tenure; and safety. The last three were the most significant ones.

The QMC then broadened its scope and changed its name to the Queensland Resources Council, and prospered after the amalgamation of the coal and mining bodies. In 1992 it had 128 members (57 full members, 19 service members, 119 associate members and 33 personal members) and 13 staff. By 2002, it had 11 staff and 152 members, with slightly fewer full members (51), many fewer personal members (2), with growth occurring in service membership (52) and associate members (47). But these two points of analysis miss a growth in staff to 15 by 1996 (before industrial relations reforms impacted) and a membership that almost touched 200 in 1999.

The transformation of the Council into a modern, professional industry association came when it came to replacing Executive Director, Michael Pinnock, who had been in the job for 23 years. The Council chose Susan Johnston, a barrister, who had formerly been Head of Environment and Land Use Planning in the Queensland Department of Premier and Cabinet, Head of the Office of Energy Management, and had led the NSW government's Review of Mine Safety. From outside the mining industry, she had tertiary qualifications in law, government and journalism.

The renaming the QMC to the Queensland Resources Council in November 2003 was a deliberate move to broaden coverage to include resources rather than just mining, so that the membership then included oil and gas producers and electricity generators. There were synergies apparent around issues like the implications of climate change for fossil fuels between energy companies and coal miners, especially through a requirement by the

Queensland government for 12 percent of electricity generation to come from gas, with a response in the development of coal seam gas.

There was a new emphasis on signing off on mine rehabilitation, and the QRC enjoyed a good relationship with indigenous groups, including an MOU with the Queensland Indigenous Working Group, and it now accepted the native title regime. The QRC developed a significant education program with part-time teachers and a more sophisticated program, delivered by teachers going into schools and talking about the resources sector, aimed at correcting a negative image of mining among youth, so in the face of a skills shortage (especially among engineers and environmental scientists) they started a Careers Awareness Campaign. This emphasis was reflected in staffing, with an increase in communication staff from one to two and a-half, and education staff from two to five, with eleven part-time teachers. In addition to education, the main issues were environment, indigenous affairs, occupational health and safety, infrastructure, industry policy.

Northern Territory

There was a small association in the Northern Territory. The Northern Territory Minerals Council (NTMC) was established in 1955—before self-government was granted to the Territory by the Commonwealth government, which was later to establish a legislated approach to Aboriginal land rights. While the Northern Territory enjoys self-government, its constitutional position is not equivalent to the states, and the Commonwealth government can over-ride any legislation.

The NTMC was the only micro-level mining association not formally affiliated with the MCA. Its membership included mineral exploration, mining, quarrying, extractive, petroleum, service, supply and specialist consultant companies and businesses. The NT Minerals Council's objectives were industry representation and promotion of the exploration, mining, minerals processing and petroleum industries in the Northern Territory, education of the public and the encouragement of the corporate responsibility of members towards the Northern Territory.

The NT Minerals Council consisted of an executive committee, supported by a small office of four professional staff, one of whom was an Education Manager. Its standing committees reflected the work program of the organisation: Education and Public Affairs; Environment; Land Access; and Health and Safety,

The Northern Territory is unique among Australian jurisdictions in that it is subject to two pieces of Commonwealth legislation involving Aboriginal land rights, being the *Aboriginal Land Rights (NT) Act 1976* and the *Native Title Act 1994.* More than 50 percent of the Northern Territory land is either Aboriginal freehold land or land under a native title claim. The granting of exploration and mining titles on this form of land tenure was subject to the procedures of the *Aboriginal Land Rights (NT) Act.* Exploration and mining title was granted over Aboriginal freehold land only after the applicant reached agreement specifying terms and compensation with the relevant land council (Northern, Central, Tiwi and Anindilyakwa) which represented traditional owners.

Most of the balance of the land the Territory area is held as pastoral leases, which may be subject to native title. The granting of exploration licenses, mining leases or petroleum permits over this land was subject to the procedures of the *Native Title Act*. Land access was therefore a major concern for the NT Minerals Council and served as a strong basis for association, especially for Aboriginal freehold land, on which access had to be negotiated with the appropriate land council, and this on-going relationship favoured action by the NT Minerals Council rather than by individual firms with individual landowners while the procedures were being decided, but the basis for association weakened. The NT Government determined in March 2000 that it would use the *Native Title Act* to process applications on pastoral land, and the first notices for mineral exploration were issued in September 2000.

The NTMC numbered among its members the local subsidiaries of national level companies and TNCs: Newmont, Energy Resources of Australia, Alcan Gove, BHP-Billiton, Woodside Energy and Xstrata. It provided a means of sectoral representation to the Territory government, but it was not a significant player on the national stage. Ultimately, however, the NTMC could not sustain an independent existence with the emphasis on individual firm negotiation with landowners, and was absorbed into the Minerals Council of Australia as MCA NT.

Part Two: The New State Chambers

South Australia

The formation of a state chamber in South Australia was first suggested in November 1978 by the state government, in the shape of the Director-General of Mines and Energy, Mr B.P. Webb, who contrasted the great mining potential of the state with its poor performance over many years.[3] His idea of a mining chamber to improve mining activity was supported by the government, the Department of Mines and Energy and the mining industry, and was discussed at an executive meeting of the state Chamber of Commerce and Industry. These parties saw the need for a group which could 'take the Mining Industry's part in dealing with the Public and with Governments on a wide range of issues, increasing awareness of our needs, importance, and potential contribution to the economy.' The formation of the South Australian Chamber was thus very much encouraged by both the government and the peak business group. The Chamber of Commerce and Industry then provided it with initial support, including free office space and services at nominal charge.

Its creation was also facilitated by AMIC, with AMIC president, Sir Frank Espie, calling a meeting of 15 people from mining companies on 19 June 1979. The meeting resolved to establish the South Australian Chamber of Minerals (SACOM) and elected its first office-bearers. Funds were advanced to it by companies, and a part-time secretary was engaged who operated out of the SACCI offices. SACOM was formally incorporated on 6 February 1980 and by 30 June 1980 it had 37 corporate members, 27 associate members and 8 personal associate members. Its membership included not just the obvious mining companies, largely from the non-ferrous sector (BHP, CRA, MIM Holdings, North Broken Hill, Pancontinental, Poseidon, Western Mining, and so on) but also a number of petroleum and gas companies with interests in the Cooper Basin (such as BP Petroleum, Delhi Petroleum, Esso, Marathon, Santos) and a number of companies involved in quarrying and extractive industries related to the construction industry. Significantly, SACOM began with a broader base than other state chambers, though it was only to incorporate 'Energy' into its title much later. To extend its reach to the artisanal opal miners of Coober Pedy, it allowed a personal associate membership to be taken up by the chairman of the mining sub-committee of the Coober Pedy Progress and Miners Association.

SACOM's starting budget was $33,000, generated by a fee structure which charged three categories of corporate members $1,400, $700 or $350—fees which were quickly increased for the 1980-81 year to $2,200, $1,100 and $550 'to enable worthwhile promotional activity to take place.' That activity was primarily in relation to the issue of Aboriginal land rights, which was noted as one of several initial 'pressing issues' requiring action.

---

[3] The details of the origins of SACOM are contained in SACOM 1980 (n.p.)

The issue was not just the adoption of the *Aboriginal Heritage Act*, which required the industry and all others to pay 'due regard' to sites of significance in accordance with Aboriginal tradition, but the government proposal to grant land rights to the Pitjantjatjara people by means of the *Pitjantjatjara Land Rights Act 1981*. It seems clear that land rights legislation proposed by the South Australian government was a significant (if not the major) stimulus for the formation of a state chamber. The Dunstan ALP government had been the first to recognise any form of land rights in Australia, with the adoption of the *Aboriginal Lands Trust Act 1966*. The first committee established by the Chamber was a Land Rights Committee, and the issue dominated the early activities of the Chamber, with a large newspaper advertisement asking Premier Tonkin that the rights of the Pitjantjatjara people be balanced against the rights of other South Australians.

In 1980 the Chamber presented its one page policy statement on land rights to the Premier, the Deputy Premier and the Minister for Aboriginal Affairs, proposing that freehold title should apply to Aborigines on the same terms as land granted to any Australian. (Mineral rights should continue to be reserved to the Crown, in other words). It endorsed the *Aboriginal Heritage Act* and recognised the need for industry to consult with Aboriginal people, but argued that the potential of the state was best achieved by preserving the existing 'tried and tested' structure of the *Mining Act*, which provided for Crown ownership of minerals, safeguards and compensation for landholders, and the vesting of power in the Crown. SACOM, in other words, did not oppose the granting of land rights; it just did not want them granted on terms that were any different to those applied to other land-owners.

Membership of SACOM in 1981 increased to 43 corporate members, and it was active on several issues, including amendments to bring the *Planning Act* into line with the *Mining Act*, but another significant issue for the Chamber emerged at this time in the form of opposition to uranium mining. The Chamber developed a uranium policy and in August 1980 established a Uranium Committee, in response to a campaign during the lead-up to the October 1981 state elections by a group called Campaign Against Nuclear Energy to get local government authorities to declare their local government areas 'Nuclear Free Zones'. It also sought an end to uranium mining, and there were several prospective uranium mines in the state, including Western Mining's large copper-uranium-gold deposit at Roxby Downs (Olympic Dam).

Opposition to uranium mining became an awkward issue for the ALP at the Commonwealth level, and it eventually developed a 'Three Mines' policy which permitted the Roxby Downs project (thanks to the marginal nature of several seats in the federal Parliament in the state), and the way in which it was addressed by the industry at various jurisdictional levels is instructive. A Uranium Information Centre was established in Melbourne to mount a national public relations defence, but the issue was of special concern for the South Australian chamber—or, at least, for those of its members (such as Western Mining, BP and Shell) with uranium prospects. The problem for SACOM was that the regulatory threat was based on the product, rather than mining as an activity, and those members mining other products were largely indifferent to the fate of uranium. The Chamber therefore introduced a Uranium Promotion Levy on those member companies involved in uranium exploration and mining to fund the uranium campaign. The Chamber was thus able to act on a specific product basis without charging (or alienating) its wider membership.

This was an important device for maintaining sectoral associability. The Chamber considered all members would benefit from the stance on uranium (SACOM 1981, 6), but recognised it would have been divisive to fund the uranium campaign from general revenue, and signalled an intention to take this approach with similar issues in future. The potential for division was also apparent in the relationship between the Chamber and the peak association, SACCI. SACOM, as we saw, had originally been sponsored by SACCI, and the agreement between the two had required SACOM members to also become SACCI members. As early as 1981, SACOM's members were objecting to this compulsion and this requirement was relaxed by mutual agreement and SACOM moved to a more independent position (SACOM, 1981: 7). The Combined Employers' Council was, however, to undertake a press and poster campaign in support of the Olympic Dam project, which would give the whole state an economic boost if approved. Coordination within the sector but across levels was also evolving, with the first of intended bi-annual meetings of a 'Presidents' Committee' (consisting of chamber presidents and their executive officers) being held in Canberra at AMIC's instigation in September 1980.

SACOM was expanding rapidly during this period. Its budget grew to $77,000 in 1980-81, thanks to increases of $200/$100/$50 in subscriptions and growing membership, and these were followed by increases of $600/300/150 in 1981-82, with the budget rising to $108,000, with an additional $38,000 being raised by the Uranium Levy. By 1982, it had committees on Education, Uranium, Land Rights and Exploration, as well as a Finance Committee and an Editorial Committee (to check all statements and materials issued by the Chamber). The Chamber was picketed over the proposed Honeymoon and Roxby Downs uranium mines, but the land rights issue became less salient. The Chamber vacated the SACCI premises at Industry House, although this 'in no way lessened the spirit of cooperation between the two Chambers' (SACOM 1982, 9). It made submissions on a Radiation Protection and Control Bill, the *Aboriginal Heritage Amendment Act* and the Commercial Arbitration Bill.

The Chamber was by now maintaining regular contact with all federal politicians from the state and both the state government and opposition and several departments, including Mines and Energy, the South Australian Health Commission, Environment and Planning, Education and the Office of Aboriginal Affairs. The close relations between the Chamber and the state government were exemplified by the fact that the State Government Information Centre helped distribute *Johnny Green's Journal,* SACOM's newsletter, named for the statue of a miner which stood watch over the historic mining town of Burra. 2,000 copies were distributed to teachers, schools, politicians and government departments.

The Chamber had mixed success on the issue of uranium mining, however, as the incoming state ALP government decided against permitting development of the Honeymoon and Beverley mines, while approving Roxby Downs, passing the *Olympic Dam Indenture Act* after a strong campaign in support by both SACOM and business more generally.

The land rights issue arose again when the first application was made under the *Pitjantjatjara Land Rights Act*—by Hematite Petroleum, which was not a SACOM member. Hematite's application to explore on Pitjantjatjara land was blocked by what it (and SACOM) regarded as a demand for 'excessively high' front end payments. While the Act made provision for arbitration, Hematite was wary of setting a precedent if it took the matter to arbitration. The opportunity was thus lost, perhaps due to the inexperience of Aboriginal negotiators seeking too much before exploration had demonstrated a resource to exploit. But the ambition of the Pitjantjatjara people was possibly encouraged by the new ALP state government, which introduced a *Maralinga Tjarutja Land Rights Bill* which the Chamber criticised as having been 'drafted by land right lawyers' (SACOM 1983, 8).

By 1983, SACOM had 42 corporate members, 26 service members and 18 personal members, and a budget of $138,000, with an additional $36,000 being spent on the uranium campaign, putting that fund into deficit.

(The currency of the debate within the ALP saw expenditure rise to $97,000 in 1983-84). Its staff was expanded to a manager, secretary and a part-time organiser. It was active on the *Maralinga Tjarutja Land Rights Bill*, the National Conservation Strategy, and legislation on occupational health and safety, sex discrimination and workers compensation. It liaised with AMIC and other state chambers to coordinate industry positions, and with other employer groups and the United Farmers and Stockowners of South Australia. It was bound by its members, to the extent that each held an effective veto over any chamber position affecting it, since it 'did not participate in any activity directly affecting a member without that member's permission' (SACOM, 1984: 4).

The mid-1980s were a time of low mineral prices, and the Chamber saw its role as being to advocate policies to 'ensure continued access to land to search for minerals and to ensure that our industry was consulted before further alienation of land took place' (SACOM 1985: 1). SACOM argued for recognition of different views among Aboriginal people in outback areas to those held by the Commonwealth Department of Aboriginal Affairs and the state minister. They sought to communicate directly with the mining industry without interference by 'unrepresentative' Land Councils, advisers and government departments. SACOM claimed that, significant sites aside, many Aboriginals were keen to have development. 'These pro-Australian aspirations were supported by the Chamber' (SACOM 1985, 4). The Chamber did not support the intention of the Anangu Pitjantjatjaraku people to apply for a petroleum exploration licence over their traditional lands, drawing attention to the accepted practice that applications were considered only from organisations with a recognised capability in petroleum exploration, and that (under the *Petroleum Act*) surface ownership or tenure carried no pre-emptive rights to tenement applications.

The issues for SACOM in the mid-1980s continued to be land rights and environment, and especially uranium, which resurfaced to the extent in 1985-86 that a Uranium Committee was constituted to deal with increased anti-nuclear activity at the time when Roxby Downs was proceeding, but the committee was disestablished in December 1987.

The Chamber was somewhat miscast at this time. Its membership was open to those engaged in 'exploration for minerals, including petroleum, or in mining, quarrying or smelting in South Australia or its vicinity' (SACOM 1986, 7). It had members from all these sectors, yet its name and logo (depicting Johnny Green, a uniquely mining symbol) did not reflect its energy or quarrying members. While it was to keep the Johnny

Green logo for another decade and a-half, it changed its name in 1987-88 to incorporate energy, becoming the Chamber of Minerals and Energy. At this time it expanded to three permanent staff plus a part-time office assistant, with a budget of $231,000, and appointed regional representatives (as a point of contact) at Port Pirie, Leigh Creek, Whyalla and Olympic Dam. It also appointed a new manager—Mr M.N. Hiern, formerly Chief Geologist in the South Australian Department of Mines and Energy.

The Chamber then fell into a state of some disorganisation. Its Annual Reports for 1987-88 and 1988-89 are held in its records only in draft form and there is then a complete gap in its holdings until 1996-97. By this time it had expanded to have five staff and had appointed former school teacher Bob Goreing as CEO. During Goering's tenure, SACOME made efforts to broaden representation on its committees and to adopt a more proactive approach to issues confronting the industry. The issues continued to be native title and Aboriginal heritage, reviews of state mining and petroleum legislation, an Inquiry by a Commonwealth Senate Select Committee into uranium mining and milling, and environmental issues, including the development of the MCA Code, greenhouse, wild rivers, parks, rehabilitation, the NEPC, NPI, oceans policy, ecologically sustainable land management, and the review of Commonwealth and state roles and responsibilities that led to the *EP&BC Act 1999*. By 1997 the budget had grown to $443,000 supporting a staff of five. Membership exceeded 60 and a two day workshop was held to develop a three-year strategic plan.

But all was not well with SACOME, as it began to sink under an explosion in committees, subcommittees and working parties. Its members were being 'participated to death', as SACOME adopted a system where there were five tiers of committees, from the Council, through 'sectorial' [*sic*] committees (Minerals Exploration, Petroleum, Extractive Industries), standing committees (Legislation and Land Access, Environmental Affairs, Occupational Health and Safety, Government and Community Relations, Industry Training), sub-committees and working parties, and committees outside the chamber. While the ambition expressed in the strategic plan might have been to involve the members in numerous deliberative committees, this explosion in the number of committees had the opposite effect.

Participating in such a number of committees was beyond the membership, and the lead had to be taken by SACOME staff. It is worth noting that poor commodity prices in the late 1990s saw the industry react in its traditional manner, and shed staff. Many of the staff shed during this period were those formerly able to contribute to a public affairs role, so SACOME was seeking greater participation at the very time when companies were less able to participate. SACOME staff, especially Bob Goering, thus feature prominently in the many committees and working parties during this period, and so the organization became staff-driven rather than member-driven. It became a professionally run organization, but it really had only one professional. Moreover, an inordinate amount of time was consumed in writing agendas, reports and minutes for this plethora of committees. While SACOME was active, questions arose in the minds of members as to just how effective this activity was. Did the generation of copious quantities of reports and submissions amount to effectiveness on the part of SACOME? It would seem that its ability to command the attention of government in fact diminished. One telling blow to SACOME was the loss of its dedicated government agency, with the absorption of the Department of Minerals and Energy into a new agency, Primary Industries and Resources South Australia in early 1998. (Two years later, a dedicated minister was again appointed, and an Office of Minerals and Energy established within PIRSA).

As Hirschman (1970) put it, the choices confronting a member of an organization with which they are unhappy are exit, voice, or loyalty. There were some signs of voice within SACOME, with an election for office-bearers held for the first time in 1997 (repeated in 1998) reflecting a growing concern with the Chamber, but some members soon began to choose exit. While the numbers of members did not reflect this immediately (corporate membership remaining constant or even growing slightly in the mid- to high 30s), by the time its new CEO Phil Sutherland, joined it in February 2001, SACOME was in trouble and running at a loss. Its budget had grown to over $600,000 and it had begun to lose members. Another loss was recorded for the 2001-02 year, and the Chamber was quite frank in its assessment of the problems that confronted it in its Annual Report:

> This was the result of a number of factors including a not insignificant number of members who chose not to renew their membership at the outset of the year, unrealistic membership subscription levels, not adjusting membership subscriptions for several years to take account of increases in operating costs, and urgent expenditure relating to the Chamber's operating environment (SACOME 2002, 2).

The Chamber had been avoiding the 'value-for-money' question by not increasing subscriptions (unchanged for six years) and deferring costs such as upgrading computing and communication systems. Its subscriptions were at the lower end of the scale of those charged by other chambers, and it now faced the challenge of seeking to increase its subscription fees and increase its membership simultaneously. Sixteen of its 58 members (corporates plus service industry) failed to renew their memberships at the end of 2002. The Chamber clearly needed to be reinvigorated if it was to survive.

One of the first changes was the jettisoning of the Johnny Green logo. Not only was this quaint and outmoded, but it excluded many members and potential members that were not miners. For those that *were* miners, an emblem featuring a man with a pick was not emblematic of modern mining. SACOME pitched itself at the resources sector, which it saw as being constituted by companies engaged in energy, extractive industries, minerals, petroleum, and infrastructure (energy and gas pipelines, energy transportation and distribution). Service industry membership was open to those industries with a client base that included the resources sector. A solely mining organization was not a viable option, because there were only about four companies actually engaged in mining in the state and about fourteen engaged in exploration. They alone could not support a sustainable professional chamber.

Sutherland had to first demonstrate the worth of the Chamber and then increase the fees. He also had to make the Chamber more visible. After initially being housed by the peak business body, it had moved to another location where it lacked visibility. It was housed in three rooms in an old building owned by the Australian Minerals Foundation—effectively consumed by another organization with no corporate visibility. Sutherland, who had a background in the Commonwealth, state and local public services, rewrote all the Chamber's promotional material and republished it with the new inclusive logo, and started to upgrade the operating systems, leasing rather than buying to save up-front costs. As he put it: 'It was a race to get upgraded operating systems in place before we went broke.' He appointed a dedicated recruiting officer, and developed a strategic plan in consultation with the members, taking care to find out what the members wanted. Then the members were able to say that activities would have to be resourced, so they were locked in and had to agree to new subscription fees to support the activity.

The membership also effectively regained control of the Chamber. The previous explosion in the number of committees meant that the staff were playing a prominent role in the conduct of their business, simply because the workload exceeded that which could be carried at a time when staff in the industry available for public affairs work was actually shrinking. The Council of the Chamber decided that all standing committees would be chaired by a member of the Council, and there were to be only nine committees: Legislation and Land Access, Minerals Exploration, Environmental Affairs, Energy, Uranium, Renewable Energy, Service Industry, Government and Community Relations, and Occupational Health and Safety. This new committee structure represented a new attempt to add 'vertical' committees for subsectors for the resources sector (energy, renewables, uranium) to those 'horizontal' committees which activities that cut across subsectors, and reflected an attempt to more inclusive to non-mining members.

SACOME also began to try to provide its members some regular, tangible service in exchange for membership. It developed a regular program of functions, including monthly breakfast briefings at a good hotel, aimed not just at informing members, but bringing them together on a regular basis. But the rejuvenation of the Chamber was assisted by the election of a (minority) ALP government, and from about 2003 SACOME had to seek much greater engagement with the government—especially because the new government had slight green tinge. For the previous eight years there had been a 'cosy and cushy' relationship with the Liberal government which did not present issues of concern to the industry. Because the Liberal government was relatively accommodating, the value of the Chamber was diminished and, as Sutherland put it 'the new government presented a raft of issues that helped sure up the relevance of the Chamber to the industry.'

Many interest groups in South Australia are under-resourced and driven by volunteers. SACOME was unique in Adelaide as it was staffed by professionals. Now it had the government engaged, and it enjoyed good relations with it. About a third of cabinet ministers knew CEO Sutherland, and it was the norm for the government to consult SACOME. SACOME signalled it was 'not afraid of a stoush and the government knows it and doesn't like it.' It was educating the new cabinet that they represented one of the few sectors that could develop remote and rural South Australia and provide a positive return on investment. It provided about 9,000 jobs, \$300m pa to state income in royalties and taxes and about \$2.2 billion in state product.

This new approach appeared to be successful. By the end of the 2001-02 year, the Chamber had 35 corporate members and 69 service members—an increase in total membership of 46 from the previous year.

By August 2004 it had 110 companies as members, including a wind energy generator and two companies interested in hot rocks as energy sources. It sought to reclaim a 'privileged position' for the sector by diversifying, putting it on a professional basis, having the members take back control, and addressing the value-for-money question.

But the decline from which it was recovering shows just how vulnerable it was, due partly to internal factors, but also to the nature of the state government, because the more accommodating nature of the Liberal government made a well-organised chamber of mines almost redundant. It had become something of an 'old boys' club' and then focused—in the absence of other imperatives—on its education function, for which it was partly funded by the Minerals Council. Most of the issues of concern were settled. The uranium issue was settled by the Coalition federal government, and environmental standards became nationalised and largely depoliticised by the inevitable executive federalism of the NEPC. And the land rights issue was no longer a salient concern. The 1998 amendments to the *Native Title Act* allowed a cooperative approach to the land rights negotiation process, and the development in South Australia of an Indigenous Land Use Agreement (ILUA) initiative became a model for the rest of Australia. The change of government to one with a more active environmental concern thus helped reinvigorate SACOME just as much as internal reform.

The 'licence to operate' for the sector in the form of access to land to prospect for minerals or oil and gas also applied to new sectors targeted by SACOME, since even wind generators and those prospecting for energy from hot rocks required access to land. Such access was first and foremost a matter within the *compétence* of the state government, and so the state level continued to be relevant for the industry. Now that it had addressed its internal problems, it had a larger membership than the Minerals Council in Canberra. But its membership was also different from that of the MCA. SACOME had only about four or five members in common with the Minerals Council, and it was the latter that was now challenged by the diminishing relevance of the Commonwealth government for the sector.

The MCA approached all state chambers in May 2004 with a proposal to establish an essentially federal industry group. This invitation was accepted by the Victorian chamber, which had been struggling with its own problems (see below), but a reinvigorated South Australian chamber with very little overlap in membership very quickly rejected the MCA proposal. One can only conclude that the fundamental reason for this was that the state level continued to hold relevance for the sector.

New South Wales

The NSW Minerals Council (NSWMC) was formed 26 April 1995 as a result of a merger between the NSW Coal Association (NSWCA) and the NSW Chamber of Mines, Metals and Extractive Industries. The Chamber of Mines, founded in 1897, had not been particularly prominent, with little new development and few issues to provide it with associability and many past provinces such as Broken Hill in decline. The reason for the continuation of two separate associations, and the reason for their eventual merger, lay primarily in the policy environment provided by state and Commonwealth governments—particularly in the area of industrial relations.

Coal organizations in NSW have a venerable history, with colliery proprietors in the north of the state signing agreements for mutual protection from 1866. There were numerous associations established, including the Newcastle Coal Owners' Mutual Protective Association (1885), the Newcastle Collieries Unanimity Guarantee Association (1887), the Associated Northern Collieries (1891), the Hunter River District Colliery Proprietors' Defence Association (1906), and the Northern Collieries Association (1916), which changed its name to the Northern Colliery Proprietors' Association in about 1942. Most of these associations were subsumed by the formation in 1922 of an industrial union to be known as the NSW Colliery Proprietors' Association (NCPA), which was not registered under the Commonwealth *Conciliation and Arbitration Act 1904* until June 1942. Those owners not members of NCPA were covered by Northern Collieries Ltd. Similar organizations emerged in the south of the state (the Southern Colliery Proprietors' Association and the NSW Coke Proprietors' Association) and the Western Coal Association.

In 1941 the NSW Combined Colliery Proprietors' Association was formed, and in 1964 became the NSW Branch of the Australian Coal Association, at the suggestion of the ACA for a merger of the various coal associations throughout Australia. The ACA, a commodity group, was formed in 1970 as a federation of the NSWCA and the Queensland Coal Association (QCA), between which organizations the secretariat rotated annually. Office files from this period indicate that the concerns of the day were the Tariff Board, workers' compensation, industrial relations, mines rescue, railways, and (from 1964) the *Clean Air Act*.

NSW shares with Victoria the characteristic of being the two most populous states in Australia, but mining is much more significant in NSW than in Victoria. Because the industry lacks any direct contact with consumers (many of whom are located in export markets) and does not sell them branded products, there is little awareness of the benefits of the industry, except in those remote locations where it is based. On the other hand, an urban, affluent population is generally supportive of the very policies which now comprised the 'problems' of land access and environmental regulation which dominated the concerns of the industry and its industry association. This and the fact that the industry was now relatively smaller than previously (measured share of market capitalisation on the ASX) meant that its structural power was diminished compared with the past. Anglo and BHP Coal moved their headquarters to Queensland, without catching the attention of the government or it electors.

Traditional concerns for the NSWCA included inflation, superannuation, rail and port charges and (especially) industrial relations. The Association was long concerned about the separate industrial relations system for the coal industry, and noted its disappointment at the failure of the Commonwealth government to make the appointment of the new commissioner to the Coal Industry Tribunal in March 1989 a joint one with the Industrial Commission to begin the process of bringing the two systems together (NSWCA 1988, iii). Environment was only a nascent issue at this stage and the dominant issue was mine subsidence. It was not until the Commonwealth Senate conducted an Inquiry into the Greenhouse Effect in 1989 that climate change began to appear on the NSWCA radar, and it registered as the second priority after industrial relations in 1990 (NSWCA 1990). The Association was particularly critical of the state and Commonwealth governments both adopting in 1990 the (non-binding) Toronto targets of a 20 percent cut to GHG emissions on 1988 levels by 2005 without any environmental, economic or social cost benefit analysis.

The NSW Coal Association undertook action at the international level on climate change, representing the Australian Coal Association at a meeting of the Intergovernmental Panel on Climate Change meeting in Sweden in August 1990 (only to find that a business statement was not permitted by the Secretariat) and the first International Negotiating Committee on Climate Change in February 1991. At the national level, it also participated in the Ecologically Sustainable Development Working Group on Energy Production in 1990-91.

The industry derived considerable benefits from the reforms of the Greiner (centre-right) Coalition state government (elected in 1988), which reformed the state rail system to achieve cost reductions, reduced port charges, removed itself from the management of the Newcastle coal loader and privatised the Port Kembla loader. Industrial relations was firmly in the Commonwealth domain, however, and the Commonwealth government resisted calls to transfer the Coal Industry Tribunal to the mainstream IR system. The Commonwealth also retained export controls, but reform began to occur at the state level, where the NSW government commenced a review of the *Coal Mines Regulation Act* and the possible merger of the *Coal Mining Act* and the *Mining Act.* Legislation to merge the two acts was introduced to state Parliament on the eve of the 1991 election.

In 1991, together with the Commonwealth, the state government initiated a review of the Joint Coal Board, established in 1948 over concerns with the reliability of supply of black coal to other states, which were otherwise dependent on the vagaries of industrial relations in the NSW coal industry. Joint legislation also provided for a Coal Industry Tribunal with a single member, from which there was no appeal. In a quasi-corporatist move typical of the Hawke era, the Commonwealth also established the Australian Coal Industry Council following an Industry Commission inquiry in to the industry and a report by the NSW Task Force on Coal Development Strategies. (See NSWCA 1991, 1). The Industry Commission Mining Inquiry had recommended sweeping reforms, including: the disbandment of both the Joint Coal Board and the Coal Industry Tribunal; the abolition of the compulsory R&D levy; the abolition of export control and export duty; the exit of government agencies from marketing; a streamlined approvals process; the subjecting of new and existing declarations of national parks to cost-benefit analysis; the reform of restrictions on foreign investment; greater competition in rail transport, and between rail and road; the introduction of foreign competition into coastal shipping; and the abolition of local government rates based on mining output.

The continuation of the CIT was a sore point for the NSWCA, as its abolition had been recommended not just by the Industry Commission review, but by two earlier reviews in 1983 and 1989. The Association was in no doubt as to the reason the ALP government had failed to act on these recommendations, claiming that 'the Federal Government has continued to bow to union pressure to maintain this body to deal separately with coal industry industrial relations matters' (NSWCA 1991, 7). But the Commonwealth government's IR reforms helped facilitate change in less direct ways. The introduction of enterprise bargaining ushered in an era of 'enterprise unions' rather than craft unions (such as the Federated Engine Drivers' and Firemen's Association, or FEDFA, whose members worked across many sectors and enterprises), and union amalgamations followed. The United Mineworkers' Federation of Australia sought to become the mining industry union, and (because it also represented workers outside the coal industry) this began to soften union opposition to the proposal to fold the CIT into the mainstream IR system. The continued existence of the Australian Colliers' Staff Association (ACSA) was entirely due to the persistence of the CIT. The UMFA secured single union coverage of greenfield mining sites from 1991, and by 1993 the amalgamated Construction, Forestry, Mining and Energy Union (CFMEU) was formed with mining and energy divisions.

Not surprisingly (given the amalgamation of the *Coal Mining Act* and the *Mining Act* in 1991), the NSWCA and the NSW Chamber of Mines established a closer relationship in 1991, but with both co-location and merger being rejected for the time being. Direct links between the two were established at the committee level, however. A merger had been recommended in a 1989 report commissioned by a number of companies (NSWCA 1991, 46), but a number of NSWCA members remained unconvinced. The merging of the *Coal Mining Act* and the *Mining Act* increased associability at the full sector level, but merger was held back by the existence of separate IR systems and was not possible until the IR systems were folded together. IR was a significant part of the NSWCA's operations at this time: in April 1991, it had 19 staff, five of whom fulfilled an IR function (two OH&S, and none an environment role). The NSWCA was overwhelmingly an employer association.

But the NSWCA was undergoing change. As its Executive Director, Meredith Hellicar, put it (NSWCA 1993, 2), 1992-93 was a watershed year in all areas of activity as it continued to move 'away from its roots as an internally focused "employer association" towards its goal of being an externally focussed "industry association".' After the 1991 Kelman Review of the Joint Coal Board, legislation was passed by both governments, removing its role in development issues and focusing it solely in workers' compensation and health and rehabilitation. Progress on the CIT had to wait until 1994. Meantime, the question of a merger between the NSWCA and the Chamber of Mines was considered again in 1993, but the option was again rejected, on the grounds that NSWCA needed to 'maintain the momentum of the coal industry reform agenda' (NSWCA 1994, 14)—which was overwhelmingly now about industrial relations. But close liaison continued between the two, and between the NSWCA and AMIC, the Queensland Minerals Council, and the Business Council.

Finally, the Commonwealth minister, Laurie Brereton, announced in April 1994 that the CIT would be absorbed into the IR mainstream. Only then, once the two associations were brought under the same IR system, did the two merge in April 1995. Then in May 1996, the incoming Howard Coalition government introduced the *Workplace Relations Bill*, permitting individual employment contracts and prohibiting secondary boycotts.

The NSW Minerals Council began with a slightly smaller staff establishment (19) than the old Coal Association had had (21 in 1994), but it must be borne in mind that it no longer had to carry its five IR staff. And this staff establishment now serviced 61 full members, 33 associate members and 17 individual members (NSWMC 1996, 29) compared with the Coal Association's 28 full and 12 associate members. Interestingly, the associate membership included Tasmania's sole coal producer, the Cornwall Coal Company, which by this route gained access to the Australian Coal Association.

The Minerals Council continued its involvement in the remaining coal industry authorities (the JCB, the Mines Rescue Board and the Mines Subsidence Board), but increasingly the matters with which it dealt came to be dominated by OH&S, environment and a number of land access issues (native title, exploration, conservation reserves, world heritage and forests). In May 1996 the Commonwealth government reduced the relevance of the national level by removing export controls on all minerals (except uranium). The importance of the state government in defining property rights and the basic operating conditions of the industry was underscored in 1997 when it passed legislation to acquire coal rights (uniquely) retained by landowners.

Most of the land access and environment issues (project approval, pollution control) were also within the *compétence* of the state government, but this was being complicated by the evolving federal situation, with the development of NEPMs in the NEPC and the commencement in late 1996 of the review of the *Environment Protection (Impact of Proposals) Act* which was to result in the *Environment Protection and Biodiversity Conservation Act 1999*. Climate change was primarily within the *compétence* of the Commonwealth government, and the NSW Minerals Council made a significant input into the development of the National Greenhouse Strategy and the National Sustainable Energy Policy through its participation on the National Greenhouse Advisory Panel. And together with the Minerals Council of Australia, it worked with the Greenhouse Challenge Office to develop a mining industry workbook to assist companies to sign cooperative agreements.

The NSWMC represented industry on several statutory boards and committees, including the Joint Coal Board, Mine Subsidence Board, Mines Rescue Board, Coal Industry Long Service Leave (Funding) Corporation, and the Coal Mining Qualifications Board. Among the 19 state government committees on which it represented the industry in 1998 were the Mine Safety Council, Blue Mountains World Heritage Community Reference Committee and the Resource and Conservation Assessment Council. And it represented the industry on four Commonwealth government committees, including the Native Title Liaison Committee. It also participated in various industry bodies, including the Australian Industry Greenhouse Network (NSWMC 1998, 24).

Land rights assumed importance when Commonwealth legislation made greater provision for state government responses to native title. The *Native Title Amendment Act* adopted by the Commonwealth Parliament in July 1998 incorporated numerous improvements to native title procedures, including a higher threshold test, the removal of the Right To Negotiate (RTN) on mining lease renewals and the ability to develop effective agreements with Aboriginal groups. It also allowed potential for the establishment of state native title administrative regimes and replacement of the RTN process on pastoral leases with an alternate state regime. In September 1998 the NSW Parliament adopted the *Native Title Act (NSW)* to make consequential changes to the state legislation, and to validate numerous potentially invalidated mining and farming leases which had been approved between January 1994 and 26 December 1996 — effectively between the *Mabo* and *Wik* decisions.

The RTN process under the original *Native Title Amendment* had effectively made native title a matter for negotiation between individual firms and specific groups of traditional owners, thus effectively removing the matters from the sectoral level to the individual firm level. The 1998 amendments not only referred many matters to the states, but ultimately provided a role for sector groups and Aboriginal land councils in negotiations. Thus the NSWMC and the NSW Aboriginal Land Council signed a Protocol for the Negotiation of Agreements for Exploration and Mining. With the state government, these parties then entered into protracted negotiations to develop a state Low Impact Exploration Regime.

Industrial relations policy continued to shape the industry, and the industry association. The *Workplace Relations Act (C'wealth) 1996* enabled companies and individual workers to enter into individual employment contracts without the intervention of unions or industrial associations, and thus posed a direct threat to the strength of unions by diminishing their relevance. In response, many unions sought to take actions to demonstrate their continuing relevance or to compete with other unions for a declining share of potential membership. The new legislation allowed the NSWMC act as facilitator and represent companies in two major reviews of the main industry industrial award, the Coal Mining Industry (Production and Engineering) Consolidated Award 1997. These produced a simplified award and resulted in removal of impediments to an enterprise focus to industrial relations. The seniority award provisions were removed on the grounds they were non-allowable by the Australian Industrial Relations Commission. These had inhibited companies from recruiting or retaining employees based on merit and returned the management of such issues to the enterprise level (NSWMC 1998, 16-17).

The dynamic industrial relations field after the 1996 Act also saw competition between unions, with the ACSA seeking to retain restrictive provisions under the exceptional circumstances provisions of the *Workplace Relations Act* as part of its effort to demonstrate its continued relevance, and the CFMEU again seeking to extend its coverage to construction work on mines at the expense of the Australian Workers Union (NSWMC 1999, 17). The CFMEU also undertook an (unsuccessful) High Court challenge to the award simplification provisions of the *Workplace Relations Act.* The Commonwealth government also finally in 1998 confirmed its intention to withdraw from joint arrangements covering the Joint Coal Board.

These reforms brought substantial gains for the industry. There was a steady decline in strike action in the coal industry, from a peak of 7.2 working days lost per employee in 1996 to 2.5 days per employee in 1999. In New South Wales, the peak of 9.4 days per employee occurred in 1997-98, with the Rio Tinto disputes (NSWMC 2003, 22). This fell to 0.7 days in 2000-01 and 0.2 days per employee in 2001-02. There was also a substantial rise in productivity (output per employee) of 56 percent in NSW (and 63 percent in Queensland) in the three years to June 2000 (NSWMC 2000, 16).

The CFMEU continued to try to demonstrate its relevance in new ways, lodging an application with the AIRC in May 2001 to vary the hours clause of the industry award. The CFMEU was joined by the ACTU in what became known as the ACTU Hours Case, which the unions lost, though the Commission did develop a new clause dealing with overtime. In 2002 the CFMEU used the Federal Court to try to overturn existing superannuation arrangements, but lost and had costs awarded against it (NSWMC 2003,

22). The NSWMC represented the industry in these actions, but industrial relations was becoming a much less significant issue.

Occupational Health and Safety, Exploration and Resource Access (land rights and conservation reserves), Environment (planning and approval, sustainable development) and Finance and Infrastructure were now the priorities of the Council. A survey of members in 2002 in developing the business plan revealed what members saw as the important issues for the Minerals Council: regulation; the community and the environment, including planning and approvals; community relations; land access and native title; mining legislation; rail reform; OHS risk management; workers' compensation; and cost reduction strategies (NSWMC 2002, 23).

The permission of the state government to develop mineral resources became problematic in 1996, with the refusal of development approval for the Lake Cowal gold project in western NSW, which would have used cyanide extraction (NSWMC 1996, 4). While cyanide contaminated water breaks down and becomes harmless after a period of weeks, a damaging television program drew attention to substantial bird kills at a nearby gold mine, where insufficient effort had been made to deter wading birds from using the tailings dam.

The NSWMC participated fully in the NEPM process and the development of the *Environment Protection and Biodiversity Conservation Act,* and it continued the high level of activity over climate change previously evident with the NSWCA. But issues such as Lake Cowal and climate change marginalised it in the politics of a state with a particularly 'green' premier in Bob Carr, who was more enthusiastic about responding to the climate change issue than the Commonwealth government, despite the heavy dependence of NSW on coal for its electricity supply (over 90 percent). The state is dominated by urban Sydney, where there is seemingly little awareness of the significance of mining to the prosperity of the state. With output of over $7b pa and likely investment anticipated by 2010 of $5-10b, mining was the largest industry in the state, about twice the size of agriculture. Despite this, it had ceased to have its own senior minister, the Department of Mineral Resources having been subsumed by the Department of Primary Industry, a substantial change from the 1980s, when the premier, Neville Wran, held the portfolio himself. His successors (Premiers 'Bob' Carr and Morris Iemma) were available to the industry only through intermediaries.

Success harmed the NSW Minerals Council, to the point that it faced a challenge to regain its former influence. The reform of industrial relations made possible the merger which brought NSWMC into being, but continued IR reform had diminished it relevance as an industrial association and it had to constantly struggle to carve out this role, which its Executive Director foreshadowed in 1993, but which has still not been assured.

The NSWMC had three categories of membership: Ordinary, Associate and Individual. Ordinary membership included coal, metalliferous and other mineral and extractive material producers, exploration companies and companies developing new mining projects. Associate membership catered for minerals companies with no current production or exploration facilities in New South Wales or no planned projects, service companies, equipment suppliers, educational institutions, etc. There were in April 2004 36 Ordinary, 29 Associate and 11 Individual members. Ordinary Membership declined from 61 in 1996, whereas Associates roughly held steady. Its staff declined from 19 in 1996 to 12 in 2004, compared with 21 in the NSWCA alone in 1994.

The Council was funded by membership subscriptions, the fee scale for Ordinary Members varying according to the size of the operations. A separate scale of fees existed for Associate and Individual Members. The Council's policies and programs were developed and co-ordinated through a number of Committees and Task Forces. The peak policy Committee was the Executive Committee[4] which was comprised of twenty chief executives or senior executives of ordinary member companies. The Executive was elected to represent the diversity of the industry in terms of size, location and activity.

It lost some members through consolidation of ownership, but some also because of the declining relevance of industrial relations, and the NSWMC was less able to 'piggy-back' other activities on the strong associability IR once provided. It was quite definitely (in Duverger's (1959) terms) a 'non-exclusive' group, which existed not solely for the purposes of securing political influence, but securing another collective good through the industrial relations system. It was now struggling as an exclusive

[4] The other major committees of the Council included the Coal Committee, Environment Committee, the Exploration and Resource Access Committee and the Occupational Health and Safety Committee.

group—focused solely on the political protection and advancement of shared interests.

In 2003 Executive Director, Dr Nikki Edwards, formerly with the Plastics and Chemicals Industry Association (PACIA—now Chemistry Australia), noted that when compared with the chemicals industry, there was less of a tradition of the CEOs who make up the NSWMC's deliberative bodies speaking with the collective voice of the industry. Yet this was increasingly what they had to do if they were not to be picked off with firm-oriented policy decisions. There was a need, especially in the NSW context outlined above, to develop a new sophistication in an industry where production-oriented executives liked to promote their companies by showing their impressively-sized 'holes in the ground'. In Edwards' view, this was like the meat industry promoting itself by showing pictures inside slaughterhouses.

The NSW Minerals Council developed close working relations with the Minerals Council of Australia, other state mining associations and other major industry associations, aimed at both ensuring appropriate co-ordination on policy issues and minimizing duplication of effort. But the NSWMC was not ready to accept the suggestion of the MCA in May 2004 that they form a single federal association. It was participating in the 'Minerals Associations Forum' established under the GMI, and was seeking to engage with the sustainable development agenda, but it clearly had some challenges in front of it.

Victoria

The Victorian Chamber of Mines was formed in 1986. It grew out of the recognition by companies in Victoria that Victorian mining laws (mostly adopted in the 1950s) were hopelessly outdated and worked against the industry; in the view of the industry, they had effectively brought a halt to mining. There was only one gold mine in operation, plus three large brown coal mines in the La Trobe Valley, but these were operated by the State Electricity Commission of Victoria, and therefore required no organization to represent them politically.

BHP, Rio Tinto (then CRA) and WMC plus a few others formed the Victorian Chamber of Mines. One insider reported that essentially WMC established the VCM and got BHP and CRA to pay. Certainly, WMC played a prominent role in the VCM: John Reynolds became Executive Director after retiring from WMC and occupied the post until 1998. (Ironically, it was said, WMC later left the VCM and left BHP and Rio with the tab). Initially, what was quite openly acknowledged was that the three largest companies (BHP, CRA, and WMC) funded the VCM and invited others to join. While headquartered in Victoria, they mined elsewhere.

The VCM grew out of the need for reform of state mining law and was essentially gold-driven. Gold mines in Stawell and Bendigo were enjoying a renaissance and were wanting to engage in activities like drilling under houses, and there was a need for an industry association to push for legislative reform to facilitate this activity. The VCM did a lot of work with the Cain ALP government and helped them develop the *Mineral Resources Development Act 1990*, which made Victoria the most progressive of all the states in facilitating mining. As a result, exploration expenditure increased from around $10m in 1990 to $52m in 1996, after which it tailed off across Australia as commodity prices dropped. It held up better in Victoria, however: by 2002 it was running at $32m in Victoria, whereas it had been halved across Australia.

The VCM did a lot of work promoting the industry. It fostered networking among companies and the interchange of best practices, but it was also engaged in educating the community. Victorian residents have tended to be in the green vanguard politically in Australia, yet there was less mining activity than in other states, so the industry employed proportionately fewer workers and had a lesser economic footprint than in other states. Victoria was also more densely populated. There was therefore a greater need to justify mining activity, not just in Victoria, but mining in Australia as a whole *to* Victorians. In 1993 it employed a teacher. A decade later the MCA had a national educational program and had started to work with investors through stockbrokers.

After 1993, with the Kennett (centre-right) government's privatisation of the energy sector, the VCM became broader and the privatised coal miners became members. The VCM was not particularly focused on the environment, but started to develop codes of practice and there was a focus on local governments through the planning approvals process. The issue drivers for the VCM were (in order) economics, environment, and social impacts. From 1995 it became involved in broader environmental issues, becoming more global in orientation and more involved in the MCA, with the President of the VCM becoming a Councillor of the MCA. It was the only state association initially to enter into a confederation relationship with the MCA. By the early 2000s, the environment was now mainstream for the

VCM, and most of what the Director Chris Fraser did was environmental in some way.

From about 1998 occupational health and safety also became a significant issue, with a high-level executive committee on safety established to work in partnership with the government. The VCM remained unhappy with the legislation and lobbied successfully for amendments, adopted late 2000. It then sought improvements to planning legislation. The MCA was used for Commonwealth issues and international issues, but the federal relationship with the MCA meant that companies that were not MCA members used the VCM to access the MCA. Brown coal miners, for example, which exported none of their output, used the VCM as a conduit to MCA and on to the Commonwealth government on climate change.

The education program became the largest work program of the Chamber, and consumed about 50 percent of the Chamber's budget. Victoria had about 25 percent of the national population, so the education program targeting this population was seen as being of national significance, and for this reason the MCA made a contribution to costs. So too did the state government, which made for a delicate relationship between the Chamber and the government. They were careful to keep their educational material entirely factual, and attempted to maintain a complete separation between politics and education.

The VCM became the Victorian Minerals and Energy Council (VMEC) in July 2001, reflecting the fact that the main products in the state were mineral sands, gold and coal. Of the large companies, all but Rio withdrew from membership (BHP-Billiton withdrawing in 2002), so VMEC became effectively composed of small companies. Membership subscriptions accounted for less than half its revenue in 2002 and raising revenue was an effort, with VMEC running at a loss and at a watershed in terms of its long-term financial viability. But the government was telling the Chamber they wanted to deal with them and not with individual companies, and encouraging them to continue and doing what it could to achieve this. The Victorian government was starting to provide some money, for example, by sponsoring a mines rescue competition and other joint work on safety.

In fact, substantial revenue was coming from both state and Commonwealth government sources. In June 2002 the Council signed an agreement for $150,000 with the Minister for State and Regional Development for the preparation of a mineral sands action plan for Victoria. In addition, the Council was granted $97,000 by the Federal Attorney-

General in June 2002 for legal advice during the negotiation of pro forma native title agreements. In late 2002 the Council gained formal recognition from the state Department of Education and Training in that its schools-based education programs had gained partnership status. As a result, $25,000 pa for three years was be provided to assist in the presentation of the programs.

Now the VMEC was being invited by the government to be partners in the development of codes and guidelines, rather than simply being invited to comment on drafts. They were involved in the drafting process, such as new dust regulations, which were likely to flow on to other states through regulatory harmonisation, but which were within the initial jurisdiction of Victoria. The Council regretted that MCA did not appear to be interested in this. Council staffing reflected the fact that the education function had become central to its operations, with an Executive Director, Office Manager, Education Manager, and a part-time Accounts Officer and three part-time Education Officers. It had working groups on Mineral Legislation, Safety, Exploration, Sustainable Development and Native Title, but education was now a core function.

The other big change was that the VMEC ceased to be a membership-driven organization. It was run initially with volunteer labour from companies who would provide work on legislation, or environmental matters. At the turn of the century companies were downsizing and rationalising. There were no longer medium-sized national companies like North Ltd and Ashton Mining, so there were no longer people available to do that work. There was a ‘hollowing out’ between the large global players and the small miners. Over half the people performing such tasks for companies were now consultants and service providers, so they could not speak for mining companies. Director Chris Fraser had to write material and then get it approved by members, rather than it being developed in committees with company representatives. In the past, committees passed policy proposals to the Executive Council for approval and it was then promulgated to companies. Fraser had a background as a mining engineer, not a public affairs specialist, whereas other chambers became staffed more by those with a policy or public affairs orientation.

The employer organization, the Australian Mines and Metals Association, handled all industrial relations issues for the industry in Victoria. VMEC did therefore not engage with unions, but was active in consulting with Victorian NGOs, such as the Victorian National Parks Association, the Field Naturalists and the Victorian Farmers Federation.

Something like 70 percent of the land in the state of Victoria was privately owned, so VMEC had to work closely with the Farmers Federation on joint agreements for prospecting and mining on farm land, jointly developing policy guidelines. The Farmers Federation was very powerful and this was one of the most important relationships for the VMEC. The VMEC also helped progress international outcomes at the state level, and took approaches developed to the state government so that outcomes were considered at state level.

The main challenge for VMEC was financial: there was a vital need to diversify its financial base to reduce its reliance on subscriptions. By 1 January 2003 the membership of the Council declined to 15 Ordinary Members, 5 Energy members, 28 Service Members, 5 Associate Members, 4 Life Members, and 4 Honorary members, a total of 61. VMEC was having difficulty sustaining itself. It could seek to cooperate with NSW and Tasmania, or become a division of the MCA. It chose to federate with the MCA, and in May 2004 accepted an invitation to become a division of the MCA—the only state chamber to do so, although so too did the Northern Territory group which no longer had much reason to engage with the government there.

Tasmania

Tasmania has a longstanding mining industry, with a number of substantial non-ferrous mines dating from a mining boom in the late Nineteenth Century, when an early chamber was focused solely on attracting capital, with capital formation always a challenge in colonial economies. Yet for most of the history of the state, the only mining industry association was a branch of the Australian Mines and Metals Association, providing services to the industry on industrial relations. From 1982, the Presidents' Committee of the AMIC included the Australian Mines and Metals Association in Tasmania (SACOM 1982, 7), but most issues of concern were handled at the firm level.

Not only did the various issues relating to the granting of exploration and mining licences not form a basis for association, but the emergence of environmental regulation also failed to do so—for good reason. The *Environment Protection Act 1973* provided a basis for the regulation of pollution, but it was notable for making provision for ministerial exemptions to be granted to environmental standards, and most large firms had such exemptions, meaning that relations between government and industry—even on environmental regulation—were effectively handled at the level of the individual firm.

The Tasmanian Chamber of Mines was formed by agreement within the minerals industry in 1985 and was viewed as the representative body for the industry within the state. It changed its name to the Tasmanian Minerals Council in 1995. By the early Twenty-first Century, it had 12 members in the 'Major Mines and Processors' category and 32 'other' members (largely service providers). The 'Major Mines and Processors' category included a mining services company (Mancala), three metals processors (Rio Tinto, formerly Comalco Aluminium (Bell Bay) Ltd, Nyrstar Hobart Zinc Smelter, and Temco), and Cement Australia Pty Ltd (owners of the Cornwall Coal Company).

The Tasmanian Minerals Council was thus the representative organisation for the exploration, mining and mineral processing industries in Tasmania, and counted among its members all of the main mines and mineral processing works, but it had few members to represent. It claimed to represent the views of the industry on a range of issues to Government — State and Federal — and the public, including the school system. As with Victoria and several other state chambers, this public educational function was important for the Tasmanian Minerals Council, behind the need to maintain access to public land for exploration and mining, for which it was considered the industry needed to demonstrate 'sustainable environmental performance, good health and safety performance and have an understanding of the expectations of the local communities.' Two of the five staff were engaged on education: in addition to Executive Director Terry Long, there was an Education Manager, Executive Assistant, Education Officer, and Administration Assistant.

Unlike other states, Aboriginal land rights were not an issue in Tasmania, because the granting of title and the historical treatment of indigenous Tasmanians meant it was highly unlikely that any would be able to demonstrate the ongoing association with the land that was necessary under the *Mabo* decision for the grant of native title. The Tasmanian Minerals Council thus enjoyed weak associability, with few potential members, and few issues before the state government providing a basis for associability.

It formed at a time of emerging environmental activity in the state, especially the closing to exploration of the South-west of the state when it was nominated and included on the World Heritage List. This action, taken in response to a hydro-electric development proposal, removed highly prospective land and gave rise to concerns over access to other areas of the state. A development in another policy domain, the Regional Forest Agreement in 1997 provided clarity over what land was available for mineral exploration.

It added an Energy Committee in 2012 and became the Tasmanian Minerals and Energy Council, and in 2015 moved its offices from the state capital of Hobart to Burnie, a small city closer to mining activity. With the development by the state government of a Tasmanian Advanced Manufacturing Action Plan, launched in 2016, the Council expanded its scope to include manufacturing, being renamed the Tasmanian Mining Manufacturing and Energy Council, building on its existing membership of mining equipment manufacturers like Caterpillar and Elphinstone. It now has 100 members.

Conclusion

The trajectory of each mining association in the Australian states and the Northern Territory shows the influence of particular events and personalities, but it also demonstrates the fundamental importance of institutional factors in changing associability at this level of governance.

In some instances (Western Australia, South Australia and Victoria, especially), state governments gave explicit encouragement by word or deed to the formation or continuation of their respective state mining association. The state government encouraged the formation of SACOM; the Victorian government did what it could to ensure the continued existence of VMEC; and the Western Australian government, at the height of its pro-development era, encouraged the industry to ever more vigorous support for the association.

Usually, however, the institutional stimulus for association came from the policy activity of the state governments with the proposal or adoption of regulatory policies that affected associability at the sector level, providing a rationale to organize beyond the individual firm (where individual licences to explore or mine were issued). These stimuli varied, but usually included potential restrictions on access to land in the form of land rights or environmental regulation. The playing out of land rights saw the relevance of the state level vary, and associability vary accordingly. Particular policy initiatives even gave rise to the formation of specific organizations on gold and uranium.

One profound effect, however, came with the reform of industrial relations law, which was decisive in allowing the somewhat belated formation of mining associations in New South Wales and Queensland that covered both coal and non-ferrous metal mining. As the trajectories of these associations show, in all but the strongest state of Western Australia, the associability of the whole sector was problematic. This was confirmed by the near disaster that almost beset SACOME (before it staged a remarkable turnaround) and the eventual failure of VMEC as a separate association. The SACOME story also demonstrates the importance of the organizational skills of individuals in producing success—a reminder that institutions might tell much of the story, but they do not capture it all. There is still some room for agency.

CHAPTER 6

MINING INDUSTRY ASSOCIATION IN INTERNATIONAL CONTEXT

The arrested development of mining industry association at the international level raises some interesting questions about interest groups in the contemporary world. The globalisation of environmental politics has been marked by something of an explosion in the number and activities of international environmental groups. Such groups are usually referred to as 'non-governmental organizations' (or NGOs), although strictly speaking they are *international* non-governmental organizations (Kellow and Murphy-Gregory 2018). But NGO (or INGO) is an acronym which, strictly speaking, applies equally to business groups, and the fact that it has become commonplace to use the expression to refer solely to environment groups (or development, human rights and other 'public interest' groups) at the international level is a good indication of just how problematic business association is at this level.

Modern politics has been characterised by a rise in importance of interest organisations as vehicles of representation and participation at the level of the nation-state, largely at the expense of political parties (Richardson 1993). Despite this increase in importance, interest groups have received relatively little systematic attention in some political systems, when compared with political parties or social movements, and even less at the international level. There has not been much research in Australia or elsewhere, for example, into changes which might have affected traditional modes of interest representation, such as the changing nature of the Australian federation and the internationalisation of environmental issues, and how (if at all) these might be linked. Most research examines interest group activity, rather than their formation, fragmentation and dissolution.

While there is an increasing number of studies of interest group formation and functioning beyond the nation-state—most particularly in the emergent quasi-federal polity of the European Union[1]—there are few studies which have attempted to bridge the sub-national to the international, to try to take account of the dynamic nature of interest association in a world as it underwent globalisation, to make sense of what factors have been driving changes in a sector and its relationships with both individual firms and peak associations, and with both significant countervailing groups (such as labour) and governance structures at different levels, which Lowi (2001) divided into macro-, meso-, and micro-levels to account for governance under globalisation.

The nature of such drivers of change has important theoretical significance for our understanding of interest groups generally. One view holds that associations emerge from society itself, and are products of the values, and capacities in society (e.g. Almond and Verba 1963; Putnam 1993). Some theorists see association being influenced predominantly by the economic incentives for organisation—'the logic of collective action'—which vary most significantly according to whether the interests for any potential group relate to public goods or private goods (Olson 1965). Successful group mobilisation, according to this view, depends upon either the pursuit of private goods or the presence of other factors which might overcome what came to be known as 'the problem of the free rider', such as the provision of additional private benefits and the use of coercion.

Others (the authors included) see the state as providing the template upon which interests coalesce to form groups. The state is the 'reciprocating agent' (Greenwood, Grote and Ronit 1992: 20), the actions of which interest groups seek to affect, but the agendas and actions of which in turn structure the incentives for group formation—what we refer to as 'associability' (see Aspinwall and Greenwood 1998; Jordan 1998; Kellow 2002; Lanza and Lavdas 2000; Schmitter 1977). As Pierson (2006) has pointed out, policies can also be regarded as institutions, and they help establish patterns of interaction by exciting the mobilisation of groups around them, forming policy networks or communities (see also Kellow 2018).

Pierson is credited with promoting a 'policy feedback' approach anchored in historical institutionalism, although he considered that this

[1] Traxler and Schmitter (1995) discuss the nature of the European polity and its implications for organised interests.

approach derived largely from work by Theda Skocpol and her collaborators from the 1980s. Skocpol pointed out that

> Too often social scientists...forget that policies, once enacted, restructure subsequent political processes. Analysts typically look only for synchronic determinants of policies—for example, in current social interests or in existing political alliances. In addition, however, we must examine patterns unfolding over time. . . . (Skocpol 1995, 58).

Pierson (1993, 600) states that David Vogel's account of the response of American business to regulatory policy in the late 1960s and early 1970s 'provides an excellent example of how policy feedback generated new structures of interest representation'. He quotes the following passage from Vogel:

> Among the most distinctive features of the regulatory statutes enacted during the first half of the 1970s was precisely that they were not directed toward specific industries. Rather, they sought to change the behavior of companies in a wide variety of different industries. This made many business executives much more conscious of their common or class interests, which in turn led to both the formation and revival of political organizations that represented firms in many different industries, such as the Business Roundtable, the United States Chamber of Commerce, and the National Federation of Independent Business (Vogel 1989, 13-14).

Sometimes, reciprocating agents (be they governments or transnational governance structures such as the European Commission) directly sponsor interest groups, but 'associability' goes beyond this to include *all* the factors (intended or not) that are conducive for the formation of interest groups. 'The state' in countries like Australia must be understood in a federal context. Interest groups exist at both the state and federal levels, and the relationships between groups at these levels is largely unexplored. Following Lowi (2001), we would expect the relationships between state and federal groups to have changed as the nature of federalism has changed. But, in addition, globalisation also placed greater importance on governance regimes at the transnational level and international organisations are also increasingly being seen as 'reciprocating agents' analogous to the state in interest group interactions. The focus of the present book is on the Australian federation and the political representation of the mining industry at state, national and international levels, and we have described the trajectories of mining industry associations at each level in some detail. This chapter seeks to make conceptual sense of interest groups in the mining sector in the context of the contemporary world, characterised by multi-level governance, mostly during the period (1990-2006) when the effects of globalisation were becoming most apparent, with some discussion of changes after this period.

How can we capture the dynamism of the relationship between interest groups and 'reciprocating agents'—the state at the national level and governance institutions at the international level? We do not wish to suggest an overly deterministic model with the state as an unchanging structural template upon which interest groups form. That seems to us to be granting undue primacy to the structural 'pole' in the structure-agency debate. But neither do we think that interest groups are solely creatures of human agency. Something between the two, something akin to Anthony Giddens' (1984) concept of structuration appears closer to what we mean. A metaphor based in molecular genetics (suggested by Jeremy Richardson) seems to capture appropriately the kind of dynamism we think exists, giving primacy to the state in providing the template for interest group activity, while still allowing for the possibility of change in the state and its policies.

Richardson (2000) has used the useful analogy that ideas in policy-making are like viruses: they can 'infect' governance processes and bring about change. We wish to extend this analogy (which we find both suggestive and infectiously seductive!) Real viruses are composed of a nucleic acid, usually RNA (or ribonucleic acid), and they infect cells, interfering with the messages being transmitted from the DNA (deoxyribonucleic acid) in the nucleus of the living cell (the chemical basis for the genetic code, or rules, contained in genes) to the ribosomes in the cell where the 'business' of cellular activity (in the form of processes like protein synthesis) is conducted. To understand the analogy, a brief explanation of the genetic basis for the 'governance' of the cell is in order.

We suggest policies are like Messenger RNA (or mRNA) and provide a means of communicating information in the form of 'commands' between the governing nucleus and the cytoplasmic 'soup' of civil society. Interest groups are then like Transfer RNA (or tRNA), being structured by the template of the policies on which they form and in response to which they change. Ideas are like the viral RNA, existing in the cytoplasmic soup of civil society, which might infect and transform cell function (or be repelled by the immune system). Stochastic 'mutations' like the Global Financial Crisis (and the COVID-19 pandemic) can also disrupt the normal. Both 'viruses' and 'mutations' might punctuate the relative equilibrium of the policy process (Howlett and Migone 2011). While leaving open the possibility that other viruses outside the 'nucleus' of the state might also 'infect' the system of governance and the structure and function of the mRNA of interest groups, we see the DNA of the reciprocating agent as providing the template upon which interest groups form. Interest groups can affect both the process of governance *and* the structures of governance, despite having their field of action structured by that system. Parties and social movements are analogues of retroviruses which are capable of reverse transcription, of changing the 'DNA' of the institutions of governance.

This metaphor allows us to capture the reflexive dynamism which is an essential part of interactions between the state and interest groups. State-centric views often fail to capture the potential for change in either policy or state structure. We wish to ascribe centrality to the state (or other 'reciprocating agents' at other levels) while accounting for the dynamism of the process, and we believe extending and filling out Richardson's views of ideas as viruses allows us to capture this while retaining the centrality of the 'nucleus' as the template upon which interest groups form. We thus grant primacy to the 'reciprocating agents' of governance institutions while providing for the possibility that tRNA, viruses and retroviruses of interest groups, ideas and parties and social movements might also change those 'reciprocating agents' and their polices. This metaphor allows us to attribute to the 'nucleus' and its means of communicating with civil society both a degree of stability and potential for change which are of approximately the appropriate order of magnitude. It is a metaphor which captures the essence of Lowi's dictum that 'policy determines politics', while allowing sufficient reflexivity to provide for the possibility that both policies and governance agencies themselves might undergo transformation.

We do not wish to stretch this metaphor too far, and will refer to it only periodically, but extending Richardson's metaphor of a virus allows us to capture both the dynamism and the reciprocity of interest group interactions with governance structures—structured by them, yet affecting their functioning and even possibly affecting their structure. We really wish no more than to use it to convey to the reader what we mean by a 'state-centric' (or 'governance-centric') approach to interest groups, and how 'associability' is changed by changes to the 'template' or 'opportunity structure' provided by the state and its policies. In so doing, we have sought to provide for the (self-evident) possibility that the state can and does change. We see states as prior, and relatively stable, but they are not immutable.

By examining how interest groups have developed and in the face of major changes in the activities of states within a federation, a national government, and the system of international governance on an issue area such as the environment we can explore the factors driving changes among interest groups—particularly, whether such factors have exerted such a gravitational pull as to dominate over any forces pushing development from below and within groups. The internationalization of environmental issues is well documented (and indicated by the growth in the number of international agreements), but the period in question also saw a substantial recasting of the distribution of *compétences* between state governments and the Commonwealth government in Australia, part of changes described at their onset as 'New Federalism' (and which included the Intergovernmental Agreement on the Environment and the reforms it produced, such as the National Environmental Protection Council/Measures). This recasting of the Australian federation and the internationalization of environmental issues are in fact linked, because the external affairs power tilted the distribution of *compétences* in favour of the Commonwealth and stimulated the subsequent redesign.[2]

The key question for us here is: 'How have mining sector interest groups in the Australian context been impacted by changes in governance regimes at the state, federal and international levels?' We suggest that there have been significant governance-centric drivers of change—changes in the 'genetic makeup' of sub-national, national, and international governance structures—as the relevance of state and national and international levels changed over the period from 1990. But, as we have seen, while the environment theme has been important, developments in other policy areas—specifically, the emergence of indigenous land rights and the reform of industrial relations—have also been significant factors in accounting for the development of mining sector associations over the decade. (The indigenous issue domestically parallels closely the alloying together of 'environment' and 'development' at the international level in the form of a 'sustainable development' agenda). Similarly, we can identify changes in the architecture of international governance structures which have been responsible for the changed associability of the mining sector at that level.

We have thus examined the utility of state-centered and society-centered conceptualisations of interest groups by studying the way in which changes in the federal constitution of the state and emerging transnational

[2] Kelemen (2004) provides a good summary of these developments in Australia and elsewhere, including the European Union.

reciprocating agencies have impacted upon the organisation of business and labour interests in the mining sector Australia and internationally. The challenges posed by new developments in environmental policy (primarily after the Intergovernmental Agreement on the Environment in the early 1990s) and the internationalisation of environmental issues in the mining sector allow us to explore the changing interactions between political action involving firms, sector groups and peak associations. We suggest that a focus on environment alone as a driver is insufficient to explain *all* the changes which we have observed. Changes in other policy areas, such as indigenous land rights and industrial relations have also been important drivers of change, perhaps not surprisingly, since they came together in the campaign against Rio Tinto we examined in Chapter One, though we must add that the international driver is best characterised as the 'sustainable development' agenda which brings together issues relating to environment, development and indigenous rights, whereas (ultimately, despite the Rio campaign) industrial relations was significant only at the nation-state and sub-state levels.

Globalization and Its Implications for Interest Groups

While there has been heightened salience for political activity beyond the nation-state, changes at the subnational level have also changed the character of the institutions with which interest groups reciprocate. Reforms to federal systems occurring simultaneously with (and partly in response to) the processes of globalisation have also constituted drivers for change as the relevance of state and federal governments has also changed. If nothing else, these changes have expanded the possibilities for political activism for firms, which can elect not only to pursue activity at the state, national or international levels, but might do so as individual firms, as members of sectorally-based associations, as members of peak business associations or as members of transnational interest groups—which themselves might be sectorally-based or peak associations and might have direct firm memberships or consist of federations of national associations. This picture is complicated still further by the widespread activities of transnational corporations which straddle both national associations and even sectors. (Many of the same corporations occur in the pharmaceuticals, chemicals and biotechnology sectors, for example). The emergence of multiple levels of governance has opened up multiple opportunities for interest group activity.

We suggest that these developments in both federal and international systems not only call for a re-examination of our conceptual understanding of interest groups but offer an opportunity to explore the relative importance of state and societal factors in their associability and activism. We consider that an examination of the trajectory evident in interest group structures and activities during the period of substantial federal reform and the emergence of enhanced global governance regimes suggests that our preference for state-oriented explanations of interest group formation and activity is justified.

In contrast to the society-centred view of interest groups, (as we have seen) scholars such as Lowi (1964) assign priority to the state and argue essentially that 'policy determines politics'. Thus, for Lowi, the central issue is how coercion is employed by the state in the policies it adopts. State action provides the template upon which interest groups form. Lowi sets out his policy typology on the basis of such differences in the deployment of coercion, and argues that for each distinctive policy type there is a distinct 'arena of power' which creates incentives for participation by individuals (or individual firms) and advantages different groups. These characteristics, for Lowi, are more theoretically significant than the nature of costs and benefits or whether the arena is one of 'transport policy' or 'environment policy' (policy *arena* before policy *area*), although issue characteristics other than use of coercion undoubtedly continue to be important in shaping the membership and nature of policy communities. This would include factors such as location in the product cycle (Greenwood, 1995: 288) and the role of ideas (as 'viruses') in policy change (Richardson, 2000). Nevertheless, there is a substantial literature supporting a state-centric approach to understanding interest groups.

Much of the literature on the role of interest groups in the policy process focuses on their participation in policy networks of various types, usually emphasizing stability and continuity of both networks and policies, rather than recognising that there are now multiple arenas in which groups might act, and the possibility that they might choose among them, possibly for strategic advantage, or use an arena to set or prevent being set precedents in other arenas (Kellow 2012; Murphy and Kellow 2013). The recent past has been characterised by policy change and interest groups have learned to exploit the multiple opportunity structures presented by multi-arena policy making (Richardson, 2000). Groups often can ignore context to some extent and choose among venues (Spill 2001), perhaps nowhere more than in the European context where an increasing number of arenas has opened up (Scharpf 2001). The European Union is held to have produced a different type of governance because of its unique multilevel structure, resulting in a series of interest group networks, organized on a European scale, that cover multiple institutional levels (Grande, 2002; Kellow and Zito 2002).

Much of the literature on interest groups, especially since Olson (1965), focuses on individual motivations to join groups or the incentives offered by groups to persuade prospective members to join or remain as members over the long term. But 'members' are often more likely to be passive 'supporters' or 'donors' and securing active participation by members is perhaps even more problematic than simply inveigling them to join and continue as passive members (Bosso 2003), and with business associations the members are firms, rather than individuals (although legally they are usually treated as persons). It seems that the nature of the governance structures with which interest groups are likely to interact—the potential 'reciprocating agents'—are of perhaps paramount importance in determining not only whether interest groups will form, but whether potential members will participate as active players.

A key alternative explanation of interest group associability is the role of the emergence of countervailing groups in interest group formation—the view that a 'common enemy', or a sudden shift in the external environment, drives actors together to form a group (Ronit 2006). Some argue that the lobbying strategies of organised interests depends not just on the characteristics of the institutional venue in question, but on the impact of oppositions from other interests in a particular venue. This view would place emphasis on factors such as the global campaign against Rio Tinto as a primary driver of changed international associability in the mining sector. Expectations of opposition from other interests is seen as being a significant factor in the decision to lobby in a given venue (Holyoke 2003). But venue selection *by* interest groups is a different matter from the formation and maintenance of an interest group. Moreover, there is little support for the hypothesis that pressure from one interest group increases or decreases with the pressure intensity of an opposing group (Ando 2003); rather, lobbying investments appear to vary according to how propitious the arena is for a group (de Figueiredo and de Figueiredo 2002).

In contrast, there is strong evidence that top-down factors, policies and governance structures, may be significant in determining the formation of interest groups, especially since we can use the quasi-experiment of the formation of new governance institutions to explore whether they impact on associability. The top-down impact of emerging European institutions resulted in convergence of business representation in France and the United Kingdom (Fairbrass 2003). The addition of venues at the European level, in other words, has had similar effects in business organization at the national level in both countries. There was a post-Maastricht lobbying boom in the European Union with the establishment of European Commission forums for interest representation. Using a simple model of informational lobbying with many lobbyists, Broscheid and Coen (2003) showed that there was a relationship between lobbying costs, the number of lobbyists, and the informational content of lobbying message, which constituted different categories of lobbying systems. Governance institutions, rather than society-centred factors primarily determined such factors, so emerging institutions at the European level facilitated the formation of supranational 'Eurogroups' by providing new opportunities for achieving influence at lower cost.

But as long as there is some reason for a group to remain active, interest groups are likely to persist at any particular level of governance as policy feedback tends to create path dependency (Pierson, 1992; 2000). A study of the EU financial services sector shows that European financial integration has not resulted in the withering away of national business associations, confirming the multilevel governance hypothesis that national associations develop direct lobbying strategies at different levels of the EU system to gain access to European decision-making process. It also suggested that national associations undertake indirect lobbying strategies (through membership in European associations) with the aim of gaining institutional access. A theory of supply and demand for 'access goods' can thus explain the extent to which national associations gain access to European institutions (Bouwen 2003). According to this view, the degree of access of business interests to the European Commission, the European Parliament, and the Council of Ministers depends upon their ability to provide the access goods demanded by that institution—typically, information that is crucial in the EU policy-making process (Bouwen 2002). One 'good' groups can provide is a reduction in the costs to governance institutions of consultation. Governance institutions want groups to form to save them having to interact with many firms seriatim, so where new institutions have emerged (such as the Commission of the EU), they frequently foster the formation of interest groups with which they can interact.

The primacy of state-centric factors appears to go well beyond economic interest groups to include green groups, which (often beginning as social movements) one might expect to be more influenced by non-state factors. For example, Hunold and Dryzek (2002) argue that the kind of context provided by state structure as it faces civil society has important consequences for what might be the appropriate strategy for the green political movement. And it seems to hold in many political systems, and to apply also with formalised systems of concertation. Montpetit (2002), for example, has argued that interest group activity is shaped by Canadian parliamentary institutions. Or, to give another example, corporatist accommodations are still to be found (Molina and Rhodes 2002), and Blom-Hansen (2001) has argued in the Danish context that corporatism can best be studied from a perspective placing politicians and agency at centre stage.

There have been refinements which have sought to integrate both state-centric and society-centric approaches. For example, Dunleavy (1988) distinguished between endogenous and exogenous groups. The membership of the latter he saw as determined largely by external factors, while the former is driven by 'Olsonian' associational logic. Neto and Cox (1997) also attempted a similar integration of institutional and society-based approaches. Lowi took issue with society-centred and (particularly) economy-centred explanations, and with attempts to interpret his typology using the nature of goods as the central organising principle (see Kellow 1988; Lowi 1988). We think our DNA/mRNA/virus metaphor captures the necessary dynamism. We would expect, then, that changes in the nature of the state or governance institutions should give rise to changing patterns in interest association, although the analysis needs to be sensitive to other factors. (For a discussion of policy typologies and policy feedback, see Kellow 2018).

By examining how interest groups have developed in the face of major changes such as 'New Federalism' and the internationalisation of environmental policy we can to explore the factors driving change—particularly, whether such factors have exerted a gravitational pull sufficient to dominate over any forces pushing development from below and within groups. The key question we have addressed, then, is this: 'How have interest groups in the mining sector in the Australian context been impacted by changes in governance regimes at the state, federal and transnational levels?'

Interest Groups in Australian Politics

One challenge in addressing that question relates to the relative paucity of literature on interest groups in Australia, the subject of our study for national and sub-national groups. While there is a substantial literature on interest groups at the national level elsewhere (especially in the United States) and a growing literature on interest groups beyond the national level (especially in the European Union), there are few systematic, in-depth treatments of interest groups in Australia (particularly on associability), and there are some matters relating to the Australian context which require clarification.

While there have been numerous studies of business in Australia (for example, Bell 1993; Galligan and Singleton 1991) and of unions as political actors (for example, Rawson 1978; Simms 1997; Singleton 1990), and attempts to interpret the Prices and Incomes Accord of the 1980s in relation to corporatist theory (Gerritsen 1986; McEachern 1986; Stewart 1985), there was when we commenced little systematic study of interest groups as a political phenomenon in Australia, with most of the existing literature consisting of chapter-length studies (for example, Condon 1975; Matthews 1980, 1989, 1990, 1994, 1997; Scott 1980). Neither has there been much research in Australia into changes which might have affected traditional modes of interest representation, such as the changing nature of the Australian federation and the internationalisation of environmental issues.

Interest groups in Australia have long been influenced by the constitutional distribution of powers, such that the emergence of a national peak business group was late and remains problematic (Bell 1995) because of the long-standing relevance of the state level for peak business associations. This became apparent with the use of quasi-corporatist modes of interest mediation during the early years of the Hawke government elected in 1983, when some analysts sought to apply the corporatist label, but (in the absence of an effective business peak association) the most that could be claimed was that this was 'corporatism without business' (Kellow 1986, 13), in contrast to the 'corporatism without labour' of Japan. The shift of industrial relations increasingly to the federal level has enhanced the associability of business at in that policy area.

With the co-existence of two peak associations in the form of the (direct membership) Business Council of Australia and the Australian Council of Commerce and Industry, ambiguities remain unresolved. (There is also the Australian Industry Group, which tends to represent manufacturers). At the same time, these peak bodies must engage in an increasingly international agenda, either at the domestic level, or through the International Chamber of Commerce, while sectoral organisations such as the Minerals Council, Plastics and Chemical Industry Association, Metal Trades Industry Association, and Chemical Specialties Manufacturer's Association, also engaged in international activity at the sectoral level, and the firms which are their members are also sometimes members of direct membership international groups. Further, groups such as the Council for

International Business Affairs emerged to meet international challenges, but these functions have been subsumed by ACCI.[3]

Transnational policy demands have provided new challenges for groups, which have often been forced to develop associational forms such as direct firm membership to overcome the rigidities of federal forms of association. This raises questions about whether such groups become dominated by more powerful members—and become 'rich firm clubs'. We can point to similar issues with the direct membership form of the Business Council of Australia, compared with the more traditional structure of the Australian Chamber of Commerce and Industry. There is a need to make sense of interest groups in the light of significant developments within Australia, examining the changing policy imperatives in the Australian federation and the international system, and exploring whether these have impacted upon the nature of interest association, including relationships between groups at the state level and those in Canberra, and that is in part what we have attempted to provide here.

We have affinity with Theodore Lowi's 'arenas of power' approach. Some have questioned the utility of Lowi's approach outside the US political system (Richardson and Jordan 1985, 100), but we argue the approach can be applied usefully to the study of interest groups in parliamentary systems (Kellow 1984), even if the nature of the legislature and executive in parliamentary governance creates difficulties for the application of the approach to the behaviour of legislators. It is more the impact of policy and state structure on interest groups that we wish to employ, and Eckstein (1960) used such a state-centred approach in his classic study of the British Medical Association. It therefore seems reasonable to accept Lowi's fundamental point that state action (or 'policies') are important and that 'A proper definition of policy must be built not in terms of the interests of citizens but in terms of the forms of state action and the formally expressed intentions of the state' (Lowi 1985, 69).

We note, however, that in some two-party systems (e.g United Kingdom; Australia; Canada) political parties may articulate some interests during campaigning generally but not always; this evident preference ceases if elected to government. Whereas, in many multi-party systems (e.g. France) and in some two-party systems (e.g. the United States) political parties tend to act more like interest groups, as they articulate interests rather

---

[3] There is now an International Business Council of Australia, based in Perth, that seems particularly focused on India, where it has a chapter–the first of a planned 60.

than aggregate them, that is bring together disparate interests in the form of suggesting a common good or general interest approach (Almond & Coleman 1960).

This suggests that in selected two-party systems there may be incentives for semi-aligned interest groups to develop a suite of approaches for when their preferred party is in government. Or indeed frosty relations with a favoured party may be an incentive to establish a stronger national association—if the back door is closed, knock harder on the front door.

Lowi's approach has the advantage of illuminating some of the conceptual difficulties which beset the study of interest groups, especially the dynamic relationship between individual firms and associations. Not just trade associations, but individual companies can be seen as interest groups (Jordan, 1998: 8). For Wilson, an interest group is an organisation which has some autonomy from government or political parties and that tries to influence public policy (Wilson 1990, 8). Scholars with a policy studies orientation (for example, Lindblom 1977, Scholzman and Tierney 1986) tend to want to include individual firms as well as membership groups, while others wish to restrict the term to associations which are open to membership (Walker 1991). Yet there are times when individual firms are significant political actors representing their interests (Bell and Warhurst 1992), and others when federations of other associations become active.

While Jordan (1998, 21) makes a useful distinction between pressure groups and policy participants (including non-collective bodies), Lowi's approach is suggestive of the kinds of factors which determine whether non-group, sectoral group or peak group actors will engage on any one issue (Lowi 1964, 709). What Lowi's approach says less about are the groups which exist for essentially non-political reasons, but which are occasionally stimulated into political activity—Duverger's (1959) 'non-exclusive groups'.

We note this limitation and have confined ourselves to an examination of exclusive groups. We confined ourselves in terms of research ambition to sector groups and peak associations representing business and labour, limiting ourselves to the mining sector and focusing particularly (though not exclusively) on responses to environmental issues. This includes consideration of the union movement at the peak, sectoral and firm level, since political alliances with individual firms or sector groups might be more significant than peak-level conflicts on redistributive issues. Business and unions tend to stand shoulder-to-shoulder on distributive and even regulatory issues, yet are essentially 'class enemies' on redistributive issues, and we wish to capture something of the flavour and dynamism of the way in which capital and labour organize and interact at the firm, sector and peak levels.

We have therefore considered interest group activity at the firm, sectoral and peak association levels and interactions between groups and state, national and international levels of governance. We have traced significant associational developments over a decade and a-half and at each level and explored the key theoretical question of the extent to which these changes appear to have been pushed from below by factors reflecting the 'logic of collective action' or from above by the emergence of new policy demands which have required new associational forms.

The book has examined the 'new federalism' environmental reforms in Australia and international regulation as the 'pull' factors to examine the effects of governance regimes on state chambers of mines, the Minerals Council of Australia, and the formation of the International Council on Mining and Metals. We have also reflected on relationships with state, national and international peak associations and associated labour organizations, and made some comparative observations of other sectors.

It was not immediately clear how trade unions have responded to these changes. They underwent a series of amalgamations and federal industrial relations reforms made state jurisdictions less important. The Hawke Government's Prices and Incomes Accord made unions less relevant to wage determination, and a subsequent move to wage negotiations at the level of the individual firm ('enterprise bargaining') undoubtedly weakened unions, which were historically organized as craft unions, which often largely overlapped with industrial sectors. But these reforms also weakened associability for business. Perhaps ironically, many unions sought refuge in federal jurisdiction from the industrial relations reforms of the Kennett government in the state of Victoria in the 1990s only to expose themselves to a similar program at the Commonwealth level after the defeat of the ALP Keating government in 1996. Unions have also been grappling with declining membership, and these factors have encouraged a greater degree of militancy in unions such as one with coverage in the mining industry, the Construction, Forestry, Mining and Energy Union (CFMEU—now CFMMEU in some states after mergers with the Maritime Union).

We might expect unions to make common cause with companies on site approval issues and even on issues which pose a threat to the sector which employs their members (such as climate change does for coal miners), but it is not clear whether this commonality of interest has been sufficient to overcome the heightened class-based conflict which was evident—for example, with the CFMEU campaign against Rio Tinto. An important question is whether the warring parties manage to cooperate on issues such as climate change which threaten the interests of them both.

Changing *Compétences*, Evolving Constitutions

This discussion suggests that we must take account of differences between sectors and between levels in understanding how the 'constitution' of each level might impact on associability. Now we turn to describe the changes in the constitution of governance at each level, which provide us with a kind of quasi-experiment through which we can observe how the changes impacted upon interest groups. From these we can derive some propositions as to how we think associability has changed.

The significant changes to the Australian federal system which we might expect to have impacted upon the associability of interest groups were primarily the changes associated with a reform agenda which was collectively termed 'New Federalism'. These reforms included the adoption of National Competition Policy and the establishment of the National Environmental Protection Council (NEPC), which followed the Intergovernmental Agreement on the Environment (IAE). The IAE was part of a rationalization of *compétences* in the Australian federation negotiated with the states after a decade of centralization of environmental powers to the Commonwealth under the external affairs power. It was a process completed by the adoption of the *Environment Protection and Biodiversity Conservation Act 1999,* which codified the distribution of powers between Commonwealth and the states by setting out specific triggers for Commonwealth involvement. Constituent policy measures thus reallocated *compétences* between Micro and Meso levels, not just by increasing the powers of the federal authority, but by specifying those matters which should be decided at each level.

While there has been little explicit discussion of the concept in Australia, the reshuffling of the federal deck after a decade of intergovernmental conflict on environmental issues has produced a result similar to that which would flow from the application of the European idea of subsidiarity, with issues being dealt with at the lowest level of government at which resolution is possible (see Longo, 1999). These changes have changed to the roles of state governments and thus changed the milieu within which interest groups operate.

The establishment of the NEPC, with its ability to make National Environmental Protection Measures thus circumscribed the ability of state governments to create 'pollution havens' to attract investment and has strengthened the hand of state governments faced with the prospect of 'industrial flight' should they adopt more stringent environmental standards (making less likely a 'race to the bottom'). It should be noted that the evidence for the efficacy of pollution havens or disinvestment in the face of higher standards is mixed (Leonard 1988), although it is certainly the case that state governments are subject to a higher degree of structural dependence on footloose industries than are national governments. The *Environment Protection and Biodiversity Conservation Act 1999,* however, ensured that state governments have a substantial role in approving developments.

States are considered to have more power in relation to mineral resources and other resource sectors than with manufacturing, which is more mobile. Krasner has argued that a company engaged in mineral exploitation needs access to the territory of specific countries were deposits are located, but a clothing manufacturer can operate anywhere there is cheap labour and transportation, so the state has more leverage over natural resource developers than clothing manufacturers (Krasner 1995, 268).

There is, however, a need for caution in accepting Krasner's insight into the significance of the immobility of natural resources for the relative power of business and government, for the conditions obtaining throughout the 1990s in the mining sector perhaps weakened its applicability. After the fall of communism, many nations previously closed to international capital opened their borders to investment and sought to sell many state-owned mines. Australian mining companies have become international actors, and while ore bodies are not mobile, capital most certainly is, so one could argue that globalisation has ensured the persistence of state government vulnerability to the structural power of business in this sector, as business has enjoyed a plethora of investment opportunities. Capital, not ore bodies, has been the scarce resource.

The adoption of the *National Environmental Protection Council Act 1994 (Cth)* and state equivalents, the *Competition Policy Reform Act* 1995 (and relevant intergovernmental agreements) and the *Environment Protection and Biodiversity Conservation Act 1999* had the effect of reconstituting the *compétences* of state and federal governments in Australia in relation to resource industries such as mining. On the other hand, Commonwealth legislation in relation to indigenous issues and industrial relations in the form of the *Native Title Act 1993* and the *Workplace Relations Act 1996* diminished significantly the sectoral relevance of states in these policy areas since they made the individual firm the focus of political interaction through the establishment of a 'right to negotiate' (or RTN) with the former, and individual employment contracts (with the latter). The previous role for Aboriginal Land Councils was much diminished under the *Native Title Act,* with the RTN being granted directly to traditional owners who could satisfy tests relating to continuous association with an area of land. While the passage of the legislation, which affected principles of land ownership and access at a sectoral level, was an important issue for the sector at the national level, once it was adopted, negotiations were to be conducted between traditional owners and individual firms. Amendments adopted by the Commonwealth in 1998, however, provided for state approaches to land rights, and thus had the effect of enhancing the sectoral relevance of state governments.

Similarly, the *Workplace Relations Act* diminished the relevance of the old state-based system of industrial arbitration in favour of negotiations between firms and workers. Interestingly, trade unions in Australia also conform to our governance-centred view of interest groups. While the rise of organized labour, both in industrial organizations and the political wing, the Australian Labor Party, occurred among society, the level of organization of the labour movement for the next century owed much to the passage of the *Arbitration Act 1904* (Cth) which regulated the labour market, providing benefits under numerous industrial awards. These benefits were, however, restricted to trade union members, so government legislation provided the exclusive benefits which increased the associability of trade unions significantly. The *Workplace Relations Act* was yet another step in the unravelling of this system, though much of that policy was overturned with the *Fair Work (Registered Organisations) Act 2009* when the ALP was again in power.

The adoption of this legislation occurred at the Commonwealth level, and therefore the relevance of this level was enhanced when it was under development and consideration, but the ultimate effect of these legislative enactments was to decrease the relevance of the Commonwealth level for associability at the sectoral level. Both native title legislation and industrial relations reforms were keenly contested at the Meso level, but (once adopted) made that level less relevant for sectoral groups by allowing state governments to legislate for native title processes (shifting any sectoral associability factors down to that level) and for industrial relations enhancing the relevance of the firm even more than had enterprise bargaining enterprise through moving at least some industrial relations bargaining to the level of individual contracts.

These developments came about as the result of Commonwealth legislation, so their passage led to a maintenance of, or even temporary increase in, relevance of the national level as legislation developed, but then a decline in the relevance of the national level for sector groups—at the very time that the international level was growing in relevance. Thus, there was something of a lagged 'hollowing out' of the organized sector at the national level as the international level increased (see below)—arrested by the response to the Resource Super Profits Tax proposal (see Kellow 2016). At the state level, however, we saw a shift in the basis for associability away from industrial relations (and possibly even land rights) towards environmental regulation and other bases.

In addition to this 'reconstitution' of the Australian federation, however, we must add the evolving significance of the macro (or international) level for interest groups. Here the options for participation were varied and considerable. Interest groups could opt for participation at the meso level in the development of national negotiating positions. They could participate at the international level at the sectoral or peak association level (in regulatory or redistributive arenas). Or individual firms might participate in institutions, such as the Codex Alimentarius Commission, where distinctive product-related property rights and international regulatory harmonisation might convert such fora into a distributive arena where beneficial approvals granted to patent or brand-name holders encourage participation by individual firms. The tensions between federations of national associations and direct firm forms of association seen in the European Union (Streeck and Schmitter 1991, 137; Greenwood 1995, 291) are likely to be present and possibly exacerbated in the multilateral system.

The paramount driver for enhanced associability for the mining industry at the international level was undoubtedly the emergence of a sustainable development agenda in the multilateral system, emerging first with the publication of the so-called Brundtland Report, *Our Common Future* (1987), though owing much to the earlier World Conservation Strategy. This agenda linked development concerns and environment concerns, and effectively made a concomitant commitment to furthering Third World development, the side-agreement to support by such nations for the development of multilateral environmental agreements (MEAs)—essentially replacing the failed 'North-South Dialogue' as a vehicle for wealth transfers from the global haves to the have-nots. Typically, therefore, the MEAs developed included features such as 'double standards' provisions exempting developing countries from their binding obligations, while also entailing commitments for technology transfer, capacity building or financial assistance. While the general thrust of the sustainable development agenda was therefore redistributive in nature, individual MEAs were regulatory in impact, typical of the growing dominance of concerns with 'low politics' in international relations.

Just as regulatory policies at the national level divide business into sectors, so that peak associations cannot find sufficient basis for associability, so too did most of these MEAs divide business interests into sectors, sometimes in ways not easily foreseen. For example, the Basel Convention dealt with trade in hazardous waste, and seemingly had little to do with mining and metals, until further definitional work and an attempt to extend a 'prior informed consent' trade regime into a prohibition regime threatened the interests of the non-ferrous metals sector in ways that differed from the plastics or paper sectors, or the waste management sector. Similarly, the emergence in the EU, OECD and UN of moves to regulate use not just of new chemical substances, but existing chemicals (including metals) challenged the interests of the sector at the international level (Kellow 1999). Again, this challenge differed between sectors.

With chemicals, subject to product patents, the political economy of regulation differed from the mining sector, where any patents covered production processes only. Chemical and pharmaceutical companies were indifferent to the loss of the licence to sell products which were out of patent and could be made more cheaply by generic producers. Indeed, they were often advantaged by bans on out-of-patent chemicals, since such bans help create markets for the new *patented* products they had developed. Thus, the chemical industry was a strong advocate of phasing out 'old' chemicals such as DDT under the Stockholm Convention. Indeed, regulation which increased the costs of placing or keeping products on the market through registration favours large transnational firms within the chemicals sector, because they can recover market approval costs across global markets. A miner of copper or nickel, for example, is highly limited in their ability to produce substitute products if use of their product becomes restricted. The way in which property rights (including intellectual property rights) are assigned is of considerable significance for business associability.

Property Rights and Associability

Recent developments have therefore reshuffled considerably constitutional relationships between different levels of governance and the nature of property rights in relation to mining are of fundamental importance. The mining industry examples suggest these developments in political structures have resulted in varied responses, which have affected such factors as the relationship between large and small firms, the attractiveness of different associational forms, and so on. And, especially because many mining firms are transnational corporations (TNCs), individual firms themselves are sometimes significant transnational actors. Where significant property rights attach to products rather than production processes, TNCs have a strong interest in securing both protection of their Intellectual Property (IP) and harmonisation of regulatory processes: the former will stimulate single firm activity at the Macro level; the latter will require a sectoral association. With chemicals, we find both; with biotechnology, the industry was too fragmented to have yet yielded a viable global association, although policy in the European Union provided an associational basis for a Euro-group, EuropaBio. (For a discussion of these sectors, see Clapp 2003).

Institution-centred explanations provide a superior account of these developments because, we suggest, underpinning even Olson's analysis is a key state function in the definition and allocation of property rights—a function significant when one examines interest groups in different sectors. *We hold that, even in essentially economic explanations, the key characteristics depend upon prior actions of governance institutions.* Our analysis suggests differences from chemicals (and biotechnology) for minerals, because property rights important to those sectors are assigned in different arenas and at different levels, and this has profound significance for associability in these industrial sectors.

Olson's distinction between public and private goods as the basis for differential associability stems primarily from one characteristic of public goods: lack of 'excludability'. Pure public goods are 'non-excludable', although they also exhibit another characteristic: they are 'non-rival' (Peston,1972). 'Rivalness' refers to the extent to which consumption of a good by one conflicts with the consumption of another.[4] As this suggests, goods which are initially non-rival can become rival when consumption rises, and congestion occurs. Rivalness—which Ostrom (2003, 242)

---

[4] It derives from the Latin for stream, and referred originally to one who shares the same stream with another

described as 'subtractability'—owes much to relative scarcity, since for goods in superabundance all consumption is non-rival.

Public goods (such as environmental goods) give rise to problems because absence of exclusion eventually produces 'congestion' (or rivalness). But while rivalness is a quality appearing to reside primarily in the characteristics of the good itself (particularly its scarcity), excludability derives primarily from state provision. In particular, it derives from the specification of property rights by the state and the establishment and enforcement of the rule of law to defend those rights—ultimately by the use of coercion. While exclusion is often *difficult* and sometimes costly to achieve in a technical sense, it is hard to think of any good which the state cannot render into an excludable good by law. It does so for all manner of goods not excludable in a practical sense without state action, including airspace, access to roads and the electromagnetic spectrum. It usually does so by regulating some commodity or activity or making it illegal and then issuing licences establishing 'rights' to undertake that newly 'exclusive' activity. In that way, many environmental public goods are maintained in a condition where they can continue to be non-rival. With some such goods, it is true that exclusion is more technically difficult, more expensive, or requires the state to employ greater amounts of coercion, but this definition and enforcement of property rights is a fundamental role of government. Ostrom (2003, 241), while distinguishing between public goods and common pool resources (which are generally rival), notes both the centrality of exclusion and the role of the state in achieving it, stating that it 'depends both on the technology of physical exclusion devices, such as barbed wire fences and electronic sensing devices, as well as the existence and enforcement of various bundles of property rights.'

Not all policies, of course, allocate costs and benefits, and Lowi later (2009) used the dichotomy of H.L.A. Hart (1961) between Primary Rules (that impose public and private duties) and Secondary Rules (that provide facilities). The restrictions on conduct that duties comprise can be considered to include 'costs', and powers conferred by Secondary Rules can be considered as incorporating 'benefits', and duties and powers might be public *or* private, so that Lowi's typology can be represented on these dimensions, rather than a public choice approach (which he resisted—Lowi, 1992). (See Kellow 2018 and Table 6.1). The fundamental point is that policy characteristics structure interest group associability.

		PRIMARY RULES (Duties)	
		Public	Private
SECONDARY RULES (Powers, Facilities)	Public	**Redistributive**	**Public Interest Regulatory**
	Private	**Distributive**	**Private Interest Regulatory**

Table 6.1 Representation of Policy Types

Property is inherently a social institution. As Hite (1979, 78) stated, it moderates conflict that might otherwise emerge over nature's bounty when there is more than one individual and there are limits to that bounty—or scarcity. Jeremy Bentham (1931, 113) put it thus: 'Property and law are born together and die together. Before laws were made there was no property; take away laws, and property ceases.' Hite pointed out there are some things that are not property because there is no compelling social need to extend the laws of property to include them.[5]

While some rights, such as riparian rights with respect to water, existed in common law, their continuation is at the discretion of the state. Indeed, prospecting rights on federal land in the United States partly evolved as customary rights during the gold rush in California (only recently acquired by the US and with little government presence). The concept of a 'miner's right' derived from a mix of Spanish, German and Cornish law and

[5] The two examples Hite gave were air and sunshine — ironically, both have seen such an extension, under the establishment of tradable emission permits and the recognition given in California by the *Solar Rights Act 1978*.

practice (Umbeck 1977). According to Lacy (1995), miners simply took possession based on laws they promulgated themselves from previous experience under laws and practices in England, Germany and Mexico in the form of 'mining district regulations', consensual bylaws of groups of individual miners. For example, 'Californian mining law 109 prescribed the posting of notice upon a tree, stake, or mound of rocks, identifying the occupier of the land' (Ryan 1974, 108-109). The miner's right in California referred to the land and the right to mine that land, whereas in the earlier Australian setting it was a document that gave the bearer the exclusive right to mine in a specific place as well as additional usufructary grazing rights and voting rights (Victoria 1861, 1). However, the Californian 'right' was not a legal document. The Californian customs spread to Nevada and elsewhere and were eventually codified by the *General Mining Act 1872*. We argue that associability differs between sectors such as mining and chemicals and — to a lesser extent—biotechnology primarily because of the way in which property rights differ in significance between these sectors.

Whether goods possess the crucial characteristic of excludability depends (for all practical purposes) not upon some inherent characteristics of the good itself, but upon the prior specification by the state of rights of access to enjoy the good. As noted above, some such rights of enjoyment existed in common law and predate historically the emergence of the nation state and the market economy, but they are upheld and enforced by the state, and were accepted and enforced by pre-state systems of governance. One can imagine some state of nature where property rights are not dependent upon government defining and upholding them, but for all practical purposes we operate in a context where goods are rendered public or private by government policies, and this definition can change as the result of state action. For example, roads were often operated as toll roads (private goods) and then public roads (public goods) became the most common form. More recently, in response to the need to regulate access and finance additional infrastructure, toll roads have again become more common.

This fundamental role of governments in defining property rights and making other provisions without which markets could not operate was spelled out long ago by Adam Smith and others but is often overlooked by economists, and many political scientists in the strict pluralist camp, as noted by Lowi (1993). We suggest that, even with the apparent contrary interpretation provided by public choice theory, the case for the primacy of institutional explanations is compelling, because of the priority of the state in defining whether or not goods are excludable and using its coercive powers to achieve exclusion. Olson's analysis — in other words — might be correct in identifying coercion as one way of overcoming the free rider problem, but it ignores the point that excludability itself entails use of coercion by the state, and the manner in which it is applied in defining private property rights can be subsumed within an institutional account such as Lowi's, categorising policies according to how the state employs coercion.

Attempts to employ public choice theory to distinguish between types of public policies, while having some explanatory power, therefore incorrectly 'write out' the state from the equation by failing to recognise the prior role of the state in defining the very theory-relevant characteristics at the bottom of such explanations. Zysman (1994, 243) put this more directly than most: 'Markets do not exist or operate apart from the rules and institutions that establish them and that structure how buying, selling and the very organization of production takes place.' Economic explanations are inescapably institutional explanations.

Much environmental policy consists of government interventions which redefine and reallocate property rights. This is most apparent with the recent trend towards the use of market-type incentive systems, such as the creation of tradable emission permits, but it is also inherent in the granting of non-tradable permits in the form of licences granted under more conventional regulatory schemes. Both these approaches can be characterised as Regulatory policy (in Lowi's terms). We grant, however, that policies might conceivably also take Distributive form, the use of subsidies, for example, or Redistributive form such as the granting of tradable rights without payment of costs, and thus the conveyance of property from public ownership into the ownership of the capitalist class. (The granting of mining rights is inherently Distributive—a matter of concern to individuals and individual firms).

Sustainable development not only raised questions about the ability of mining companies to gain rights access to the land they needed, especially in developing countries where indigenous peoples might have to be displaced, but the agenda also gave rise to numerous regulatory challenges to the products of mining that provided a basis for sectoral associability. The UN Conference on Environment and Development at Rio in 1992 did not go well for industry in general, but it went especially badly for mining. Although it was only 'noted' rather than agreed to by governments, Agenda 21 developed at Rio was to assume hegemonic importance in later international politics, as its various texts were invoked as authority for particular actions. Chapter 19 dealt with chemicals and, *inter alia,* called for the phasing out of chemicals which were toxic, persistent and bioaccumulative. Virtually every metal met these criteria, and the industry saw a need to engage better at the sectoral level in such processes if its interests were not to be adversely affected. The proposed amendment to the Basel Convention which could have restricted trade in metal scrap and residues alerted the sector to the possibilities, and the metals industry was subsequently much more focused as the International Forum on Chemical Safety was established and negotiations proceeded on the Rotterdam Convention (on prior informed consent for trade in chemicals, or PIC) and the Stockholm Convention (on persistent organic pollutants, or POPs) (Kellow 1999).

Much work on metal toxicity and risk was commenced by commodity associations (such as the International Copper Association, and similar commodity associations for lead, nickel, zinc and so on), but the same principles applied across the sector and this commodity-by-commodity approach was resulting in duplicated and dissipated effort. And the need for more effective global engagement was underscored by the looming 'Rio+10' conference, the World Summit on Sustainable Development (WSSD), to be held in Johannesburg in 2002. If that was not enough, the World Bank in 2001 commenced an Extractive Industries Review, which was later to recommend that the Bank immediately cease investing in coal mining and phase out investing in oil projects in four years—a recommendation the Bank was later to reject (although adopted later at the behest of the Obama Administration), but it certainly focused the collective minds of the industry.

We now move to interpret our case studies of mining industry association at each level in the light of this theoretical discussion.

The Development of Mining Industry Associations

1. The Macro level: The Global Response

The absence of an international sector group reflected primarily the absence of a regulatory regime that might have served as the basis for association. There was a tentative response to the internationalization of environmental issues represented by UNCED in Rio in 1992, especially the foreshadowing of moves to regulate toxic metals such as lead, with the formation of the International Council on Metals and the Environment (ICME). The regulatory threat was weak, and the industry response was commensurately weak, with a reluctance by companies to invest substantial resources or authority in ICME.

The international hazardous waste regime (a Basel Convention amendment threatening trade in metal wastes) exacerbated the need to engage more effectively in international regulatory arenas, especially as the anniversary of Rio approached in the form of WSSD in Johannesburg in 2002, as did the prospect of the World Bank's Extractive Industries Review established in 2001

In response to these developments, the CEOs of three leading transnational mining companies, Rio Tinto, Phelps Dodge and WMC Resources, initiated the Global Mining Initiative, including a review of mining industry associations. From this, the International Council on Mining and Metals was formed in 2001 to continue ICME's work on metal toxicity, but also to extend its work on the sustainable development agenda that threatened to jeopardize access to land for exploration and mining that was seen as a threat to the 'license to operate' for the industry. Significantly, climate change was left off the agenda as it would have divided the sector, although this issue was added later in the decade.

The decisive factor in the formation of ICMM was the common concern with securing access to ground (the 'licence to operate') and the importance of reputation in ensuring development approvals. Raising standards of corporate behaviour through the adoption of codes of conduct in response to these threats, first by national associations such as the Minerals Council of Australia (MCA), and later by ICMM, were self-regulatory attempts to forestall, or at least minimize, externally imposed regulatory approaches. Like any regulation, however, these self-regulatory codes could be more easily met by larger firms, which were also more focused on protecting the collective global reputation of the industry to ensure continued access to mining prospects. The membership of ICMM was therefore dominated by the larger TNCs, especially those that produced several metals, and therefore less likely to find adequate representation through an international commodity organization focusing on marketing rather than production.

ICMM remained a direct firm membership organization (with provision for participation by national associations), and the nature of its activities made membership attractive only for the large multi-national, multi-metal corporations. While it did initially attract single metal producers operating in a single jurisdiction, in the form of Phelps Dodge (US) and Codelco (Chile), both these corporations resigned their memberships after the first year (though rejoined later). The Brazilian iron ore company CVRD (now Vale) joined ICMM only after it diversified, when it acquired nickel producer Inco in October 2006. There was a similar pattern with other mergers and acquisitions. Teck and Cominco merged in 2001 to form TeckCominco, which then became an ICMM member. Barrick Gold acquired Placer Dome in January 2006 and then joined. Freeport-McMoRan acquired Phelps Dodge in March 2007, rendering the Phelps Dodge resignation irrelevant. Noranda merged with Falconbridge in 2005 only for the Swiss-based mining company Xstrata to take over the merged corporation in 2006. Xstrata (now part of Glencore) then joined.

2. The Meso Level: The Nation state

The trajectory of the Minerals Council of Australia (MCA) also reflects institutional factors, from its initial formation at the initiative of the Commonwealth government. Until the 1960s, there was no national mining industry association, because there was no reason for one to exist: the Commonwealth had no policy measures to provide a basis for association. The industry was able to secure the concessions it sought from the Commonwealth without political organization, partly due to its historic connections with the Liberal Party of Australia, and to an extent, ongoing connections through fund-raising. A chilly connection soon after resulted in some of the mining sector shifting its allegiance to a reconfigured Country party, now renamed National party. The Joint Coal Board was formed to ensure continuity of supply, but with the development of large coal resources in Queensland this became redundant. The Commonwealth established a Coal Industry Tribunal to regulate industrial relations in the sector, and the Australian Coal Association was formed to represent the industry in response (with the Coal Associations of NSW and Queensland as its members).

There were some efforts at association at the commodity level within Australia. Mount Isa Mines (MIM) was the leading player in the Copper Producers Association of Australia, which operated as a domestic cartel, taking advantage of import controls, until the adoption of the *Trade Practices Act 1974* made cartel activity illegal. The Association then went out of existence (Tsokhas 1986, 135). In 1962, MIM and other Australian producers formed local Lead Development and Zinc Development Associations to promote the use of these metals in Australia, while their international equivalents sought to coordinate promotion and marketing plans. There was some discussion in the sector of forming an association in 1963, but nothing came of this.

The Australian Mining Industry Council (AMIC) was formed in 1967 at the direct instigation of the government. The scope of AMIC was limited to metals miners, to the exclusion of the coal industry, which was kept apart by having its own set of institutional factors (the originally state-constituted Joint Coal Board and Coal Industry Tribunal). From about 1990, associability increased with the emergence nationally of environmental issues and the land rights issue in the wake of the *Mabo* decision establishing native title over unalienated Crown land—until the *Native Title Act* decomposed the issue to the level of the individual firm, and then the 1998 amendments increased associability at the state level. With environmental issues, several High Court decisions enhanced the *compétence* of the Commonwealth government, but the IGAE in 1992 marked the commencement of a return of powers to state governments, culminating in the adoption of the *Environment Protection and Biodiversity Conservation Act 1999*. AMIC was concerned over the potential denial of access to land on environmental and Aboriginal land rights grounds and was initially stridently combative in its approach to the government on these issues.

Individual companies with a global presence began to develop a more sophisticated approach to such issues, however, led by Rio Tinto subsidiary CRA (which had lost its Panguna copper mine on Bougainville to separatist conflict) and BHP (which had run into problems with the impact on landholders and the environment of its Ok Tedi mine in Papua New Guinea). There was thus a growing dissonance between the positions of the leading companies and the harder AMIC position, and the softening began to be reflected in AMIC thinking, especially after it appointed a new Executive Director in 1994, from the federal bureaucracy. He instituted a review of AMIC, which subsequently changed its name to the Minerals Council of Australia and adopted a structure which freed it from making consensus decisions.

The development of an Environmental Code was favoured by (and favoured) larger firms, but associability at the national level declined markedly by 2000, and membership of the Minerals Council along with it, to the point that it represented only about 20 of the largest mining companies. There were a number of inter-linked reasons for this shrinking presence. For example, industrial relations reforms moved conflict to the level of the individual firm, although the separate existence of a specific industrial association as a sectoral response to the old IR system largely quarantined the Minerals Council from the effects of this set of reforms. The Commonwealth government secured IR reform in the coal sector, and once the Coal Industry Tribunal system was brought into the IR mainstream in

1994, not only did IR become less salient at the national level, but the greatest impact of this reform came at the state level, removing the reason for the existence of separate state coal industry associations and encouraging the formation of single chambers of mines in NSW and Queensland. (The Australian Coal Association was eventually absorbed into the Minerals Council). In May 1996 the Commonwealth government also reduced the relevance of the national level by removing export controls on all minerals (except uranium).

A very powerful illustration of our point here was provided by the (bungled) introduction in 2010 of a resources rent tax, which galvanised the sector so that it could contest the issue. By 2013, the Minerals Council had 52 full members and 44 Associate Members—more than double the membership at its lowest point

3. The Micro Level: The Australian states

While the state chambers of mines have traced different paths in their recent histories, institutional factors have again been the fundamental drivers, with various policy changes in environmental regulation, industrial relations and Aboriginal land rights impacting differently on each state organization (and state governments often playing even more significant roles, encouraging formation in South Australia and continued existence in both strong chambers such as Western Australia and weaker ones such as Victoria). State mining chambers, while they have had their problems, continue to provide relevance for companies, and attract high levels of membership—particularly by juniors (although most, like the Minerals Council of Australia, are supported by local branches of TNCs).

After its formation, AMIC worked cooperatively with Chambers of Mines in Queensland, Western Australia and the Northern Territory, but there were no longer state chambers in New South Wales, Victoria, South Australia or Tasmania. Most had had chambers at federation in 1901, but these acted to try to attract capital investment, always a problem in colonial economies. State committees of AMIC were established in NSW, Victoria and South Australia, and the Victorian state committee also represented Tasmania. Each of these states saw the establishment of a state chamber, in each case stimulated by the emergence of a regulatory agenda providing associability previously absent, when the granting of exploration and development approvals was largely a matter of distributive policy (granting property rights to the individual firm).

At the time AMIC was formed there were state chambers only in Queensland and Western Australia. Even then, Queensland had a chamber in name only, as it was not formally incorporated, and operated essentially as a creature of the state's predominant miner, MIM, which provided virtually all the resources for the Chamber. There was precious little environmental regulation at this time, and until 2000 environmental regulation of mining was undertaken by the Department of Mines and Energy rather than the Environmental Protection Authority that had been established in 1994—a classic case of regulation by a captured agency. (The minister was even from Mt Isa and was a former MIM employee). The key relationship between mining business actors and government was that relating to the granting of property rights—first to explore and then to exploit. Given the pro-development orientation of most Australian states, this was not a conflictual relationship: it was essentially a matter of distributive policy where individual firms were the predominant political actors, since the benefits were distributed at the firm level. Only with the increasing regulation of mining activities did a genuine chamber of mines representing the sector make sense.

The Western Australian Chamber of Mines began as predominantly a gold mining organization in 1901. The Chamber grew, particularly with the development of iron ore, bauxite and nickel mines through the 1960s mining boom and then oil, petroleum and natural gas, resulting in the formal renaming as a Chamber of Minerals and Energy. Today the Chamber covers exploration, processing, downstream value adding and refining of over 40 different types of mineral and energy resources in Western Australia. By the time of the 'resources boom' at the time of the 1981 federal election, Western Australia was a diverse mineral-rich state with a strong chamber of mines: it dealt with various taxation issues, workers' compensation, manpower and training, and safety, but it was also engaged with the emerging environmental agenda on issues including coastal zone management and national parks.

In addition to the emergence of the (Regulatory) environmental policy agenda in the 1970s, land rights were particularly important for Western Australian mining companies as the state had both high mineral prospectivity and a substantial Indigenous population, and the Chamber lobbied actively against a legislative approach to the issue. When the High Court *Mabo* decision imposed a new set of property arrangements, the Chamber was active in seeking to minimise its adverse impact on the state, even persuading the state government to attempt a separate legislated approach to the problem (ultimately futile, on constitutional grounds). The

Chamber has continued to enjoy high associability and expanded to include energy companies among its members. It attracted a substantially larger membership than the MCA and included many smaller companies — though much of the heavy lifting was done by subsidiaries of the TNCs that dominate both ICMM and the MCA.

In New South Wales, the formation of a sector-wide industry association was hindered by policies that continued, until 1994, to provide strong separate associability for the coal mining industry. Associability for the NSW Combined Colliery Proprietors' Association was provided by both the unique industrial relations framework of the Coal Industry Tribunal (CIT) and the Joint Coal Board (see Simms 1981). The Proprietors' Association became the NSW Coal Association in 1964 and federated with the Queensland Coal Association in 1970 to form the Australian Coal Association. The Commonwealth government resisted mounting calls to transfer the CIT to the mainstream IR system and also retained export controls, but reform began to occur at the state level, where the NSW government reviewed and then merged the *Coal Mining Act* and the *Mining Act* in 1991. The ALP Commonwealth government then ended the separate CIT system in 1994, and there was no longer a reason for a separate coal association and the NSW Minerals Council was formed in April 1995.

The new NSW Minerals Council continued its involvement in the remaining coal industry authorities, but increasingly the matters with which it dealt came to be dominated by OH&S, environment and a number of land access issues (native title, exploration, conservation reserves, world heritage and forests). The continuing importance of the state government in defining property rights and the basic operating conditions of the industry was underscored in 1997 when NSW passed legislation to acquire coal rights (uniquely) retained by landowners since the colonial era. Most of the land access and environment issues were also within the *compétence* of the state government; and adoption of the *Native Title Amendment Act 1998* and the *Environment Protection and Biodiversity Conservation Act 1999* returned further matters to the state.

The formation of the South Australia state chamber was initiated in November 1978 by the Director-General of Mines and Energy to enhance the development of mining, very much encouraged by both the government and the peak business group in response to both the emergence of Aboriginal land rights and (especially) the emergence of nuclear issues with the development of a massive copper-gold-uranium mine at Roxby Downs.

The Victorian Chamber of Mines formed in 1986 out of the need for reform of state mining law and was essentially gold-driven. The VCM sought to educate the community, an effort by mining companies to create a favourable image of mining among those who were not obviously beneficiaries from the mining sector, which had a lesser economic footprint than other states and was also more densely populated. There was therefore a greater need to justify mining activity, not just *in* Victoria, but mining in Australia as a whole *to* Victorians, with the MCA making a contribution to costs. The state government also provided funds for the education program, helping to keep the VCM viable.

While the VCM was therefore supported by many of the large mining houses based in the state — but with no operations in the state — there was very little reason for a mining chamber to exist in Victoria, and it eventually ceased to have an independent existence. The VCM became the Victorian Minerals and Energy Council (VMEC) in July 2001, reflecting the fact that the main products in the state were mineral sands, gold and brown coal. Most large companies withdrew from membership, so VMEC struggled and became effectively composed of small companies. But the government wanted to deal with VMEC and not with individual companies and encouraged them to continue, doing what it could to achieve this. The government started to provide more financial support, for example, by sponsoring a mines rescue competition and other joint work on safety. By 1 January 2003 the membership of the Council had declined to 15 Ordinary Members and 5 Energy members, and in May 2004 it accepted an invitation to become a division of the MCA—the only state chamber to do so (though joined by the Northern Territory chamber).

For most of the history of Tasmania, the only mining industry association was a branch of the Australian Mines and Metals Association, providing services to the industry on IR. From 1982, the Presidents' Committee of the AMIC included AMMA in Tasmania, but most issues of concern were handled at the firm level. Not only did the various issues relating to granting exploration and mining licences not form a basis for association, but the emergence of environmental regulation also failed to do so because the *Environment Protection Act 1973* regulating pollution made provision for ministerial exemptions to be granted to environmental standards, and most large firms had exemptions, meaning that relations between government and industry were effectively handled at the level of the individual firm.

The Tasmanian Minerals Council was formed only in 1985. Aboriginal land rights were not an issue in Tasmania, because the granting of title and the historical treatment of Indigenous Tasmanians meant it was highly unlikely that any would be able to demonstrate the ongoing association with the land necessary under *Mabo* decision for the grant of native title. The TMC thus enjoyed weak associability, with few potential members, and few state government issues providing a basis for associability. It formed at a time of emerging environmental activity in the state, especially the closing to exploration of the South-west of the state when it was included on the World Heritage List. This action, taken in response to a hydro-electric development proposal, reserved highly prospective land and raised concerns over access to other areas of the state. The Tasmanian association has survived by adapting, adding energy companies and ultimately manufacturing, stimulated by a state government initiative.

Conclusion

The trajectories of mining industry associations at each level strongly suggest that the important stimuli for change have been primarily institutional in nature. While we must always allow some room for human agency (leadership, for example), the major drivers have undoubtedly been institutional.

The alternative explanation might be that 'countervailing groups' have shaped the trajectory of mining industry associations, but changes in groups in other industrial sectors such as chemicals and biotechnology facing similar countervailing groups at all levels suggested a very different pattern. These other sectors did not show similar developments to those of mining sector groups at all levels of governance, with both unions and peak business groups all being influenced somewhat differently by their own institutional constraints.

This analysis helps to answer a puzzle that stems from a comparison between the chemicals sector and the mining industry. There is no chemicals sector organization at the state level in Australia because there is no reason to organize there. The key property rights for that sector are competitive, defined by patent law and the rights to sell after regulatory approval on grounds of efficacy and safety by national governments The granting of access to land by state governments (unlike prospecting and mining rights for mining) is of little importance. Even pollution regulation has been 'nationalised' in Australia through the adoption of National Environmental Policy Measures. While the chemical industry organized nationally for much of its history to secure tariff protection, and though regulation on efficacy or risk continues to provide additional reasons for Meso-level organization, the transnational nature of the dominant corporations has made the Macro level and the international harmonization of regulation a much stronger basis for associability for chemicals. The same pattern is apparent with the recently emerged biotechnology sector, because the property rights at stake are essentially the same, though the highly fragmented nature of the sector has limited global associability. An international biotech industry association has proved elusive: one emerged for WSSD in Johannesburg in 2002, but it never thrived and disappeared from 2007.

We have examined here the utility of an institution-centred conceptualisation of interest groups by studying the way in which changes in the federal constitution of the state and emerging transnational reciprocating institutions, including policies, have impacted upon the organisation of the mining sector. We have used the challenges posed by regulatory developments faced by the mining sector to explore the changing interactions between firms and sector groups. A focus on environment alone as a driver is insufficient to explain *all* the changes we observe. Changes in other policy areas, such as Indigenous land rights and industrial relations have also been important drivers of change, though we must add that the international driver is best characterised as the 'sustainable development' agenda which brings together issues relating to environment, development and indigenous rights, whereas IR was significant only at the state and sub-state levels.

While we would caution the need to allow for agency, for the skill or otherwise of the people involved in business associations, we would argue for the primacy of institutions in structuring associability for business groups. But our research shows that associability varies across levels in multi-level governance systems as the incentives for collective action provided by policies-as-institutions changes. This supports the more general findings of Schofer and Longhofer (2011) and of Eising (2004) in the EU (see also Grande 2002). The mining industry has faced similar countervailing groups to those that have campaigned against chemicals (and biotechnology) but its associations demonstrate different trajectories, thanks to institutional

differences. As indicated by studies of policy feedback, institutions (and policies as institutions) matter for interest groups, and the most significant factor affecting associability for sector groups appears to be the manner in which institutions at each level of governance define and modify significant property rights for that industrial sector.

BIBLIOGRAPHY

Allen Consulting, *Options for a Global Industry Association Structure for the Mining, Minerals and Metals Sector. Report to the Global Mining Initiative,* September 2000.

Almond, Gabriel, and Sidney Verba. *The Civic Culture*. Princeton, N.J.: Princeton University Press, 1963.

Ando, Amy Whritenour, 'Do Interest Groups Compete? An Application to Endangered Species' *Public Choice* 114, no.1-2 (2003): 137-159.

Anon. 'Australian Mineral Cos Must do More for the Environment', *Asia Pulse*, December 9, 2001.

Anon. 'Dispossessed Dayaks Slam Rio Tinto Mining Methods at Stopwork Meeting, *Newcastle Herald*, February 3,1998, 4.

Anon. 'Global Union Campaign Claims Rio Tinto Abuses', *Australian Financial Review*, May 25, 1998,4.

Anon. 'Unions use offshore big guns to battle Rio Tinto on home turf', *The Australian*, February 27, 1998, 40.

Anon. 'Minerals Council takes issue with Opposition', *Australian Mining*, October 10, 2001,
http://www.miningaustralia.com.au/articles/06/0c007f06.asp

Arthur D. Little, Inc. *Review of Industry Associations; Final Report to the Global mining Initiative Representatives.* Reference 70050, March 2000.

Aspinwall, M., & Greenwood, J., *Collective action in the European Union: interests and the new politics of associability*. London, Routledge, 2013.

Atkinson, M.M. and Coleman, W.D., "Policy networks, policy communities and the problems of governance." *Governance*, 5 No.2 (1992): 154-180.

Australian Associated Press Financial News Wire August 21, 2002.

Australian Associated Press General News. December 11, 2002.

Australian Associated Press, July 24, 2002.

Australian Associated Press, June 7, 2000.

Australian Bureau of Statistics. (Annual). Employee Earnings, Benefits and Trade Union Membership, Australia. ABS Series 6310.0

Australian Financial Review, August 23, 1990.

Australian Financial Review, August 30, 1990.

Australian Financial Review, September 7, 1990.

Australian Financial Review, November 1, 1991.

Australian Financial Review, February 6, 1992.

Australian Financial Review, October 11, 1994.
Australian Financial Review, November 25, 1996.
Australian Financial Review, November 15, 1997.
Australian Financial Review, May 25, 1998.
Australian Financial Review, June 23, 1999.
Australian Financial Review, July 10, 2000.
Australian Financial Review, July 11, 2000
Australian Financial Review, October 12, 2000.
Australian Financial Review, October 13, 2000.
Australian Financial Review, November 28, 2000.
Australian Financial Review, September 3, 2001.
Australian Financial Review, October 10, 2001.
Australian Financial Review, August 22, 2002.
Australian Mining Industry Council. (1990) "Shrinking Australia: Economics and Land Access." *Mining Review* (July 1990): 17-23.
Australian Mining Industry Council. 1992 Annual Report.
Australian Mining Industry Council. 1975. Annual Report.
Australian Mining Industry Council. 1979. Annual Report.
Australian Mining, October 10, 2001.
Australian, 23 October 2016.
Australian, November 18, 1996.
Australian, December 10, 1996.
Australian, December 18, 1996.
Australian, February 27, 1998.
Australian, 22 September 2017.
Bell, S. and J. Warhurst, "Political Activism Among Large Firms," In S. Bell and J. Wanna, *Business–Government Relations in Australia*, Sydney: Harcourt Brace Jovanovich, 1992.
Bell, Stephen. 'Between the Market and the State: The Role of Australian Business Associations in Public Policy.' *Comparative Politics* 28 No.1(1995): 25–53.
Bentham, Jeremy. 1931. *The Theory of Legislation.* (C.K. Ogden, ed., Richard Hildreth trans.) New York: Harcourt Brace & Co.
BHP, *Industry Association Review.* 19 December 2017.
Blom-Hansen, Jens "Organized Interests and the State: A Disintegrating Relationship? Evidence from Denmark" *European Journal of Political Research*, 39(3) (2001): 391-416.
Bosso, Christopher J, "Rethinking the Concept of Membership in Nature Advocacy Organizations" *Policy Studies Journal*, 31 No, 3 (2003): 397-411.

Bouwen, Pieter. "Corporate lobbying in the European Union: the logic of access." *Journal of European public policy* 9, no. 3 (2002): 365-390.

Bouwen, Pieter. "Lobbying in de Europese Unie: Is er nog toekomst voor nationale belangengroepen?." *Res Publica* 45, no. 4 (2003): 673-696.

Broscheid, Andreas, and David Coen. "Insider and outsider lobbying of the European Commission: An informational model of forum politics." *European Union Politics* 4, no. 2 (2003): 165-189.

Brundtland, G.H., M. Khalid, S. Agnelli, S. Al-Athel and B.J.N.Y. Chidzero, *Our common future*. Oxford: Oxford University Press, 1987.

Burton, Bob, 'WWF Signs $1.2M Partnership With Rio Tinto.' *Mining Monitor*, 5 No. 1 (March 2000): 9.

Carroll, William K; Carson, Colin, 'The Network of Global Corporations and Elite Policy Groups: A Structure for Transnational Capitalist Class Formation?' *Global Networks*, 3 No.1 (2003): 29-57.

Chamber of Minerals and Energy, Western Australia, *Annual Report* 1992

Chamber of Minerals and Energy, Western Australia, *Annual Report*, 1993

Chamber of Minerals and Energy, Western Australia, *Annual Report*, 1994

Chamber of Minerals and Energy, Western Australia, *Annual Report*, 1995

Chamber of Minerals and Energy, Western Australia, *Annual Report*, 1996

Chamber of Minerals and Energy, Western Australia, *Annual Report*, 1997

Chamber of Minerals and Energy, Western Australia, *Annual Report*, 1999

Chamber of Minerals and Energy, Western Australia, *Annual Report*, 2000

Chamber of Mines of Western Australia, *Annual Report* 1981.

Chamber of Mines of Western Australia, *Annual Report* 1982.

Chamber of Mines of Western Australia, *Annual Report* 1983

Chamber of Mines of Western Australia, *Annual Report* 1984

Chamber of Mines of Western Australia, *Annual Report* 1985

Chamber of Mines of Western Australia, *Annual Report* 1988

Clapp, Jennifer. "Transnational corporate interests and global environmental governance: negotiating rules for agricultural biotechnology and chemicals." *Environmental Politics* 12 No.4 (2003): 1-23.

Clow, S. *The International Nickel Trade*. Sawston: Woodhead Publishing 1992.

Condon, C. "Urban Pressure Groups" in ed. R. Lucy (ed.), *The Pieces of Politics*. South Melbourne: Macmillan, 1975.

Courchene, Thomas J., "Glocalization: The Regional/International Interface." *Canadian Journal of Regional Science* 18 No.1 (1995): 1-20.

de Figueiredo, John M and Rui J P de Figueiredo Jr (2002) "The Allocation of Resources by Interest Groups: Lobbying, Litigation and Administrative Regulation" *Business and Politics*, 4 No. 2 (2002): 161-181.

Deutsch, Karl W. *The nerves of government: models of political communication and control*. New York: The Free Press, 1963.

Douglas, M. *Risk and blame*. London: Routledge, 2002.

Dow Jones Commodities Service, December 10, 1996.

Dow Jones International News, October 11, 2000.

Dunleavy, P., "Group Identities and Individual Influence: Restructuring the Theory of Interest Groups" *British Journal of Political Science* 18 (1988): 21-50.

Duverger, Maurice. *Political parties, their organization and activity in the modern state*. London: Methuen, 1959.

Eckstein, Harry *Pressure Group Politics: The Case of the British Medical Association.* Stanford: Stanford University Press, 1960.

Eising, R., "Multilevel governance and business interests in the European Union." *Governance* 17 No. 2 (2004): 211-245.

Eurometaux. (n.d.) European Non-ferrous Metals Association. https://eurometaux.eu

Euromines., (n.d.) European Association of Mining Industries. http://www.euromines.org

External Environmental Advisory Group, *Annual Report 2000-01*, Minerals Council of Australia Website, http://www.minerals.org.au/downloads/pdf/EEAG01Report.pdf

Fairbrass, Jenny, "The Europeanization of Business Interest Representation: UK and French Firms Compared" *Comparative European Politics*, 1 No. 3 (2003): 313-334.

Galligan, B. *Utah and Queensland Coal: A study in the micro political economy of modern capitalism and the state*. Brisbane: University of Queensland Press, 1989.

Galligan, B. and G. Singleton, eds., *Business and Government Under Labor*. Melbourne: Longman Cheshire, 1991.

Gerritsen, R., "The Necessity of "Corporatism": the case of the Hawke Labor government." *Politics*, 21, No1 (1986): 45-54.

Giddens, Anthony. *The constitution of society: Outline of the theory of structuration*. Berkeley: Univ of California Press, 1984.

Gottliebsen Robert 'Oresome prospects' *Weekend Australian* (3-4 June 2000): 52

Gottliebsen Robert 'Master of mine games' *Weekend Australian* (5-6 October 2002): 46.

Grande, Edgar. "Institutions and Interests in Europe: Interest Groups and Governance in a System Structured by Multiple Levels." *Foro Internacional*, 42 No.2 (2002): 293-316.

Greenwood, J., Grote, J.R., and Ronit, K. eds., *Organized interests and the European Community* (Vol. 2). London: SAGE Publications Limited, 1992.

Greenwood, Justin. "The Pharmaceutical Industry: A European Business Alliance that Works" in Justin Greenwood ed. *European Case- book on Business Alliances*. London: Prentice- Hall, 1995.

Griffith, Ernest S. *Congress: its contemporary role.* New York: New York University Press, 1956.

Hart, H.L.A. *The Concept of Law.* New York: Oxford University Press, 1961.

Hawke, Bob. *The Hawke Memoirs*. Sydney: Mandarin Books, 1996.

Henderson, Ian 'Reith sets up shop in Beazley's yard' *Weekend Australian* (3-4 June 2000): 32.

Henning, D. H. "Natural resources administration and the public interest." *Public Administration Review*, 30 No.2 (1970): 134-140.

Henry, Adam Douglas. "Ideology, Power and the Structure of Policy Networks." *Policy Studies Journal* 39 No. 3 (2011): 361-383.

Herald Sun, October 13, 1997.

Hirschman, A. O. *Exit, voice, and loyalty: Responses to decline in firms, organizations, and states*. Cambridge: Harvard University Press, 1970.

Hite, James C. *Room and situation: The political economy of land-use policy.* Chicago: Nelson-Hall, 1979.

Hoffman, Stanley. "Obstinate or Obsolete: the Fate of the Nation State and the Case of Western Europe." *Daedalus* 95 No.3 (1966): 862-915.

Holyoke, T.T., "Choosing battlegrounds: Interest group lobbying across multiple venues." *Political Research Quarterly*, 56 No.3 (2003): 325-336.

Howlett, Michael, and Andrea Migone. "Charles Lindblom is alive and well and living in punctuated equilibrium land." *Policy and Society* 30, no. 1 (2011): 53-62.

Hunold, Christian, and John S. Dryzek. "Green political theory and the state: Context is everything." *Global Environmental Politics* 2, no. 3 (2002): 17-39.

ICEM. *Rio Tinto—Behind the Façade.* Brussels: ICEM, 1998.

ICEM. *Rio Tinto—Tainted Titan.* Brussels: ICEM, 1998.

ICMM The Mining and Metals Industries: Progress in Contributing to Sustainable Development, Working Paper, 27 February 2002.

ICMM Response to the Draft MMSD Report – 16th April 2002a.

International Copper Association. *Annual Report* 1993.

International Institute for Environment and Development. Breaking New Ground: Mining, Minerals and Sustainable Development (Final Report of the MMSD Project). 2002.

International Market Insight Reports, September 19 1997.

Jordan, Grant. "What drives associability at the European Union level? The limits of the utilitarian explanation" in Justin Greenwood and Mark Aspinall eds *Collective Action in the European Union and the New Politics of Associability*. London: Routledge, 1998.

Kamat, S., "The privatization of public interest: theorizing NGO discourse in a neoliberal era." *Review of international political economy*, 11 No, 1 (2004): 155-176.

Keating, Tom. "Domestic Sources of Canada's Foreign Policy." *International Journal* 39 No,1 (1983/1984): 146-170.

Kelemen, R. Daniel. *The Rules of Federalism: Institutions and Regulatory Politics in the EU and Beyond.* Cambridge, Mass: Harvard University Press, 2004.

Kellow, Aynsley. "The policy roles of bureaucrats and politicians in New Zealand." *Politics*, 19 No. 2 (1984): 43-53.

Kellow, Aynsley. "Electricity planning in Tasmania and New Zealand: political processes and the technological imperative." *Australian Journal of Public Administration* 45, no. 1 (1986): 2-17.

Kellow, Aynsley. "Promoting elegance in policy theory: Simplifying Lowi's arenas of power." *Policy Studies Journal* 16, no. 4 (1988): 713.

Kellow, Aynsley *The Internationalisation of Environmental Issues: Implications for the Mining Industry.* Report for MIM Holdings Ltd. 1994.

Kellow, Aynsley. *International Toxic Risk Management: Chemicals, Ideals, Interests and Representation* Cambridge, Cambridge University Press, 1999.

Kellow, Kellow, Aynsley. "Baptists and bootleggers? The Basel Convention and metals recycling trade." *Agenda: A Journal of Policy Analysis and Reform* 6, no. 1 (1999): 29-38.

Kellow, Aynsley. "Norms, interests and environment NGOs: The limits of cosmopolitanism." *Environmental Politics* 9, no. 3 (2000): 1-22.

Kellow, Aynsley. "Comparing Business and Public Interest Associability at the International Level" *International Political Science Review* 23 No. 2 (2002): 175-186.

Kellow, Aynsley. "Multi-level and multi-arena governance: the limits of integration and the possibilities of forum shopping." *International Environmental Agreements: Politics, Law and Economics* 12, no. 4 (2012): 327-342.

Kellow, Aynsley. "Learning from the RSPT mistakes: is reform still possible?" *Australian Journal of Political Science* 51, no. 1 (2016): 134-149.

Kellow, Aynsley. "From policy typologies to policy feedback." In Eds H.K. Colebatch and R. Hoppe, *Handbook on Policy, Process and Governing*. Cheltenham: Edward Elgar Publishing, 2018.

Kellow, A., & Hannah Murphy-Gregory (Eds.). *Handbook of Research on NGOs*. Cheltenham: Edward Elgar Publishing., 2018.

Kellow, Aynsley, Theodore J. Lowi and Marian Simms (2000) 'Interest Groups in Federal and Global Context: The Case of Environmental Policy and Australia'. Paper Presented to the IPSA World Congress, Quebec. August 2000.

Kellow, Aynsley, and Marian Simms. "Policy change and associability: The Australian mining sector." *Australian Journal of Public Administration* 72 No. 1 (2013): 41-54.

Kellow, Aynsley and Anthony R. Zito "Steering through Complexity: EU Environmental Regulations in the International Context" *Political Studies*, 50 (2000): 43-60.

Kelly, Paul, *The end of certainty.* Sydney: Allen & Unwin, 1992.

Kettl, D. "The Transformation of Governance: Globalisation, Devolution, and the Role of Government." *Public Administration Review* 60 No.6 (2000): 488-497.

Korten, David C. *When Corporations Rule the World.* London, Earthscan, 1996.

Krasner, Stephen D. "Power politics, institutions and transnational relations." In Ed. T. Risse-Kappen '*Bringing transnational relations back in: Non-state actors, domestic structures and international institutions.* Cambridge: Cambridge University Press, 1995.

Lacy, John, C. "The Historical Origins of the United States Mining Law and Proposals for Change." *National Resources, Energy and the Environment Law* 10 No.1 (1995): 13-20.

Lanza, O and Lavdas, K. "The disentanglement of interest politics: Business associability, the parties and policy in Italy and Greece" *European Journal of Political Research* 37 No. 2 (2000): 203-235.

Leonard, H.J., *Pollution and the struggle for the world product: Multinational corporations, environment, and international comparative advantage*. Cambridge: Cambridge University Press, 1988.

Levy, David L. and Daniel Egan "Capital Contests: National and Transnational Channels of Corporate Influence on the Climate Change Negotiations" *Politics and Society* 26 (1998): 337-361.

Lindblom, Charles E. *Politics and Markets,* New York, Basic Books, 1977.

Littlewood, George (2000) "The Global Mining Initiative" Address to Mining 2000, Melbourne September 20, 2000.

Longo, Michael. "Subsidiarity and local environmental governance: A comparative and reform perspective." *University of Tasmania Law Review* 18, no. 2 (1999): 225-246.

Lowi, Theodore J. "American business, public policy, case-studies, and political theory." *World politics* 16, no. 4 (1964): 677-715.

Lowi, Theodore J. "Why is There No Socialism in the United States? A Federal Analysis." *International Political Science Review* 5 (1984): 369-380.

Lowi, Theodore J. "The State in Politics." In Ed. R.G.Noll, *Regulatory policy and the social sciences.* Berlin: de Gruyter, 1985.

Lowi, Theodore J. 'An Assessment of Kellow's "Promoting Elegance in Policy Theory"' *Policy Studies Journal* 16 (1988): 725-728.

Lowi, Theodore J. 'The state in political science: How we become what we study'. *American Political Science Review*, 86 no.1 (1992): 1–7.

Lowi, Theodore J. "Rights and Risks in the History of American Government." in Ed. Edward J. Burger Jr, *Risk,* Ann Arbor: University of Michigan Press, 1993.

Lowi, Theodore J. "Our Millennium: Political Science Confronts the Global Corporate Economy." *International Political Science Review* 22 no.2 (2001): 131-150.

Lowi, Theodore J. *Arenas of Power*. (Edited and Introduced by Norman K. Nicholson). Boulder, CO: Paradigm Publishers, 2009.

Manheim, Jarol B. *The Death of a Thousand Cuts: Corporate Campaigns and the Attack on the Corporation.* Mahwah, NJ: Lawrence Earlbaum, 2001.

Marsh, D. and Rhodes, R.A.W. *Policy networks in British government.* Oxford: Clarendon Press, 1992.

Matthews, T. "Australian Pressure Groups" in Eds. Henry Mayer and Helen Nelson, *Australian politics: a fifth reader*. Melbourne: Longman Cheshire, 1980.

Matthews, T. "Interest Groups" in Eds. Rodney Smith and Lex Watson, *Politics in Australia*. Sydney: Allen & Unwin, 1989.

Matthews, T. "Federalism and Interest Group Cohesion: A Comparison of Two Peak Business Groups in Australia." *Publius* 20 (1990): 105–128.

Matthews, T. "Employers' Associations, Corporatism and the Accord: The Politics of Industrial Relations" in Eds. S. Bell and B. Head *State, Economy and Public Policy in Australia*. Sydney: Allen & Unwin, 1994.

Matthews, T. "Interest Groups," in Ed Rodney Smith *Politics in Australia* (3rd ed). Sydney: Allen & Unwin, 1997.

McEachern, D., 1986. Corporatism and business responses to the Hawke government. *Politics*, 21 no.1 (1986): 19-27.

MetalWorld, www.metalworld.com, accessed 15 September 2004.

Minerals Council of Australia *Australian Minerals Industry Code for Environmental Management*. February 2000. http://www.minerals.org.au/downloads/pdf/Code2000.pdf, 2000.

Minerals Council of Australia *Annual Report 1997*

Minerals Council of Australia *Annual Report 1998*

Minerals Council of Australia *Annual Report 1999*

Minerals Council of Australia *Annual Report 2000*

Minerals Council of Australia *Annual Report 2001*

Minerals Council of Australia. Australian Minerals Industry Code for Environmental Management: Third Progress Report, *Minerals Council of Australia Website,* http://www.minerals.org.au/downloads/pdf/thirdcodeprog.pdf November 2001.

Minerals Council of Australia, (1998) *Minerals Industry Survey Report 1998*, Minerals Council of Australia, http://www.minerals.org.au/downloads/pdf/mis_1998.pdf

Minerals Council of Australia, (1999) *Minerals Industry Survey Report 1999*, Minerals Council of Australia, http://www.minerals.org.au/downloads/pdf/mis_1999.pdf

Minerals Council of Australia, (2000) *Minerals Industry Survey Report 2000*, Minerals Council of Australia, http://www.minerals.org.au/downloads/pdf/mis_2000.pdf

Minerals Council of Australia, (2001) *Minerals Industry Survey Report 2001*, Minerals Council of Australia, http://www.minerals.org.au/downloads/pdf/mis_2001.pdf

Minerals Council of Australia. (2001) *Australian Minerals Industry Code for Environmental Management: Second Code Progress Report*, November 2001, Minerals Council of Australia Website, http://www.minerals.org.au/downloads/pdf/REPORT.pdf

Minerals Council of Australia. (2002) *Minerals Industry Survey Report 2002*, Minerals Council of Australia, http://www.minerals.org.au/downloads/pdf/2002_mis.pdf

Mining Monitor 'WWF Signs $1.2M Partnership With Rio Tinto', *Mining Monitor*, 5 no.1, (2000). http://www.mpi.org.au/mm/editions/mining_monitor_vol5no1.pdf

MMSD Assurance Group, Minutes of First Meeting Selsdon Park, 21-23 May 2000.

Molina, Oscar; Rhodes, Martin "Corporatism: The Past, Present, and Future of a Concept" *Annual Review of Political Science*, 5 (2002): 305-331.

Montpetit, Eric (2002) 'To Be Done with Lobbying: How Canadian Institutions Influence the Action of Interest Groups' *Politique et Societés*, 21 No.3 (2002): 91-112.

Moody, Roger (2001) *Sleepwalking with the enemy – or waking the truth*, Mines & Communities Website: http://www.minesandcommunities.org/Charter/sleepwalk2.htm

Murphy, Hannah, & Aynsley Kellow "Forum shopping in global governance: understanding states, business and NGOs in multiple arenas." *Global Policy*, 4 no.2 (2013): 139-149.

Neto, O.A. and G.W. Cox "Electoral Institutions, Cleavage Structures and the Number of Parties" *American Journal of Political Science* 41 (1997): 147-174.

New South Wales Coal Association, *Annual Report*, 1990.

New South Wales Coal Association, *Annual Report*, 1991.

New South Wales Coal Association, *Annual Report*, 1993.

New South Wales Coal Association, *Annual Report*, 1994.

New South Wales Minerals Council, *Annual Report*, 1996.

New South Wales Minerals Council, *Annual Report*, 1998.

New South Wales Minerals Council, *Annual Report*, 1999.

New South Wales Minerals Council, *Annual Report*, 2000.

New South Wales Minerals Council, *Annual Report*, 2002.

New South Wales Minerals Council, *Annual Report*, 2003.

Newcastle Herald, February 3, 1998.

Olson, Mancur. *The Logic of Collective Action.* Cambridge, Mass.: Harvard University Press, 1965.

Ostrom, Elinor "How Types of Goods and Property Rights Jointly Affect Collective Action." *Journal of Theoretical Politics* 15 No.3 (2003): 239-270.

Ottaway, Marina. "Corporatism Goes Global: International Organizations Nongovernmental Organizations Networks and Transnational Business." *Global Governance* 7 No.3 (2001): 1-22.

Peston, Maurice. *Public goods and the public sector.* London: Macmillan, 1972.

Pierson, P. "When effect becomes cause: Policy feedback and political change." *World Politics*, 45 (1992): 595-628.

Pierson, P. (2000). "Increasing returns, path dependence, and the study of politics." *American political science review*, 94 No.2 (2000): 251-267.

Pierson, P. "Public policies as institutions." in Eds. I. Shapiro, S. Skowronek & D Galvin (Eds.). *Rethinking political institutions: the art of the State.* New York: NYU Press, 2006.

Platts International Coal Report, August 26, 2002.

Plowman, D. *Holding the Line: Compulsory Arbitration and National Employer Co-ordination in Australia.* Cambridge: Cambridge University Press, 1989.

Putnam, Robert. *Bowling Alone: The Collapse and Revival of American Community*. New York: Simon & Schuster, 1993.

Queensland Minerals Council, *Annual Report* 1991-2

Queensland Minerals Council *Annual Report* 1992-3

Queensland Minerals Council *Annual Report* 1993-4

Queensland Minerals Council *Annual Report* 1997-8

Queensland Minerals Council *Annual Report* 1998-9

Queensland Minerals Council *Annual Report* 2000-1

Rawson, D. *Unions and Unionists in Australia*, Sydney: George Allen and Unwin, 1978.

Reimann, Kim D. "A View from the Top: International Politics, Norms, and the Worldwide Growth of NGOs." *International Studies Quarterly* 50 No.1 (2006): 45-67.

Richardson, J. J. (2000). "Government, interest groups and policy change." *Political studies*, 48 No.5 (2000): 1006-1025.

Richardson, J. J. Ed. *Pressure groups*. Oxford: Oxford University Press, 1993.

Richardson, J.J. and Jordan, G., *Governing under pressure: the policy process in a post-parliamentary democracy*. Oxford: Oxford UP, 1985.

Richardson, Michael, "Australia Will Speed Mining Projects: New Approach Entails a Shift from Labor's Pro-Aboriginal Stance." *International Herald Tribune,* 2 November 1991.

Riddell-Dixon, Elizabeth. *Canada and the International Seabed: Domestic Determinants and External Constraints.* Kingston, Montreal, London: Magill-Queens University Press, 1989.

Rodman, Kenneth A. "'Think Globally, Punish Locally': Nonstate Actors, Multinational Corporations, and Human Rights Sanctions" *Ethics and International Affairs* 12 (1998):19-41.

Ronit, K. (Ed.). *Global public policy: business and the countervailing powers of civil society*. London: Routledge, 2006.

Ryan, Barry. "The Law Surrounding 'Miner's Right': Origins of the Mining Law of Queensland" Paper read to the Queensland Law Society 27 June 1974.

https://espace.library.uq.edu.au/view/UQ:210103/s00855804_1973_1974_9_5_101.pdf. (Accessed 24 April 2016).

Sandbrook, R. "UNGASS has run out of steam." *International Affairs*,73 No.4 (1997): 641-654.

Satchwell, Ian. 'Australian Minerals Industry Code for Environmental Management.' *Australian Journal of Environmental Management* 4 No.1 (1997): 6-7.

Scharpf, Fritz W. "Notes toward a Theory of Multilevel Governing in Europe" *Scandinavian Political Studies*, 24 no.1 (2001): 1-26.

Schattschneider, E.E., *The semisovereign people: A realist's view of democracy in America*. New York: Holt, Rinehart, 1960.

Schlozman, K.L. & Tierney, J.T. *Organized interests and American democracy*. New York: Harper & Row. 1986.

Schmitter, P.C. "Modes of interest intermediation and models of societal change in Western Europe." *Comparative Political Studies*, 10 no.1 (1977): 7-38.

Schofer, Evan, and Wesley Longhofer. "The Structural Sources of Association." *American Journal of Sociology* 117 No.2 (2011): 539-585.

Scott, R. (ed.) *Interest Groups and Public Policy*. South Melbourne: Macmillan, 1980.

Simms, Marian. "Bureaucrats and Businessmen: The Changing Composition of Boards and Commissions from Chifley to Menzies." *Australian Journal of Public Administration*, 40 no.3 (1981): 254-263.

Simms, Marian, "Trade Unions" in Ed. Rodney Smith, *Politics in Australia* (3rd ed). Sydney: Allen & Unwin., 1987.

Singleton, Gwyn. *The Accord and the Australian Labour Movement*. Carlton: Melbourne University Press, 1990.

Skocpol, Theda. *Protecting soldiers and mothers The political origins of social policy in the United States*. Cambridge: Harvard University Press, 1995.

Skocpol, Theda. *Diminished Democracy: From Membership to Management in American Civic Life*. Norman: University of Oklahoma Press, 2003.

South Australian Chamber of Minerals and Energy, *Annual Report*, 2002.

South Australian Chamber of Minerals, *First Annual report for the Year to June 1980.*

South Australian Chamber of Minerals, *Annual Report*, 1981.

South Australian Chamber of Minerals, *Annual Report* 1982.

South Australian Chamber of Minerals, *Annual Report*, 1983.

South Australian Chamber of Minerals, *Annual Report*, 1984.

South Australian Chamber of Minerals, *Annual Report*, 1985.

South Australian Chamber of Minerals, *Annual Report*, 1986.

South Australian Chamber of Minerals and Energy, *Annual Report*, 2002.

Spill, Rorie L "Choosing among the Branches: Strategic Advocacy by Interest Groups" *The American Review of Politics*, 22 (2001): 375-395.

Stewart, Randall G. "The Politics of the Accord: Does Corporatism Explain It?" *Politics* 20 (1985): 26- 35.

Streeck, W. and Schmitter, P.C. "Community, market, state–and associations? The prospective contribution of interest governance to social order." *European sociological review*, 1 No.2 (1985):119-138.

Sydney Morning Herald, June 27, 1990.

Sydney Morning Herald, August 30, 1990.

Sydney Morning Herald, September 28, 1990.

Sydney Morning Herald, June 5, 1996.

Sydney Morning Herald, December 7, 1996.

The West Australian, October 14, 1997.

Traxler, F., & Schmitter, P. C. "The emerging Euro-polity and organized interests." *European Journal of International Relations*, 1 No.2 (1995); 191-218.

Tsokhas, Kosmas. *Beyond dependence: companies, labour processes and Australian mining*. Melbourne: Oxford University Press, 1986.

Umbeck, John. "The California Gold Rush: A Study of Emerging Property Rights." *Explorations in Economic History* 14 (1977): 197-226.

Underdal, A. *The politics of international fisheries management: The case of the Northeast Atlantic*. New York, NY: Columbia University Press, 1980.

United Nations Research Institute for Social Development (UNRISD) 1997. Globalization and Civil Society: NGO Influence in International Decision-Making. *Discussion Paper No. 83*, April.

Uren, David (2000) "Unions hit campaign trail" *Weekend Australian* 27-28 May, 2000, 37.

Victoria. *Government Gazette* 52 No.3 (April 1861): 1.

Vogel, David *Fluctuating Fortunes: The Political Power of Business in America.* New York: Basic Books, 1989.

Vogel, D. "Trading up and governing across: transnational governance and environmental protection." *Journal of European public policy*, 4 No.4 (1997): 556-571.

Walker, J.L., *Mobilizing interest groups in America: Patrons, professions, and social movements*. Ann Arbor: University of Michigan Press, 1991.

Waters, Malcolm. *Globalization*. London: Routledge, 1995.

Weekend Australian, 27-28 May 2000.

Weekend Australian, 3-4 June 2000.

Weible, Christopher M. "Beliefs and Perceived Influence in a Natural Resource Conflict: An Advocacy Coalition Approach to Policy Networks." *Political Research Quarterly* 58 No. 3(2005): 461-475.

Weiler, Joseph H.H. "The White Paper and the application of Community law", in R. Beiber, D. Dehousse, J. Pinder and J.H.H. Weiler (eds), *One European Market?* Baden-Baden: Nomos, 1988.

Wilson, G.K., 1990. "Corporate political strategies." *British Journal of Political Science*, 20 No.2 (1990): 281-288.

Wilson, James Q. *Political organizations.* New York: Basic Books, 1973.

Windmuller, J. and Gladstone, A. Eds. *Employer Associations and Industrial Relations: A Comparative Study*. Oxford: Clarendon Press, 1984.

Zysman, John. 1994. "How Institutions Create Historically Rooted Trajectories of Growth." *Industrial and Corporate Change* 3 No.1 (1994): 243-283.